Social CRM
FOR
DUMMIES®

by Kyle Lacy, Stephanie Diamond, and Jon Ferrara

WILEY

John Wiley & Sons, Inc.

Social CRM For Dummies®

Published by
John Wiley & Sons, Inc.
111 River Street
Hoboken, NJ 07030-5774
www.wiley.com

Copyright © 2013 by John Wiley & Sons, Inc., Hoboken, New Jersey

Published by John Wiley & Sons, Inc., Hoboken, New Jersey

Published simultaneously in Canada

For general information on our other products and services, please contact our Customer Care Department within the U.S. at 877-762-2974, outside the U.S. at 317-572-3993, or fax 317-572-4002.

For technical support, please visit www.wiley.com/techsupport.

Wiley publishes in a variety of print and electronic formats and by print-on-demand. Some material included with standard print versions of this book may not be included in e-books or in print-on-demand. If this book refers to media such as a CD or DVD that is not included in the version you purchased, you may download this material at http://booksupport.wiley.com. For more information about Wiley products, visit www.wiley.com.

Library of Congress Control Number: 2012952204

ISBN 978-1-118-24249-0 (pbk); ISBN 978-1-118-28313-4 (ebk); ISBN 978-1-118-28421-6 (ebk); ISBN 978-1-118-28704-0 (ebk)

Manufactured in the United States of America

10 9 8 7 6 5 4 3 2 1

WILEY

About the Authors

Kyle Lacy is Senior Manager of Marketing Research & Education at ExactTarget. In this role, Kyle leads an effort to build and distribute an ongoing research series that sets aside theories and assumptions about consumer online preferences. This series instead focuses on solid data collected through a combination of focus groups, experiential research, and online surveys.

Kyle is the author of three books, *Twitter Marketing for Dummies*, *Branding Yourself,* and *Social CRM for Dummies.* Prior to joining ExactTarget, Kyle co-founded a marketing technology company, helping over 350 clients build and deliver digital marketing experiences. You can follow him on Twitter at @kyleplacy or visit his blog at KyleLacy.com. He lives in Indianapolis, IN, with his wife, Rachel, and their dog-like cat, Harley.

Stephanie Diamond is a thought leader and management marketing professional with over 20 years of experience building profits in over 75 different industries. She has worked with solopreneurs, small business owners, and multibillion dollar corporations.

For eight years, Stephanie worked as a Marketing Director at AOL. During her tenure, subscriptions grew from fewer than 1 million to 36 million. She had a front row seat to learn how and why people buy online. While at AOL, she developed, from scratch, a highly successful line of multimedia products that brought in an annual $40 million dollars in incremental revenue.

In 2002, Stephanie founded Digital Media Works, Inc. (MarketingMessage Mindset.com), an online marketing company that helps business owners discover the hidden profits in their business. She is passionate about guiding online companies to successfully generate more revenue and use social media to its full advantage.

As a strategic thinker, Stephanie uses all the current visual thinking techniques and brain research to help companies to get to the essence of their brand. She continues this work today with her proprietary system to help online business owners discover how social media can generate profits. You can read her blog at www.MarketingMessageBlog.com.

Stephanie's other books include *Prezi For Dummies, Dragon Naturally Speaking For Dummies,* and coauthor of *Social Media Marketing For Dummies.*

Stephanie received a BA in Psychology from Hofstra University and an MSW and MPH from the University of Hawaii. She lives in New York with her husband and her Maltese named Colby.

Jon Ferrara, a social entrepreneur at heart, founded GoldMine Software and lead the company until it was sold ten years later. GoldMine helped pioneer the Sales Force Automation (SFA) and Customer Relationship Management (CRM) markets, and GoldMine was used by millions of companies.

After realizing that social media was going to forever reshape customer engagement, Ferrara entered the start up world again when he noticed a distinct lack of any products that effectively combined relationship management, social listening, and engagement with sales and marketing. Jon founded Nimble to create an social business platform to fill this gap.

Dedications

Kyle Lacy: To my wife, Rachel, and to all the digital marketers of the world who are pushing to drive change in their organizations.

Stephanie Diamond: To Barry who makes all things possible. And to my family for their love and support.

Jon Ferrara: To the man who taught me the meaning of relationships, customer engagement and Social Selling, my father, Angelo Ferrara. He taught me the power of listening and engaging customers, nurturing relationships and staying top of mind with customers. To the woman who has taught me the importance of being present with family, friends and who teaches me on a daily basis the importance of art and soul development, my wife, Arleen Ferrara. To my children who on a daily basis teach me about myself and enable me to grow as a human being.

Authors' Acknowledgments

Kyle Lacy: I often say that social media is multiple minds building a creative community, and this book is no different. I couldn't have written this book without the help of some extremely special people. First off, thank you to Amy Fandrei and Rebecca Huehls for their absolutely angelic patience during the writing of this book. I would also like to thank my coauthors, Jon Ferrara and Stephanie Diamond.

I would like to thank the people in my life and my community who helped me gain the knowledge, experience, and insights to product this book. I have two families in my life. My immediate family and my ExactTarget family. Thanks to my wife Rachel Lacy for her patience and love while writing this book. I would be remiss not to thank my parents and siblings for building my understanding of what it truly means to build community.

Also, thank you to all the Social CRM, CRM, social media, and digital marketers who helped form the ideas in this book. There are too many to name, but you know who you are. Thanks for providing content that helps drive change instead of irrelevancy.

Stephanie Diamond: It has been my distinct privilege to write this book. I want to offer thanks to my coauthors, Kyle Lacy and Jon Ferrara, and the *For Dummies* publishing team at Wiley for lettting me coauthor this book for their audience of smart readers.

The following people were especially important in creating this book, and I offer very sincere thanks:

To the great creative group at Wiley, Acquisitions Editor Amy Fandrei, Senior Project Editor Rebecca Huehls, and Technical Editor Alison Zarrella. They helped make this project a reality.

To Matt Wagner, my agent at Fresh Books, for his continued hard work and support on my behalf.

Finally, thanks to you for choosing this book to learn about social CRM. I wish you enormous joy on your exciting journey into this up-and-coming trend.

Jon Ferrara: To the greater CRM/SFA community of users, analysts, editors, and VARS who have supported and inspired my entrepreneurial quests, especially to the GoldMine and Nimble communities.

Huge thanks to Kyle Lacy and Stephanie Diamond for bringing me in to help with the book they wrote. Much appreciation to Amy Fandrei, Chantal Kowalski, and Jen Webb from Wiley Publishing for their support, assistance, and guidance during the course of this project.

Publisher's Acknowledgments

We're proud of this book; please send us your comments at http://dummies.custhelp.com. For other comments, please contact our Customer Care Department within the U.S. at 877-762-2974, outside the U.S. at 317-572-3993, or fax 317-572-4002.

Some of the people who helped bring this book to market include the following:

Acquisitions and Editorial

Sr. Project Editor: Rebecca Huehls

Acquisitions Editor: Amy Fandrei

Copy Editor: Heidi Unger

Technical Editor: Alison Zarrella

Sr. Editorial Manager: Leah Michael

Editorial Assistant: Annie Sullivan

Sr. Editorial Assistant: Cherie Case

Cover Photo: © Grady Reese/iStockphoto; © Mark Bowden /iStockphoto; © Yunus Arakon /iStockphoto; © Mathias Wilson /iStockphoto; © Stígur Karlsson / iStockphoto; © Jacob Wackerhausen / iStockphoto

Cartoons: Rich Tennant (www.the5thwave.com)

Composition Services

Project Coordinator: Sheree Montgomery

Layout and Graphics: Carrie A. Cesavice, Jennifer Creasey, Joyce Haughey, Andrea Hornberger, Christin Swinford

Proofreaders: BIM Indexing & Proofreading Services, Jessica Kramer

Indexer: Valerie Haynes Perry

Publishing and Editorial for Technology Dummies

 Richard Swadley, Vice President and Executive Group Publisher

 Andy Cummings, Vice President and Publisher

 Mary Bednarek, Executive Acquisitions Director

 Mary C. Corder, Editorial Director

Publishing for Consumer Dummies

 Kathleen Nebenhaus, Vice President and Executive Publisher

Composition Services

 Debbie Stailey, Director of Composition Services

Contents at a Glance

Table of Contents

Introduction

Greetings reader, welcome to the new world of social business and *Social CRM For Dummies*. Pat yourself on the back for picking up this book! You are about to enter a world of customer-focused technology that will revolutionize the way you support and market your business. In our very humble opinion, it's an exciting time for all.

Social CRM (that is, customer relationship management) responds to dramatic changes in the business world. Over the past 23 years, we have witnessed an extreme transformation in how customers deal with brands. Much of the change is directly related to the Internet and the development of social media. Extend a hand and welcome social consumers with social technology at their fingertips! With social media, customers can speak, share, and build opinions and thoughts around *your* brand.

Whether you are an executive of a global business or the owner of a small business, the idea of digital communication is extremely important to your business strategy. The last five years have seen a massive growth in marketing automation, customer service, and sales support technology. And it is forever changing . . . daily.

Although the rapid changes social media has brought can feel exhausting, it's absolutely imperative to have a finger on the pulse of the CRM and social CRM world. *Social CRM For Dummies* is your guide to entering this world. In this book, we help you understand where your business is, where you want your business to be, and how to steer your business toward that goal.

About This Book

If you deal in any aspect of customer communication — internal or external — this book is for you. Whether you're an executive or small business owner, this book will give you an in-depth look at the world of social business and social CRM.

The world of customer relationship management is absolutely massive. The changes in the industry from software development to cloud-based computing have created a scenario of constant development for everyone in the marketing industry. We wrote this book to help you gain traction in the ever-changing world of social CRM. This book deals with communication. Period. Communication is (or should be) at the center of every business entity.

There is a saying out there, "Relevance is in the eye of the beholder." Relevance is exactly why we decided to write this book. The customer deems you relevant if and only if you speak to them as an individual instead of the mass. We are in a world where personalization is king and the rest? Just details. Welcome to the world of social CRM. Enjoy the ride.

Also, this book doesn't look good gathering dust on a bookshelf. Use it!

Foolish Assumptions

Many authors make assumptions about their readers. How are we to judge? Here are some simple assumptions we have made about you. Feel free to use a pen and put check marks next to the one(s) that apply to you:

- ✔ You are innovative and want to change the way you do business in the digital age.
- ✔ You have used at least one social networking site in your lifetime, such as Twitter, Facebook, LinkedIn, Yammer, or Chatter.
- ✔ You have some business experience running a small business or working in an enterprise-level organization.
- ✔ You love your customers and posses an innate desire to cater to their every need.

We also assume that you have some basic web skills, such as knowing how to use Google.

Conventions Used in This Book

We have some consistent things happening throughout the book that you need to be aware of. Consistency equals success right? In this book, those consistent elements are called conventions.

- ✔ Italics are used to indentify and define new terms.
- ✔ If you have to type something, you will find the words are **bolded** to keep things clear and concise.

✔ URLs, code, Twitter handles, or e-mail addresses within a paragraph appear in a special font. A URL looks like this: `http://www.dummies.com` (and if you're on an electronic device, clicking or tapping the URL will take you to that website). A Twitter handle, such as Kyle's, looks like this: `@kyleplacy`.

How This Book Is Organized

The idea of shifting your business to focus more on the consumer can be a daunting task. We have written a wide variety of ideas from strategy to software, which is why this book is broken down in parts and sections. We organized the book in the *For Dummies* way because it is perfect for quick reviewing and reading. If you want to know about certain software for marketing automation, you can go directly to that section. Perfect right?

Let's take a look at how each section is organized and detailed.

Part 1: Welcome to the World of Social CRM

This is your complete guide to understanding the beginning of CRM and social CRM. From humble beginnings, the world of data management has shifted dramatically over the years. This is where you learn from where we have come and where we are going.

We define the changing world of the consumer as well as the technology. If you just read Part I of the book (which we don't recommend), you'll have a full understanding of what it means to be a true social business.

Chapter 1 introduces you to the impact social media is having on businesses and how that connects to customers' personal use of social media. You also find out how to connect where CRM was to social CRM today and in the future. Chapter 2 introduces you to the fundamental elements of social CRM, such as multiway communication, collaboration with customers, and customer engagement. You also find out how social CRM supports business's core needs, such as retaining customers, finding leads, offering customer support, and more. Chapter 3 introduces the challenges social CRM poses and strategies that can help lay the groundwork for your social CRM initiatives. Chapter 4 is your guide to the social customer's habits and best practices for approaching the social customer via social media.

Part II: Building Your Social CRM Strategy

Simply put, Part II moves from the 20,000-foot view in Part I to the ground level. Chapter 5 helps you formulate your overall social business strategy, from internal matters (such as finding the right person to lead your social CRM initiative and adjusting business processes) to external strategies (like initiating co-creation with your customers). After you have a better understanding of your big-picture strategy, you're ready to start working within your organization to implement your social CRM plan. Chapter 6 focuses specifically on how to adjust your marketing strategy, Chapter 7 digs into the nitty-gritty of social technology, and Chapter 8 explains how to help your sales team adjust to a social CRM business model. In Chapters 9, 10, and 11, you discover ways to reach out to customers, including creating customer loyalty and advocacy programs, delivering customer service via social media, and effectively reaching out to customers on mobile technologies.

Part III: Developing a Social and Collaborative Business

Employees are customers too! This section details the different ways your employees are affected by social CRM. How do you truly create a social business that thrives under the new technology? (We in the biz call it the Zappos effect. More on that later.) Discover strategies for turning your business into a social organization in Chapter 12. Then, in Chapter 13, you discover different methods and technologies for implementing that strategy.

Part IV: Measuring the Impact of Social CRM

We highly recommend this section for those of you who love analytics and Excel spreadsheets. Success is not only grounded in strategy, but also in measuring the success of a project or campaign. It is imperative to understand the world of analytics and measurement. It will define your campaigns, technology, and business moving forward. Chapter 14 introduces ways you can deal with the massive influx of data that social CRM can bring. You also find help deciding what social media metrics are important to your overall social CRM strategy. Chapter 15 looks ahead to emerging technologies that are likely to become more mainstream in social CRM, including emerging consumer technologies as well as the future of mobile and embedded technology.

Part V: The Part of Tens

This is almost like the tradition of Thanksgiving or watching the IU Hoosiers' basketball games before March Madness. Simply tradition. Every *For Dummies* book has a Part of Tens, which in this case sums up the different types of software and/or technology you should use on your social CRM journey. For example, we detail the different tools to use for sales support, customer service, and marketing automation. When you're ready to start researching software that can support your social CRM strategy, this Part of Tens is for you.

Icons Used in This Book

We love icons as long as they are not on a PowerPoint slide deck at a conference. We use icons in the book to highlight important points. Here's a breakdown of what the icons mean.

The Tip icon gives you suggestions, shortcuts, and tricks to better enable your business to be more social and engaged.

Yes, it is a bomb. No, it doesn't mean you are dead. The warning icon is simply a warning. It highlights points where your business needs to stay alert and cautious in order to keep your social CRM initiatives on track.

The Remember icon is used for the awesome factoids that will basically change your life. Go back to these over and over to keep your social CRM project focused on sound planning and results.

The majority of this book is geeky. When we are over-the-top geeky, you see the Technical Stuff icon. You can ignore these tidbits, but we think you'll find them useful when you're ready go beyond the basics of social CRM.

Where to Go from Here

Go forth into the world of customer communication, increased collaboration, and support scenarios. Sounds fun already right? So, where do you start?

If you already understand how and why the world is changing due to technology, feel free to skip Part I and jump directly to Part II. However, it is extremely imperative that you truly understand where the business world is truly moving in regards to customer communication and technology.

If you have a specific topic in mind that you want to know more about, check the Index or the Table of Contents. Then flip to that chapter, section, or page. That, friends, is the beauty of the *For Dummies* guide.

If you have any questions regarding social CRM or customer communication, feel free to check out Kyle's blog at www.kylelacy.com or Jon's website at Nimble www.nimble.com. If we have important updates to this book, you can find them online at www.dummies.com/go/socialcrmupdates.

You're ready. Enjoy the ride.

Part I
Welcome to the World of Social CRM

The 5th Wave · By Rich Tennant

"Just how accurately should my social media presence reflect my place of business?"

In this part. . .

This part is your bird's-eye view of social CRM. You find out where CRM has been, what social CRM looks like today, and where social CRM is likely headed a few years from now. We help you understand basic priciples of social CRM, and in doing so, you may begin to develop a picture of what your business's social CRM strategy might look like. No big change comes without a few challenges, so we help you understand the common ones and offer tips to help you work through those successfully. You also find an introduction to social customers: their habits, their preferences, and their reasons for interacting with brands in the social sphere.

Chapter 1

Implementing the New Social Business

In This Chapter

▶ Defending the new social media model

▶ Looking at the history of CRM

▶ Defining what it means to be social

Welcome to the new social business. Many of you may read this opening line with surprise, thinking, "What do you mean the *new* social business? We've been talking about being a social business for years. At least a decade!" Yes, businesses have been talking about being social for decades, but technology has finally reached a point where implementing social media is now part of the overall strategy. We can discuss the idea of being a social business until we're blue in the face; however, it's time to act, time to take charge!

The new social business represents a fundamental shift in business management that impacts both a salesperson who keeps track of consumer information using a technology and the management of customers' Facebook profiles via a database.

As a business owner, marketing executive, or professional, you're just now jumping into the world where you can connect the data, interactions, and customer information between sites like Facebook and your customer database. That's the new idea behind a social business. It's what this book is about: social media data and interaction married with business data that has been collected for years within different software and management technologies.

See, that is cool.

In this chapter, you look at what makes the combination of social media, marketing communication, and technology worth your investment.

Accepting the New Social Change

Many companies have issues with change, which could be associated with the speed at which technology changes or fear of making the wrong decisions. However, we believe that the issue with change management isn't the fear of a new strategy. The issue lies within a business's organizational structure. When *hasn't* a marketer enjoyed talking about a shiny new object?

Many organizations have trouble moving into the future of technology and marketing because of fragmentation. Their technology is isolated in silos, so to speak, and various systems don't always work together. Thus the company's marketing strategy tends to be associated with the specific channel, like social media and mobile. Instead, you want the technology change to be associated with the brand or company.

The issue? Businesses that want to thrive need to change by moving toward a new approach to marketing and organizational management. Given the new era of hyper-connected and empowered consumers, customers demand this change. Marketers must embrace the changing landscape to understand unique consumer needs and preferences.

Before we jump into the technology and strategy, we focus on making the case for this change, because acceptance is critical. Everyone in the business, from senior leadership to part-time customer service representatives needs to accept that this social change is happening. Without overall acceptance, you'll struggle to fully implement the social strategy within your business. After employees are on board, your business is ready to implement strategies and technologies that build social media within your database.

Defending the business side of social media

We all understand that "being social" is and always will be a staple to the success of any business. Whether you're talking in the town square or attending a meeting at the local bank, you're building relationships with individuals to drive interaction and sales to your business. Business structures, government regulations, product road maps, competitive environments, and sales pipelines are different from one business to another. However, the idea of being social remains the same. The social business is the one that will succeed in the generations to come.

To make the case for social business and the change that comes with it, you need to go beyond the superficial platitudes. People are tired of hearing,

"Social media is the best thing ever! Social media will change your business and revolutionize sales."

To make the case for social business, we suggest you focus on changing coworkers' perception of the fundamental idea of sales and customer communication. This change happens when you use the data behind social media to drive interactions with customers.

To encourage acceptance of the new social change, start with the understanding behind the personal side of social, the human side of social, and then move on to the business side.

- ✔ **Personal side:** The personal side of the brand is the personality of the company. What are people saying about the company? How do you bring out the personality of the brand?

  As humans, we are social. Well, the majority of us are social, right? The human race thrives from building and maintaining long-lasting relationships because of our ability to be social. We strive to connect. Period.

- ✔ **Business side:** After addressing the personal side of the brand, you're ready to tackle the business side. In the new social business, the business side focuses on the return on investment of social media and defines it by transactional information.

The following sections offer more details about these two fundamentals for acceptance and building a strategy around social change.

Understanding the personal side of social media

Marketing, as a concept, was and is built around the connection between two individuals — except for one difference. Marketing wants to use that same connection to build a relationship between a product and a consumer. Advertising executives of the olden days sat in smoke-filled rooms and tried to define what it means for a brand to be social and to see that branded product by using the personal side of a product. There's only one problem with that scenario: A product isn't human. Or is it?

The personal side of a product and brand is the complete set of interactions happening around that product or brand by the consumer.

You want to use this personal side of social, the human side, to drive interaction between customers and employees. Promotional items and coupons are for the business end of this deal. The personal side of social is between humans using technology to interact with each other.

Until recently, businesses haven't been able to fully understand the personal side of the social business. However, technology and concepts surrounding social CRM have helped define what it truly means to be social.

Defining the business side of social media

What do you value as a business? If you haven't formally listed a set of values, don't worry; you can determine what you value pretty easily by defining your strategy. However, it's an important question to answer before moving into the world of social CRM. The business side of social is defining those measurements in order to understand what you need to do to be successful. This side also determines the budget and amount of resources that you need to allocate in order to make a transition to the social CRM world a successful one.

Connecting CRM History to Today

CRM (customer relationship management) became part of the business world when business leaders decided they needed a better way to manage their contacts and customers through software. The idea of CRM is pretty straightforward: It's the management of customer interaction with a brand or company. Many of you may think of CRM in the context of sales; however, CRM now touches almost every aspect of your business.

Traveling dirt roads to the computer screen

Imagine yourself owning a small store in the wild, wild West. You have customers, and they love to buy hard tack and flour. How do you keep track of their purchases? In the past, store owners used the ledger system to track purchases, and they remembered certain points about their customers. In a small town with a small group of people, it was easy to remember that Marge's husband was Bill. But what happens when the town grows? You expand your business and offer more locations, with more products and more customers. The mind is a powerful thing, but it's hard to manage the names, faces, and relationships of thousands of customers.

The mind turned to notes and, beginning in the 1950s, the Rolodex. Ah, the trusty Rolodex. Spin through the names and find the next customer; add more customer information as that becomes available. It made remembering customer information easier; however, the elements of the earth (fire, wind, water, dirt) weren't kind to the paper Rolodex, and the desktop computer changed everything.

Welcoming the power of computing

The business world started witnessing the first hint of the CRM revolution in the late 1980s. This was based on the introduction of the server architecture and wide adoption of the desktop computer (fueled by major players like Apple and IBM). Simply put, the computer offered much more power and memory than thousands of Rolodex cards. Can you imagine sorting through all that ink and paper? No way.

The computing revolution brought forth companies like ACT! and GoldMine that released their own software platforms that helped individuals and large businesses manage hundreds of thousands of contacts.

The early nineties witnessed many companies such as Siebel Systems and Oracle building massive databases and ushering in the term SFA (sales force automation). SFA helped sales organizations streamline their sales processes and increased productivity. Think Rolodex on major steroids. The computing and software revolution led to the adoption of a data and networking strategy called CRM (customer relationship management).

Crafting the CRM Definition and Philosophy

As witnessed from this chapter, it's the power of computing that truly drove the innovation within companies all over the world. The software provided by ACT! and GoldMine would change the very nature of customer relationships. This revolution eventually laid the red carpet for future companies, including Salesforce, Marketo, ExactTarget, and Nimble. Before we get into the future, let's break down the philosophy and definition of CRM.

Optimizing customer relationships

The year was 1995, and the research firm Gartner coined the first definition of CRM: "Customer Relationship Management is a business strategy with outcomes that optimize profitability, revenue, and customer satisfaction by organizing around customer segments, fostering customer-satisfying behaviors, and implementing customer-centric processes."

Gartner also introduced the Eight Essential Building Blocks of CRM, a list that gives us an excellent starting point for this book.

- ✔ **Vision:** What's your company's vision? Are you including your mission statement and goals in your marketing strategy? They also apply to the CRM philosophy of driving customer-centric data and communication.

- ✔ **Strategy:** What's your strategy for reaching the customer? How do you manage the relationship before and after the sale?

- ✔ **Valued customer experience:** In this customer-centric world, experience is paramount to everything else. By using CRM to manage your contacts, you're creating a truly valuable experience for your customers. You're remembering their needs and wants!

- ✔ **Organizational collaboration:** Do your employees work together and share data? Collaboration is the key to success in many organizations.

- ✔ **Processes:** Are your sales processes streamlined? Do you use software to manage the data and development of prospects?

- ✔ **Information:** CRM allows you to store information that would otherwise be lost to paper, trash cans, and spilled milk.

- ✔ **Technology:** Do you build technology into your overall marketing strategy? Allowing great technology behind CRM is essential to success.

- ✔ **Metrics:** Data is king in the world of CRM. Are you managing your metrics effectively?

These eight building blocks are just the beginning to developing the CRM strategy. You must also take into account the social and business side of CRM, which (as discussed earlier) allows your company to truly be customer centric. A customer-centric strategy involves using computing power to optimize customer relationships. Remember Marge? Imagine managing sales data for five thousand different Marges?

Predicting the future of CRM

At the time of this writing, many experts were coining the future of CRM as social CRM, otherwise known as CRM 2.0. We still have a long way to go as far as perfecting the idea of customer relationship management is concerned. The future will be owned by the individuals, companies, and software platforms that focus on the idea that customers are the center of all strategies. That's what social CRM is truly about.

In this book, we touch on many subjects, from customer service to marketing; however, every aspect of your business is now involved in the future of CRM. The social business and an evolving CRM platform is just the next evolution in this customer-centric world.

Chapter 2

Meeting the New Kid on the Block: Social CRM

*A*t the time of this writing, Facebook surpassed the one billion users mark. Let's break it down real fast: One billion people are either using or signed up for the social networking site. That's one billion, with a *b*. This monumental accomplishment isn't just a huge user base for the social networking giant. It shows a fundamental shift in the way people are communicating with each other and brands. It shows that the social side of business is going to be more important in the future than ever before.

Social media is just one ingredient to a successful social CRM strategy, but it's a fundamental ingredient. This new customer relationship management mandate presents new challenges for any business owner. However, it ultimately enables you to truly know your customers and their preferences. In this chapter, we help you get acquainted with this new kid on the block. You might just find out that this paradigm shift to social business isn't so overwhelming.

Defining Social CRM

There are many forms and definitions surrounding the idea of social CRM. The basic idea is that multiple business units interact using the social web (social media). You have the ability to overlay the traditional CRM model with social data that builds better relationships for the future. The official definition is best given by our friend Esteban Kolsky in his presentation Three Reasons You Will Do Social CRM:

Social CRM is a philosophy and a business strategy, supported by a system and a technology, designed to improve human interaction in a business environment.

It's about more than just changes and advances with communication methods, social media monitoring tools, and CRM software. Social CRM represents a real paradigm shift in the way businesses conduct everyday business. It really is all about the customer. True customer-focused approaches must guide marketing, product development, and customer service. Today's social customer, empowered with knowledge and an eager audience, can intimidate and confuse many businesses.

We want to guide you on best strategies for reaching out to the social customer and help you understand ways to harness data about this ever-evolving customer. In this new era that's riddled with social networking platforms and abundant information sharing — in real time — old ways of managing customer relationships just don't cut it anymore. And that is the fundamental idea behind the CRM philosophy.

Using social media for CRM

Customers, more now than ever, influence the way that companies conduct business. Customers don't run your business but they do determine how you engage them. Listening to customers' suggestions and indicators for preferred communications methods through social monitoring tools like Google Alerts and TweetDeck just makes good business sense. Social CRM requires that you learn a new way of customer relationship management — listening and adjusting your business messages to maximize profitable opportunities. You can still run business as usual, but don't miss opportunities to hear what your customers are really saying about and to you through their social networks.

Customers want to engage on a social level with brands, similarly to how they communicate with friends and family. For example, Facebook users can tag photos, comment on posts and photos, and make recommendations to connect with a company, product, or brand. That's a good thing — at least it's better than sending your company unsubscribe or do-not-contact messages.

With social media, businesses can have more channels where they can reach customers in a less in-your-face manner. Businesses just have to get up to speed with adjusting and personalizing their messages to varying audiences on varying channels, including Twitter, Facebook, Pinterest, Foursquare, and so on. Managing the social channels is the fundamental idea behind social CRM.

Accepting multi-way communication

The rise of mobile devices and the extremely tech-savvy consumer is taking communication cross-channel and not just one way . . . in real time. Brands need to adapt.

Gone are the days of megaphone-broadcasting your targeted messages and moving on to your next targeted message. Also, two-way communications like a good ol' phone calls and one-to-one e-mail aren't the end-all, be-all (though still very effective.) You have to listen and accept the fact that your customers are talking (about you) on multiple channels. Consumers beat enterprise to the social scene and started the conversations, putting businesses in a position to react and try to catch up. Accepting that customer communication is multi-way gives your brand a better chance to proactively intercept and engage these conversations.

Social media strategies often have been an afterthought to traditional marketing plans instead of being integrated in a brand's overall messaging strategy. The approach is often something like this: "Hey, we should probably try this social media stuff. Get Bob's assistant to set up a Facebook page and see what's up with Twitter." What do you get with that approach? Anything but integrated marketing. Communication channels increase and evolve at a wink of an eye in today's social business.

Moving from brand speak to real conversations

If you're a seasoned marketer reading this, you're more than familiar with brand speak. For those less familiar with the term, *brand speak* is the idea that mission statements and boardrooms can and should define the conversation between a brand and the consumer.

With stringent and hard-set brand speak in place, the consumer isn't in control. Remember we just talked about giving control to and collaborating with your customers. To implement social CRM strategies, your organization must move from brand speak to real conversations.

Of course, you'll always have an agenda for these conversations. That's just human nature. However, you have to train yourself to really listen so you can adjust your messages in a way that your audience will actually hear them. So put your ear to the ground using social media monitoring tools and Google Alerts and you might learn these things:

- ✔ How your customers perceive your brand
- ✔ What your brand advocates want more of from you
- ✔ What your unsatisfied customers want to see fixed
- ✔ How your audience wants to be reached — its preferred channels
- ✔ What brand speak your customers do want to hear

This doesn't mean that you shouldn't have a plan to carry brand messaging. You most certainly should, but your plan has to be flexible and malleable in order to adopt the changes that your customers request.

Discovering the Social CRM Fundamentals

The definition of social CRM is complete only if we also include the fundamental elements of a successful social CRM strategy. While the entirety of this book is about being successful at implementing a social CRM strategy, we also want to touch on two main elements: influence and community.

The influence of the customer is extremely important to the success of any social CRM strategy. This is important when managing customer expectations and building the strength of customer advocates within their respective communities.

Employee and customer influence within communities are truly a fundamental part of a successful social CRM platform, which plays on the elements of community and influence between your customers and employees.

Focusing on community building

In order to build a successful social community, a business must first understand how and why consumers engage with their brand through social channels. Studies have shown that a vast majority of Facebook Page fans are either current or past customers. This means that your fans have already interacted with your business through another channel — your storefront, website, e-mail, telephone line, and so on. All this indicates that the social media ecosystem is a breeding ground for community building between fans and past fans. It's the perfect mix of people! The following are examples of community building:

✔ **Posing questions:** People are more apt to respond to a question than comment on a statement. Giving fans two options in a question can elicit responses, too. When you're trying to engage the social community, you can ask questions that may generate ideas for future content.

✔ **Repurposing content from fans and followers:** Fans and followers are part of the community element of your brand. The content they create on social media sites can help fuel the content for your brand. After all, your customers are your best salespeople, right?

✔ **Promoting contests:** Photo contests have gained great popularity on Facebook. Many people are proud of their photos and are more than eager to share them. See an example of Peet's Coffee in Figure 2-1.

✔ **Creating cross-channel marketing:** If a certain piece of content is gaining engagement on Facebook, it's a good bet that it'll catch e-mail subscribers' attention, too. This idea works in reverse. Listen to what your customers like and use that content to help fuel other avenues of your marketing initiative, such as e-mail.

Now, if you get a transaction somewhere in that mix, bonus! However, with community building, transactions can't be the main aim, and that's a tough pill to swallow for much of enterprise that clings to the way things used to be.

Figure 2-1: An example of community engagement with a photo contest from a brand with a loyal following.

Giving influence to your customers

When we say "giving influence to your customers," we don't mean you have to turn your entire business over to them. Customers own and define their own personal experience with a brand, and companies can learn to optimize these experiences. You determine who you are as a company — your mission, your philosophies — but each customer has a personal and individual experience with your brand.

Customers are telling businesses when, where, and how much they will purchase and have embraced a variety of channels to do so. Social sharing sites like Pinterest and social shopping sites like Glam exemplify the idea of community building around commerce.

Glam Media (www.glam.com), which proclaims to be "the leading curated social media platform company," is a content promotion company that focuses on lifestyle topics like fashion, food, and parenting. Glam helps brands build a loyal base of writers who enjoy the brand's products. Glam's blog writers are paid based on the advertisements attracted to their pages, and advertisers become attracted to a blog after an audience (consumers) is generated. So the consumers determine where the advertising dollars will go and distinguish what content is actually valuable.

Collaborating with customers

Fundamental to the social business is collaboration with customers. This is about creating a place where customers can define the conversation and start building and deepening an understanding of the brand. Your best salesperson is your happy customer. Use it to your advantage.

Determining the value of a customer goes beyond loyalty. A repeat customer can drive profits but a repeat customer who also sends your brand referrals can more greatly affect your bottom line. Who doesn't love raving fans? A customer's value goes well beyond just what she buys. Companies need to take into consideration that customer's potential to generate profitable new customers. What a customer may say about your brand and his or her willingness to refer new customers to you definitely holds value and expands upon customer loyalty.

Incentivizing your socially engaged customers is great way to turn them into brand advocates. Here are few examples of incentives that you can offer to customers:

✔ **Earn a $20 credit to your account when your next referral subscribes.**

✔ **Refer three friends to buy the same deal you just did, and your purchase is free.** That's how LivingSocial encouraged its customers to promote a deal, as shown in Figure 2-2.

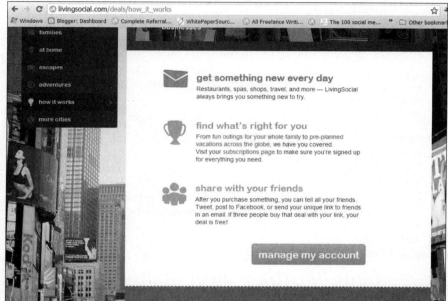

Figure 2-2:
An example of incentivized referrals from popular group-couponing site LivingSocial.

Wherever your customers are talking is where you should be listening and collaborating. With review sites, social media, and search gaining popularity and usage from customers, it's critical for you to be listening to what your customers are sharing on these sites. Many consumers turn to review sites for recommendations on just about any type of service on the fly.

Understanding the Differences in Social and Traditional CRM

Because you picked up this book, we're guessing that you've already heard of CRM. If you need a refresher on how we define traditional CRM, visit Chapter 1 or take a look at Figure 2-3. In this section, we outline the key differences between traditional and social CRM.

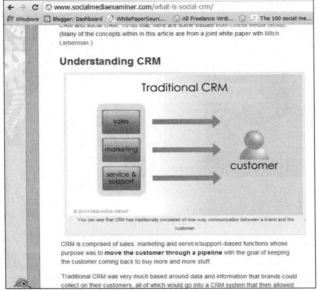

Figure 2-3:
Social
Media
Examiner
depicts
traditional
CRM.

Social CRM is a strategy. It's a philosophy, not just software and technologies to gather and manage customer data, though such technologies support social strategies. On the other hand, traditional CRM aims to move customers through a pipeline with the desired end result of repeat business and incremental sales. Typically, marketing, sales, and customer service departments manage and maintain the CRM system. Traditional CRM largely is a customer data bucket. Any and all information that can be collected about a customer is dumped into the CRM bucket, with intentions to better target customers. It was and still remains very effective and valuable at doing exactly that. However, traditional CRM is most effective when a business determines the media for reaching its customers — media that the business controls.

Customers' preferred communication channels are evolving and greatly varied. Customers hang out in online media that your business doesn't control, they're constantly influencing their own experience with your brand, and they're in control of their experience with brands. Customer influence over a brand drives the socialization of business and changes in CRM. Businesses used to own the media in which they would interact with their customers. Now, customer relationships take place in media outside of a business's control. Customers determine where and when to engage with businesses in social CRM.

Shifting from selling to relationship building

Sales strategies for your product, service or idea used to encompass a flashy brochure and a salesperson with an agenda. Then your customers got online and started talking to each other, using referral sites like Angie's List (www. angieslist.com) and Yelp. They detailed their experiences with your brand for others to read, and rated you amongst your competition.

Prior to making a purchase, consumers turn to these referral sites to ask their network for recommendations and an insider's knowledge of a brand. No longer do your customers rely on your biased brochure or sales force to learn what you really have to offer. They tap into a social network of people with similar interests to get a less biased opinion of your service or product.

With all that talk taking place — out of your control — it becomes paramount to build and maintain good relationships with your customers. Happy customers can become your brand advocate, offering personal experience that speaks volumes compared to agenda-riddled corporate literature.

Everything social is public

We've all heard the horror stories of major brand, celebrity, and politician missteps on Twitter. Oprah has apologized on Twitter. The White House's Communications Director received major grief for chatting up sports on Twitter while much of the world was watching historic events in Egypt in 2011. In Figure 2-4, you can see the tweet that led to Chrysler's public Twitter apology. So the big guys make mistakes, too. You can learn from their blunders.

Sure you can delete a tweet or a post, but there's no saying who saw it first and maybe even grabbed a screen shot. Social media is primed for quick, impulsive messages. You must remember that it's all public, open for the world to see. Resisting the urge to tweet and post like firing loose cannons will prove to save you from embarrassment and apologies down the road. Even if you delete a tweet or post, it still lives on out in the cyber world on some server somewhere. It never really goes away.

Also, freedom of speech reigns supreme online. While you might politely ask a customer to remove an unfavorable comment or post, that customer may not be inclined to do so.

A Lesson from Chrysler: Tweet With "#&@&ing" Care

MARCH 9, 2011 BY JD RUCKER | 30 COMMENTS

+1 0 | Like 141 | Tweet 278 | Share 134

I find it ironic that Detroit is known as the #motorcity and yet no one here knows how to f_ _ _ing drive

about 3 hours ago via web   Reply Retweet

ChryslerAutos
Chrysler Autos

Mistakes. They happen. If they didn't, humanity would be boring.

On social media, mistakes happen way too often. The ease of the medium has made it to where Tweets and Facebook updates can be sent to thousands of people in seconds without much.

Figure 2-4:
Chrysler had to issue a public apology for this Twitter misstep.

Defining new metrics of success

Success or failure is preceded by goals and expectations. Traditional CRM carries easily quantifiable, clear-cut goals and desired outcomes. The first goal is to get a decent ROI on the CRM technology just adapted by the organization. The next goal is to get incremental value from new and established customers.

With social CRM, another change of perspective is required. Your ideas regarding success metrics need a significant shift to big-picture ideas. Determining social CRM success doesn't have clearly outlined transactions generated from CRM interactions. Your success and positive changes will occur over time, not overnight. Approaching social CRM really requires an organization to adopt a new cultural philosophy.

Did you just gasp? Consider these ideas of success and evaluate where your organization stands:

- Word-of-mouth referrals
- Positive online feedback
- More deeply engaged customers — across multiple channels

Customer-focused objectives become paramount with social CRM and require whole organizations to get behind the philosophy and live it. A strategy with perhaps only the marketing department cheering on the sales team to engage customers doesn't work. You must put a top-down strategy in place to launch successful social CRM. The organization's leaders must guide this long-term change of a customer-centric culture. Not everyone will or can get on board overnight — so understand that you should be both patient and persistent. It's the long-haul goal of customer engagement that will keep the cultural shift on track.

Aiming for customer engagement

We want to make sure that we illustrate true customer engagement as something more than a coined term used in social media and a metric on many social networking sites. Customer engagement goes far beyond that. Customers can engage with a Facebook post, once or maybe twice. You may get a retweet or comment on your blog. Is that customer engagement? Sure. Is it enough to define success for your brand? We don't think so. Fully embracing social CRM fosters something much more than one-off interactions.

The customer engagement we're talking about is when customers become involved in the overall experience of your brand. The motives for this ongoing involvement with your brand are determined by your customers, each with their own set of reasons. Your business may never know all the reasons for a customer's engagement, but you'll need to know enough to continually foster that involvement. Your customers are selecting the ways in which they will engage. Some customers want to keep you at arms length, and others may invest more time building a relationship with your brand. However, that can't be the end-all, be-all goal of social CRM either.

Recognizing the Benefits of Social CRM

Social CRM presents some pretty significant changes and shifts, organizationally, technically, and strategically for companies, but it isn't for nothing. The business environment is changing whether you like it or not, so why not take a look at the up side of the social CRM shift. Here are just a few key benefits of implementing a social CRM strategy:

- Locating where your customers prefer to communicate
- Educating consumers in the ways they like to hear new information
- Engaging social customers, who can carry and share your messaging to their extended networks
- Receiving constructive feedback on your brand so you can make strategic adjustments

✔ Identifying new opportunities and generating leads

✔ Reducing customer support costs with targeted monitoring software

When you see the benefits, both short and long term, it makes good business sense to implement the necessary changes to get the social CRM ball rolling. You have to remember that you won't realize all the benefits overnight and the approach to social CRM requires long-term ideas and patience.

Increasing customer retention

A customer-centric social CRM strategy should naturally form stronger customer relationships — if you're really listening — through traditional and social media. Truly understanding the customer by using data (both social and traditional) will build the success of customer retention. By monitoring your customers' online behaviors and conversations around your brand, you can seize the opportunity to intercept conversations that, for instance, misrepresent your brand or that may identify a disgruntled customer.

Gathering user data such as profile information, buying habits, demographics, and so on primes you for an opportunity to respond in a fashion that fits that individual customer. Listen. Then give 'em what they want. People like to talk to like-minded people. If you identify the reason for a potential customer cancellation or negative social conversation, you can adjust your communication style to be more like that customer's. You'll have a better chance of earning trust from that customer, and then the right to ask for them to stay with your brand.

We've all heard people say, "Please don't judge us on our mistakes but instead on how we handle our mistakes." It's true. Mistakes happen, and the vast majority of the human race understands that. You increase your odds of retaining customers when you know more about them and meet them where they prefer to communicate.

Generating leads

Cold calling and a canned sales pitch won't cut it with today's social customer. Relationship marketing and trust are the way to increased leads. The added benefit of farming leads with social CRM is identifying new customers in a more qualified way.

When you're listening to social conversations about your brand, you can identify potential customers who've already raised their hands to say that they have a need or interest in either your brand or brands like it. You may find conversations where potential customers are explicitly asking for help — help that you have the right to offer when you keep a customer-centric approach.

Keep these tips in mind when looking to generate leads with social CRM:

- ✓ **Relevancy:** Once you've identified an opportunity to engage, be sure that your response truly is relevant to the conversation and not just loaded with your own agenda.

- ✓ **Intent:** Enter the conversation with the intent to help solve a problem, not sell a product.

- ✓ **Timeliness:** Messages are short-lived on Twitter and Facebook (a matter of minutes.) You need to seize your opportunity in the real-time moment and let missed opportunities be missed. Coming to the party late isn't quite fashionable in these online social occasions.

Converting leads into customers

The speed at which you can turn a lead into an actual customer increases with social CRM. Mainly, you've identified where and how your customers prefer to interact. Also, you've learned a great deal more about your customers personally by engaging with them on a social level.

These new layers of customer (or potential customer) relationships empower your sales team to tailor its approach to customers. People buy from people they like. Customer-centric social CRM strategies help build trust and rapport to turn leads into actual customers, speeding up your pipeline.

Identify the customers' need/pain and offer them a relevant, helpful solution. Then you've earned the right to ask for the transaction or desired outcome that benefits both the customer and your brand.

Reducing customer support costs

Social media users have a lower tolerance for bad service, and these customers tell others about their experiences. An American Express study (the 2012 American Express Global Customer Service Barometer) showed that social media users tell 67 percent more people about their experiences (good or bad) than they did in 2011.

So customer support is a big deal, right? These social customers also like self-service support online, which can reduce your customer support costs. First, you have to identify your customers' most requested information and common trends related to your brand. Before investing in a whole new software suite, determine if your business infrastructure is in place to handle the changes. Evaluating how social CRM will address your customer service needs can bring opportunities to the forefront. Remember that social CRM is strategy and philosophy supported by software and technologies. Getting the right infrastructure in place to have productive interactions with your customer will prove to make your next social CRM-related technology purchase a wise investment.

Identifying innovative ideas

Who better to help create your brand's next great thing than the people who already know, love, and champion you? Social CRM's customer centricity identifies innovative ideas when your ears are to the ground. Consider the following on how to *crowdsource* (gather information from a crowd) innovative ideas from the social landscape:

- ✔ **Listen and observe.**
  - *What do your customers like about your brand?*
  - *What have your customers identified as areas for improvement?*
- ✔ **Keep an eye on the competition.**
  - *Have the competition's customers commonly posed questions about the same feature over and over again?*
  - *What are the favorite characteristics of your competition's brand that fans are chatting about in social media?*
- ✔ **Ask for the ideas.**
  - *Are customers using your products in creative ways?*
  - *Have your customers modified or enhanced your product on their own?*

Watch for images and photos of your brand on sites like Pinterest (http:// pinterest.com) to see how customers are using your product. You can also establish your photo contest on Facebook or Twitter, showcasing creative uses.

Chapter 3

Overcoming Challenges to Social CRM

In This Chapter

▶ Tapping into social CRM best practices

▶ Preparing a plan of action

▶ Setting goals for a social CRM program

Clearly, there are many benefits to using social CRM to gain more information about customers. However, this new information can lead to other challenges that you must be prepared to face.

Adapting to this flood of information can be overwhelming. A company must make organizational, technological, and strategic shifts to fully integrate social CRM into an organization of any size. As a fairly new process for businesses, social CRM guidelines are still being developed. In this chapter, we outline current challenges in social CRM and provide best practices for overcoming these obstacles.

Understanding the Challenges of Social CRM

One of the biggest challenges in social CRM is the speed at which new technology, communication channels, and customers adapt to each other. Social CRM is a major shift in the way companies perceive and interact with customers. Monitoring technology can't always keep up with changes and additions to social media platforms, and we can't always predict customer adoption and use patterns of new social media channels. Frankly, we don't *know* what we don't know until we experience it personally.

Integrating social CRM into your organization requires flexibility as both businesses and customers adjust and adapt to the social CRM process. Here, we identify some of the most common challenges you may face. Later on, we provide strategies for preparing for and overcoming these challenges.

Here are the top five challenges of social CRM:

- ✔ **Creating a company-wide shift to customer centricity.** If your organization isn't used to focusing on customers, adjusting to social CRM can take some time. This is especially true for larger companies. In the following sections, we outline how to get everyone on board with the social CRM philosophy. In Chapter 13, we will explore how to integrate social CRM into your company's ecosystem.

- ✔ **Accepting that reaping the benefits of social CRM requires patience.** It's easy to get excited about new processes and systems to help grow your business. Just keep in mind that as with most things, social CRM isn't a quick fix or overnight system shift. It takes time to collect data, train employees, and help customers adjust to a new way of interacting with your organization. Have patience and faith that you'll see the benefits of social CRM soon — just not the very first day you implement it.

- ✔ **Sifting through the overload of information generated in social media.** Social CRM provides more data than most organizations could ever want or need, and that isn't necessarily a good thing. Knowledge is power, but only if you can easily access it and know what to do with it. Determining what's valuable enough to add to a social CRM system and what you can ignore presents a challenge to many organizations. We cover this briefly in this chapter, as well as more in-depth in Chapter 14.

- ✔ **Meeting customers in media that your company doesn't own.** Most executives have to adjust their thinking to adjust to utilizing communication channels outside of their company's own online real estate. Company websites and toll-free numbers are safer, but that isn't necessarily where your customers are. They're using Facebook, Twitter, and whatever the next social media technology may be. For social CRM to be successful, you need to go where the customers are.

- ✔ **Adjusting brand-speak to actual conversations.** Customers don't respond well to industry and company jargon. Many brands struggle to speak to customers in a language that customers understand, but corporate speak won't fly on Facebook. A conversational tone is key when you're communicating through social media, where customers also chat with their friends.

Establishing Best Practices and Guidelines

Every customer or group of customers is unique. Couple that with the fact that each brand approaches social media differently, and it becomes difficult to define hard-set best practices for all businesses. This can be frustrating for business leaders who have long loved sets of rules that can apply to all. In social CRM, those ideas are thrown aside, leaving brand leaders grasping for examples of mapped success.

What worked for one brand or business may not work for the next in social strategies. To establish best practices, you must know your brand's audience. This means understanding the following about your audience:

- ✔ Preference for communication
- ✔ Threshold for humor
- ✔ Motivations for interaction with a brand

For example, both Arizona Iced Tea and Red Bull are canned, caffeinated, and nonalcoholic beverages. Though a small segment of both brand's audience overlaps, each has customers that vary greatly. Attempting to apply social media strategies that work well for Red Bull's rowdy, energetic customers probably would turn off many of Arizona Iced Tea's loyal drinkers. Each brand's customers require different messages to get them to engage with a brand. The technology is often the same between many audiences — most people use Facebook, Twitter, Foursquare, blogs, and so on. However, the strategy and messaging must vary greatly. Blanketed messaging is doomed to fail.

As you develop the best practices and guidelines that suit your customers, remember that the end result has to be quality conversations with social consumers, not a transaction. Social CRM best practices are based on listening to customers' preferences and then adjusting brand messages to better reach them — and then listening again. For more help with developing internal policies for engagement, flip to Chapter 13.

Building a Social CRM Team

Before drawing out a plan on paper, take stock of what you have available to dedicate to implementing a plan of social CRM attack. What resources — such as personnel, budget, and existing technologies — do you have available to tackle establishing an integrated social CRM strategy and plan? Your plan can be as small or large scale as you want it, limited (of course) by your resources. You can also adjust and expand it as you dig into how the social CRM philosophy will affect your day-to-day business. The important thing is that you make a start.

Work with what you have and what you can comfortably add to the mix. Here are some organizational questions to ask before developing a central plan and procedures:

- ✔ Who will lead the social CRM implementation?
- ✔ How many additional team members can we add to the team?
- ✔ How many hours can each team member commit each week to the new project?
- ✔ Who will communicate the new procedures to the whole organization, departments, and individual team members?
- ✔ Which departments are the main internal stakeholders for social CRM strategies?

Building an infrastructure to implement and manage a social CRM strategy will pay off greatly in the long run. Also, identifying an owner for the social CRM implementation and maintenance will help to create urgency, accountability, and follow-up for updates and analysis. Approaching this new social business philosophy requires patience and long-term planning. You need to put procedures in place throughout each department to support the overall organizational goal of becoming a truly social business, embracing new technologies.

Training Your Employees

It's extremely important that all employees understand the purpose of implementing social CRM within their systems and daily procedures. The social aspect of customer communication is the key to the future of the business. Getting everyone on board to shift the focus to social business will take training.

Social CRM is all about the customer. We'll remind you of that again and probably again a few more times. Your employees are your internal customer when it comes to social CRM. Providing them with clear benefits for a social CRM system may limit the resistance you meet.

The challenging part about training employees on a new social CRM system is that it's two-part training:

✔ **Understanding the social customer:** Employees must know the social customer to engage the social customer. Learning consumers' communication preferences is vital to social CRM success, and you must train employees well in this area.

✔ **Embracing the new technology:** Inevitably, some individuals resist social media monitoring. Getting your employees to buy into social business is key to convincing them to embrace the software solution you choose. As with any data system, what you get out of it is only as good as what you put into it. It's crucial that your staff is universally trained on expectations for data entry and the like.

We dig deeper into employee training in Chapter 13, but it's important to begin thinking about who should manage your social CRM now. Keep them in mind as you read through this book.

Prioritizing Activities and Resources

In order to build a sustainable and scalable social CRM program, you must prioritize activities with dedicated resources in mind. We've talked a lot about the philosophy of social CRM, social business, and the social customer. Also, we've reiterated that an approach to this new philosophy requires patience for long-term outcomes. You're building relationships, not just grabbing for transactions.

Implementing a social CRM system doesn't have to overwhelm your organization's resources or budget. It requires some prioritizing in order to start. Determine the best place to spend your time and money by considering what your customers are showing you. The following questions can help you start prioritizing tasks associated with implementing your social CRM plan:

✔ **What are the top five social media channels that reach your audience?** It isn't possible to actively engage on every social media site, so take stock of where the majority of your customers already are, and follow them there. This will likely include well-known sites like Twitter and Facebook, but you may be surprised to find other niche networks as well. Don't be afraid to join these, even if they aren't mainstream — they could end up being a better fit for your brand.

✔ **When do your customers interact most regularly throughout the day?** You might think that your customers check social media first thing in the morning, but step back and get inside their heads for a moment. Are they at work? Driving kids to school? They may prefer to engage with your brand in off hours. Experiment with different times to publish content, and don't feel confined to traditional office hours.

✔ **Within your organization, who interacts the most with your customers?** If it isn't the same team responsible for social CRM, find these people. Talk to them. Chances are that they'll have great customer insight. Knowing the most common questions they're asked can help you better prepare the social team.

✔ **Where have you identified a need to expand your social media strategies?** Look at what competitors are doing, as well as brands you'd like to emulate, and then make sure that you have a real need to take on a new task or expand into a certain site — don't go there just because it's what everyone else is doing. For instance, if you primarily create text-heavy white papers, Instagram or other photo sites may not be for you.

✔ **Are niche social networking sites reaching your ideal customer?** Smaller, targeted sites can be great, but only if your customers are actually on them. Beware of sites that are too niche. Sometimes, Facebook really is the best place to be based on sheer numbers alone.

✔ **How are your customers engaging socially?** Notice whether they're asking questions or perhaps commenting on a particular type of content more often?

For instance, if you discover that your photographs attract more interactions than other types of content, dedicate staff who can capture more, interesting photos. Or perhaps your audience engages with product updates or how-tos. Begin analyzing your current social media content to look for patterns of response and engagement, and build on what you find. Adapt to your customers' desires by providing more of the content they engage with or share, and phasing out posts that don't elicit a response.

After considering these questions, brainstorm and ask numerous questions to determine how your resources will be best put to use in social CRM.

Establishing Your Social CRM Goals

Even though we keep saying that you'll see social CRM's benefits over time, not overnight, you should still establish goals for a long-term strategy.

Here's the main question: Why do you want a social media and social CRM strategy?

Your strategy will vary drastically depending on how you answer that question, and your answer might lean toward one of these two approaches to social media:

- ✔ **Relational:** If your answer is something like this, "We want to improve our communication with our customer and enhance our support offerings," you have more of a relational approach to social media.

- ✔ **Transactional:** If your answer is something like this, "We want to leverage social media as a marketing tool to drive more business," you have more of a transactional approach to social media.

We believe that social CRM is about interactions — relationships more so than transactions. If you make improving customer communication a priority, transactional business objectives will naturally follow. Lead with customer service goals, and sales will follow. With social CRM, customer support and marketing go hand in hand. If you lean toward the transactional approach, keep that in mind as you read this book and think about how you can shift your focus.

Keep in mind that social CRM is still evolving. Take time to plan out your goals, using what you've learned from past marketing initiatives and business strategies, and don't set yourself up for disappointment with unrealistic goals. The goals that follow provide a good starting point, and we clarify them further throughout this book.

- ✔ **Get employees on board.** Inspiring your employees with your new social business model should be your first priority. Take the time to provide proper training, and make sure your employees fully understand the value of social CRM and what it means for the organization. They should view social CRM as an exciting new opportunity, not a chore they must perform. Chapter 12 can also help with this.

- ✔ **Listen to customer feedback.** Make sure you're really listening to your customers' feedback, not just monitoring conversations. Set goals about what you want to do with the information you collect. Think about how you will use it to improve your organization and customers' interactions with you, both online and off. Chapter 4 explores this in greater detail.

- ✔ **Start social conversations.** Don't just wait for customers to come to you. Strike up conversations with them first! This can greatly improve customer perception and interaction with your brand. The more conversations you start, the more you have, which means more data for you to learn from. Chapter 7 includes many ideas for starting and building social conversations.

- ✔ **Collect social data.** One of the great benefits of social CRM is that it helps you segment your audience. You can easily identify who opens e-mails, clicks your Facebook ads, replies to your tweets, and comments on your blog posts. Collect, filter, and apply that data to better reach your customers where and how they want to be reached. In Chapter 14, we explain data collection and measurement in greater detail.

These are all realistic goals initially. As you learn your own best practices, you can then establish more goals. Just keep in mind that in order to establish clear goals, you need a full picture of your audience. Start with basic goals to gather this information, and refine from there.

Keep your goals flexible. You may find that they change as social media platforms evolve or your business grows. Create goals you can build on. For instance, a goal of replying to 25 percent of social conversations may be a great starting point, but you should revisit it periodically and aim for higher percentages. Let your goals grow with your organization, and with social media as a whole.

The social CRM process of a business consultant extraordinaire

Brian Vellmure, principal and cofounder of management consulting firm Initium, outlines his process for creating a customer-centric social CRM and the opportunities it presents. (Chapters 4 and 9 expand on his ideas.) Social CRM is a five-step process, as follows:

1. **Understand who your customers are, what they value, who they interact with. Segmentation plays a key role here.**

2. **Find out how they interact and set a plan to engage with them in the context of their preferred communication channel(s).**

3. **Focus on communicating with them in a way that is relevant and helpful in assisting them to achieve their goals.**

4. **Present and/or create or co-create new products or services that help them accomplish (or do better) the jobs they are trying to do.**

5. **And finally, deepen the value of your relationship over time by repeating the cycle over and over again.**

This basic process should be at the core of any customer-focused strategy. Social media doesn't change these ideas. However, here are five ways that your organization can leverage social technologies during this process:

✔ Use social analytics and social network analysis to better understand your customers and prospects. Aggregate demographic, psychographic, and socialgraphic data.

✔ Use listening and monitoring tools to extend reach beyond where and how you've been able to listen and engage before. Add social as an additional interaction channel.

✔ Capitalize on new social media platforms by being the first to try out new sites. This allows you to communicate in new and/or more relevant ways with your customers. Align your business with emerging social media sites before your competitors do.

✔ Utilize internal communications systems within your organization to streamline information, product developments, and service developments to all employees. This could be through a company newsletter, closed social media site, or other messaging platform your company chooses to use. For more ideas, turn to Chapter 13.

✔ Increase engagement with existing customers on new channels in a way for the world to watch and observe. Be everywhere your customers are and enable them to share what they love (or don't love) about you to their networks.

Chapter 4

Courting the Social Customer

. . . .

. . . .

The entire social CRM world revolves around the social customer, and it's this social customer who led corporations into the new paradigm of social business. Consumers are more educated, savvy, demanding, and active than ever before. Businesses must adapt to meet the needs of these social customers.

Empowered with a network of knowledge, the social customer has forever changed the way business is conducted. Businesses need a strategy to harness the buying power of consumers online. In this chapter, you get a clearer picture of the who, what, when, where, and how of social customers. You learn about their habits and communication methods. This knowledge is essential to building a strategy to reach social customers.

We discuss the media that social customers use and how they use them. This chapter also provides insight into social motivations and behaviors so that you can better approach social customers and ultimately earn their trust to do business together.

Exploring the Habits of the Social Customer

Facebook's rapid growth caught many businesses off guard. "Hey, I guess we need a Facebook page," echoed across quite a few marketing departments. Then it was, "Jon in IT says there's a whole lot of chatter on Twitter." It seems there's always a new social media platform to explore, but without an understanding of these social media sites and a strategy for utilizing them, businesses are lost. Misguided social pages can be found across the web. Many businesses have been merely reacting to the phenomenon of customers gaining control of the marketplace and media, learning as they go, but they were missing an understanding of the evolving social customer. Here are some questions that might have remained unanswered for these businesses, including yours:

✔ Who are these people, demographically speaking?

✔ What interests these customers most?

✔ When does this social customer engage online?

✔ Where are *your* customers?

✔ How are consumers engaging with one another in new media?

Enterprise didn't and still doesn't control the multiple channels where the social customer is influencing business. Taking a look at consumers' habits gives businesses — enterprise and small alike — a chance to be in the middle of the social conversation.

Looking at customers' buying patterns

Marketers have long thought that consumers gathered several brands for consideration and then went through a narrowing-down process until one brand remained for actual purchase.

However, a consumer's decision-making and buying process includes far more than a bucket of options to buy. Today, consumers don't just narrow down their buying options. They add and eliminate brands during a longer period of consideration. After they make a purchase, customers' brand loyalty depends on their experience with the product and the company they purchased from or that made the product. Customers are comfortable terminating their relationship with a brand at any time. Also, throughout this process, consumers share their experiences with their social networks online.

Understanding how customers use mobile devices

Information sharing takes place in real time. It takes just a few seconds to post to Facebook, Twitter, or any other social network. With the growing number of mobile devices and smartphones, consumers have an enormous amount of data at their fingertips. More inclined to search the web straight from a mobile device or fire up an app, today's mobile consumer rarely picks up the phone to talk directly with anyone for information-gathering purposes.

Meeting social customers where they interact claims a crucial element of social CRM, and more and more, they're using mobile devices for those interactions, as follows:

- ✔ Consumers post, tweet, pin, blog, e-mail, and text from wherever they happen to be at that moment.
- ✔ Consumers rely on their mobile devices to make educated buying decisions on the fly, often instead of asking a live salesperson for help. According to a study from Google, conducted by independent market research firm Ipsos OTX, 79 percent of those with a smartphone use their mobile device to help with shopping, and 70 percent use the smartphone for help while in the store.

Having all this information constantly available in real time empowers today's consumers. Here's a quick list of a few ways that social customers use mobile devices in the buying process:

- ✔ Connect to their social network for recommendations.
- ✔ Find store information.
- ✔ Obtain and redeem coupon offers.
- ✔ Compare prices.
- ✔ Check for item availability.
- ✔ Read store and product reviews.

Mobile consumers use their devices to locate stores, restaurants, movies, and other services nearby. According the same Google study mentioned previously, 9 out of 10 smartphone users took action based on a mobile search. Smartphones make smarter shoppers. Meeting customers on their mobile devices gives you a more targeted shot at a transaction.

Think about your business, and how consumers are likely to use their phones in relation to your product or service. How can you improve on that experience? The answer may be an app, a mobile-enhanced website, or a more aggressive presence on existing mobile apps like Yelp, Foursquare, and so on. Conduct market research to see what consumers are already doing, and find out where there's a hole in the mobile market that you can fill.

Understanding the change in advertising

Individuals, not businesses, control much of the way advertising is consumed today. TV watchers can fast-forward through recorded advertisements when watching recorded shows. Mobile users can skip ads on games. Today's empowered consumers demand that ads offer attention-grabbing content, creativity, and innovation.

People still read the newspaper, watch television, and listen to the radio. Advertisers still advertise in traditional media, and many consumers still respond to those advertisements — but it isn't always the response you expect. Traditional ads often prompt the social consumer to conduct mobile searches or connect to their online social network for information. Advertising is still alive and well, but it's very different from what it was even a few years ago. A print ad is no longer a single entity. It's tied to your digital and mobile presence as well.

Permission-based advertising grows as consumers become fed up with intrusive ads. E-mail marketing laws have led the way for opt-in advertising. The good news is that this shift to consumer-empowered advertising offers more targeted messaging opportunities. Advertisers can segment audiences and hyper-focus ads to cater to individuals' preferred methods of receiving marketing messaging.

As technologies evolve and change, advertisers have to adjust quickly to stay in front of the right audiences. Channels like YouTube and Facebook empower DIY-style advertising for low budgets and high creativity. Advertisers need to tailor ads to be more personal and highly innovative to capture today's social customer.

On social networks, customers provide a wealth of information. They willingly volunteer information about their interests, relationship, workplace, and more. All this data is available for your brand to use — you just need to put it into action.

By matching psychographics (interests) with demographics (age, gender, and so on), you can finely tune your advertising strategy to reach unique segments of customers and speak to them in relevant ways. These hyper-targeted ads break through the clutter because they seem to be speaking directly to the individual customer instead of a wide range of audiences.

Recognizing how customers use social media

At the heart of social media is being social. That may sound silly to read or hear, but it's surprising how many businesses miss that point. The social customer accesses social media to connect with family and friends, seek out old friends, and make new relationships.

Often, a need for entertainment motivates social users to get online or open an app on their mobile device. Mostly, their attention is focused on the social network they're interacting with. They're alone and looking for something to grab their attention. If you plan carefully, that something may be your content, but keep in mind that a customer's primary goal isn't to view your ad. Social customers are looking, first and foremost, for human, social connections, tapping into their established networks for advice, suggestions, and recommendations. They also vent, rant, and share honest opinions through multiple channels. They may also seek product reviews and customer feedback, or offer up their own opinions. All these actions are social in nature, even if they involve your brand.

When your brand provides value in this social context, social media offers a place for your business. Consumers search social media for tangible value, such as coupons, discounts, and so on. The upcoming sections of this chapter discuss how you can influence and interact with your customers.

Influencing the Social Customer

In order to influence this new type of customer, you have to give customers what they want. Remember the social customer is empowered with knowledge. Relevancy presents the key to influencing these consumers.

Keep in mind that roughly 84 percent of a Facebook page's fans are already current or past customers. This will help you craft a more relevant approach to your social messages. Getting customers to share your content needs to be your ultimate goal, not trying to upsell them. Yes, you can sell on Facebook, but your efforts will seem hollow given the social nature of the site. Quality over quantity rings true with everything about Facebook. Having one hundred engaged fans weighs more than 1,000 fans that never share your content or return to your page.

Providing relevant content to your fan base will be the only way to mobilize them to start talking about your brand to their friends. Social CRM is about managing conversation — not about managing the customer. In the new world of social CRM, the customer is in charge. Customer-centric strategies will be your only hope for influencing conversation that actually benefits your brand. To help you craft what customer centric might mean to your business, the following sections explore why people share content and how to make your brand's content more worthy of sharing.

Knowing why people share

Word-of-mouth nods on social networking sites create strong conversion opportunities, but only a very small segment of your customers will interact with your business on Facebook. Facebook recommends aiming to convert 10 percent of your real-life customers into Facebook fans. Though that number seems low, remember it's about quality not quantity. You have to remember what your business posts are up against. Your status updates fall into a Facebook user's timeline alongside updates from their mother, brother, sister, daughter, and best friend. The relationships with those people are likely to run deeper than with any business or brand.

Again, we have to remember all things in a social CRM strategy must remain customer centric. You have to give consumers content that rivals the deep connections of personal relationships that draw them to use social media in the first place. It makes them feel something, and feel strongly enough that they want others to see it.

Creating content that people want to share

Using your own personal experience on Facebook, Twitter, and other social networks makes considering your audience's motivations seem less mystical or mysterious. You're a consumer, too. Tap into your own habits to know why others share. Here are a few questions to ask yourself that may help generate share-worthy content:

- Which content have you found compelling enough to share?

- What motivates you to take action on a post?

- What irritates you most on social media platforms?

- What types of sharing and commenting actions are you most likely to take on social media platforms?

Interactive content lends itself to, well, interaction. Motivating your fans, followers, and subscribers to interact with content and then share is more likely with photo contests, videos, polls, and questions — content that makes them feel something. Earlier in this chapter, we talk about offers and discounts motivating people to engage with your brand online. Give them a good deal and encourage them to share it or even incentivize them to do so. We've told you that's why they're looking, so delight them with what they want.

Sharing the recommendation

When Facebook users initially click Like on your page, you can prompt them to recommend your page to their friends. The same is true with Facebook Ads and other content. If you get a recommendation, they like you. They really like you!

A recommendation is a high form — if not the highest — of desired gestures from a Facebook fan. It requires consideration and significant action on the part of the user. Clicking Like on a Facebook page or ad is relatively effortless. Do you know how many pages you've liked on Facebook? Take a quick guess, without looking, and then compare your guess to the actual number. Chances are it's far more than you guessed, and that's true for most consumers. The average Facebook user likes about 80 pages. Clicking Like once is easy. Engaging and recommending is much harder.

How many of those pages did you recommend to your friends (or even visit in the last six months)? Sharing recommendations takes extra steps and effort and indicates a deeper level of engagement. Your content has to be pretty compelling to elicit that gesture. Keep that in mind when crafting messaging.

Talking to the Social Customer

Perhaps this section should be titled "Talking *with* the Social Customer." No one really likes to be talked at with a bullhorn. Listening and responding appropriately is what makes conversation an art. You have to adapt your messages to what your customers want to hear.

Armed with knowledge, the social customer requires a relevancy in social messaging. This digital diva of a customer wants offers, discounts, apologies, recognition, recommendations, more information, transparency, and entertainment. It takes a shift in the mindset of a business to reach this customer.

It's all about the customer. To implement a successful social CRM strategy, we all just have to accept that fact and grow to love it. This customer wants to be wowed, courted, heard, understood, and appreciated. Don't we all? Think of your own dating experiences and what you did to keep the attention of your would-be sweetheart. You put on your best behavior, crafted exciting outings, and cleaned up real nice. You listened to what he or she had to say about the past and future. You processed the new data and came up with a plan to win his or her heart forever.

Marketing to social customers closely resembles that courtship, but you probably didn't provide a list of features and benefits and ramble off the reasons for a second date. With social customers, you have to listen and react accordingly. Fortunately, social customers are forthright regarding what they want and don't want. Mirroring social customers' behavior can win trust. Tell them upfront what a relationship with you will entail. Show them that you're listening and help them when they least expect it. And give them gifts.

Taking marketing beyond messaging

If the social customer is in control — and he/she is — marketing has to be more than brand speak that's aimed at the customer. Social CRM, social business, and the social customer revolve around conversations that build trust. An ideal result from that trust is brand loyalty, but you've got to earn it. And today's social customer is going to make you work for it. Traditional marketing messaging isn't enough to gain that trust.

Social CRM is a philosophy and strategy. Customer centricity, when it's true and authentic, drives success in social CRM. That customer focus must reside deep in an organization, in every department. You have to convince every employee who carries responsibility for your brand to hop on board, to live and breathe this strategy. Tailored messaging can come through in the social world, but at the heart of the message you must incorporate tactics like the following:

- ✔ **Building relationships:** Transactions no longer act as the only desired result of engaging with customers in social media. Generating fans and advocates based on trust represents business done well with the social customer.

- ✔ **Solving customer issues:** Helping your customers on the social stage, with their friends and network watching, places you in the well-earned spotlight. Truly thinking of how you can assist your customer makes for a natural way to build trust and a fan.

✔ **Entertaining:** If you can provide content that evokes an emotion, you'll likely gain shares and word-of-mouth action. The social customer demands creative and attention-grabbing content.

✔ **Offering incentives:** As mentioned earlier in this chapter, people sometimes engage with your brand because they want to see if they can find a deal. When you can provide a discount or incentive, you're giving your customers what they want. That's a good thing.

Adding value for your customer up front

Offering incentives marks a significant piece of social business. The social customer has told enterprise through many studies that they want coupons, discounts, and incentives. So why do so many businesses avoid it? Perhaps it's because traditional messaging is just a habit that dies hard.

Permission-based marketing harnesses a captive audience of people who actually want to hear what you have to say. The empowered social customer can easily ignore marketing today. On Facebook, users can click an ad to remove it, as shown in Figure 4-1. Facebook then asks the user why he no longer wants to see the ad and requests information on what the user would prefer to see. That's power in the hands of the consumer.

Figure 4-1: Facebook gives advertising power to the individual user.

More and more information is becoming available about your customers' online behaviors. The unfortunate side effect is that many of them feel a bit exposed. When people feel like a target or number to be gathered, they tend to tread more lightly toward an interaction. If you can present your business like an open book with no secrets to hide, you can help the leery customers take the next step toward engagement.

Try messages like the following to add up-front value for the social customer:

- "When you like our page, you'll receive weekly coupons."
- "For up-to-date product information, follow us on Twitter."
- "We'll be running daily photo contests on our Facebook page. Great prizes await!"

Providing customer service they didn't expect

Some of the greatest social media success stories arise from unexpected, personalized customer service. One of the best examples — and one that's maybe a bit over the top — took place on Twitter, with Morton's steak house. Author Peter Shankman cried out in a tweet (shown in Figure 4-2) for a porterhouse steak amidst his weary travels through multiple airports. To his surprise, Morton's sent a representative to meet up with Shankman's arranged driver and deliver to Shankman a steak dinner, sides, and tableware. Shankman of course tweeted out the super delivery (shown in Figure 4-3) to his 10,000 Twitter followers. Big win for Morton's!

Granted, Shankman wrote a book on customer service and has an advantageous audience for any brand. However, Morton's steak house had to be listening to its social customers to realize the awesome opportunity in front of it. Small business and enterprise alike can hear opportunities to wow customers when they're primed to listen.

home, I wouldn't have time to stop for dinner anywhere, and certainly didn't want to grab fast food at either airport. When I got on the plane, my stomach was a rumbling a bit, and I had visions of a steak in my head.

As I've tweeted and mentioned countless times before, I'm a bit of a steak lover. I go out of my way to try steakhouses all around the world when I can, and it's one of the reasons, no doubt, that my trainer at my gym is kept in business. But it's all good – give and take. Over the past few years, I've developed an affinity for Morton's Steakhouses, and if I'm doing business in a city which has one, I'll try to schedule a dinner there if I can. I'm a frequent diner, and Morton's knows it. They have a spectacular Customer Relations Management system in place, as well as a spectacular social media team, and they know when I call from my mobile number who I am, and that I eat at their restaurants regularly. Never underestimate the value of a good CRM system.

Back to my flight. As we were about to take off, I jokingly tweeted the following:

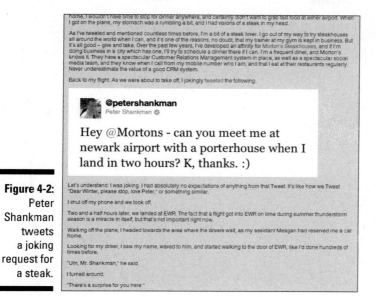

> **@petershankman**
> Peter Shankman ✔
>
> Hey @Mortons - can you meet me at newark airport with a porterhouse when I land in two hours? K, thanks. :)

Let's understand: I was joking. I had absolutely no expectations of anything from that Tweet. It's like how we Tweet "Dear Winter, please stop, love Peter," or something similar.

I shut off my phone and we took off.

Two and a half hours later, we landed at EWR. The fact that a flight got into EWR on time during summer thunderstorm season is a miracle in itself, but that's not important right now.

Walking off the plane, I headed towards the area where the drivers wait, as my assistant Meagan had reserved me a car home.

Looking for my driver, I saw my name, waved to him, and started walking to the door of EWR, like I'd done hundreds of times before.

"Um, Mr. Shankman," he said.

I turned around.

"There's a surprise for you here."

Figure 4-2:
Peter Shankman tweets a joking request for a steak.

As I say in my book over and over again, customer service is no longer about telling people how great you are. It's about producing amazing moments in time, and letting those moments become the focal point of how amazing you are, told not by you, but by the customer who you thrilled. They tell their friends, and the trust level goes up at a factor of a thousand. Think about it: Who do you trust more? An advertisement, or a friend telling you how awesome something is?

Of course, I immediately tweeted out what happened:

> **@petershankman**
> Peter Shankman ✔
>
> Oh. My. God. I don't believe it. @mortons showed up at EWR WITH A PORTERHOUSE! lockerz.com/s/130578715 # OMFG!

And sure enough, Twitter lit up like a bottle rocket. Click the image to expand it, it's worth reading.

Figure 4-3:
Steak surprise.

Part II

Building Your Social CRM Strategy

The 5th Wave — By Rich Tennant

"I'd respond to this person's comment on Twitter, but I'm a former Marine, Bernard, and a Marine never retweets."

In this part. . .

Part II is where you start figuring out how to apply social CRM ideas to your business. You find tips for choosing a person to lead your social CRM initiatives. You find guides for handling the changes social CRM will bring to key groups within your business: marketing, sales, and customer service. We also take you on a whirlwind tour of social media platforms and tools. This tour can help you understand what's available beyond Facebook and Twitter and what social sites might be a good fit for your business's social CRM strategy. In addition to social media sites themselves, you learn how social CRM can help you create or improve your customer loyalty program and how social CRM enables you to reach out to customers on mobile devices.

Chapter 5

Establishing the New Social Business Model

Creating an infrastructure to embrace the social business requires a general to lead the charge for cultural change within any organization — no matter the business size. Whether you appoint a C-level social officer or a social media specialist, you need someone to drive and motivate the social business model. You have to look at processes and roles that touch the customer experience and prepare for a major shift in the way you do business. To really get into the social game, your organization must establish an operational model to cater to the social experience, internally and externally.

The social business model goes way beyond social media monitoring and responding to customers via social channels, though those are key elements to social CRM. Monitoring will be rendered worthless unless you establish strategic processes to turn your findings into valuable insights worth turning into an actionable approach. Customer-created content continues to proliferate, and you need to get ahead of the messages, not just respond to what's being crafted.

This chapter explores what really drives the social customer's experience and what internal and external factors play into what you can and can't control. Well within any organization's means is the ability to identify and empower a role to drive and manage your social business model and its key elements, including social media strategy, processes, training, guidelines, and so on. You need a framework. A new social business plan affects the entire company, and you'll need a leader to guide a scalable integration to your current systems.

Finding the Right Person to Lead the Way

For true social CRM success, identify a social leader to drive the cultural change from sales to experience, as shown in Figure 5-1. This organizational leader will coach, mentor, empower, and support the overall social business model being deployed within your organization. With a leader in place, you'll have a better chance of creating a consistent experience for your audiences and customers. The idea is to transform your business model and culture. Then leverage technologies to support that transformation. Ultimately, you're embracing a model that will foster more direct relationships with your customers.

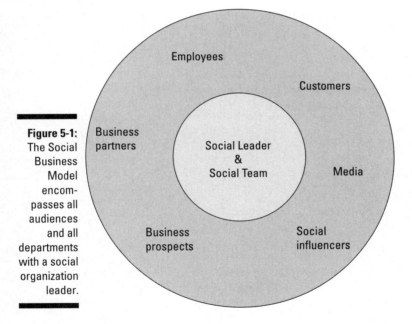

Figure 5-1:
The Social Business Model encompasses all audiences and all departments with a social organization leader.

Of course, the exact job description for this role varies by company and industry, but we can identify quite a few characteristics and skills required to be an effective social media leader:

- First and foremost, the candidate must be well-versed in all the social media platforms you currently use or are planning to join.

- The candidate should also have experience with tracking and analytics, and be open to the idea of proving social ROI and providing measurable results for campaigns.

✔ In order to lead your whole organization, your social media leader must be able to clearly communicate the benefits of social media within the organization.

✔ Additionally, the leader must be prepared to explain how each social platform works, and stay up to date on new advancements.

✔ Writing skills are essential for communicating quickly and clearly with customers, and the leader must be able to think on her feet. Social media conversations move at a rapid pace, so choose someone who can keep up.

✔ Finally, your social media leader must be well-versed in your brand, or a quick learner who's ready to jump right in and become an expert on your organization right away. Social CRM keeps brand leaders on their toes, so choose someone who can respond to customers quickly.

During the hiring process, don't be afraid to look at candidates' social media profiles and ask them about the brands they follow. Look for communications, advertising, marketing, public relations, or English majors, but don't discount other backgrounds. Prior experience is a plus, but make sure the candidate is ready to discard old habits and start fresh.

Defining Processes That Yield Insights

A social business model is driven by customers having and driving the experience with your brand. As a brand representative, you aid in moving the conversation forward, and these customer interactions altogether create an all-encompassing experience. With customer experience directing the model, you're adopting an outside-in customer approach. Your customers infiltrate your overall operating model.

But what does that operating model look like? Although each industry has variations, the following basic steps outline how to involve your customers in conversations that you can learn from:

1. **Identify the social networks on which your customers interact.**

   This will likely include the usual suspects — Facebook, Twitter, and Foursquare — but don't discount newer sites like Google+ and Pinterest, or Yelp and other review sites or forums. There are niche sites for quite a few industries as well. For instance, those in the travel industry should look at TripAdvisor and FlyerTalk. Identify a few of these more narrowly focused sites and see if your audience is active there.

2. **Listen to what customers are saying about you.**

   Before you start addressing your customers (and potential customers), listen up. What are their complaints with your business? Do they have any suggestions for improvement? And what do they love about you? Identify their pain points and favorite features to see how you can begin to give them what they want, and continue to deliver what they already enjoy.

A great way to get a feel for customer sentiment is to search Twitter for your brand name (not just your username). You can identify general themes pretty quickly. Write them down, and then do a search for broader keywords and competitors. For example, representatives for a pizza place would first search for their restaurant's name, then search for pizza and their city or state, and, finally, search Twitter for local competitor pizza chains.

3. Join the conversation.

Your Facebook, YouTube, and Twitter audience are mostly previous or current customers who like your brand. You need to evolve your typical marketing approaches into conversations to really interact with this audience. Begin by answering questions and providing suggestions to customers who are already talking about your brand. Using the search method outlined in Step 2, you can find people who are addressing you directly, as well as those who are mentioning you in passing. When replying to questions feels natural, you can begin guiding the conversation by asking questions yourself, and posting content designed to grow the conversation around your brand.

To brainstorm content around your brand, organize a meeting with many different departments within your organization. Ask attendees to write down the questions they're asked most often about your brand, or the feedback they hear from customers. The more input you can get, from a variety of sources, the better.

4. Implement customer suggestions.

Now that you know where your audience is and what they're saying, it's time to take action. Take their pain points and find ways to address them, whether it's through content or actual organizational changes. If customers are confused by what time your business closes, or angry that it isn't later, try posting your hours more clearly in social media, or experiment with staying open later on certain days. And don't focus only on the negative. Look at what customers already love and build more conversations around that. If, for instance, customers say you make the coziest slippers, use those testimonials as retweets, challenge commenters to define just how cozy with a Facebook fill-in-the-blank update, or post photos showing your socks snuggled up by a fire.

Incorporating Social Into Your Company Branding

There are two social factors key to branding your business within the new business model: humanization and personalization. Too often, a brand representative thinks she must be a faceless entity without a personality — Brand X, not Mary at Brand X.

But it's hard to have a conversation with a brand; only people can truly communicate with each other. Humanize your brand and shape how it will grow and evolve by giving it a personality. Technology allows us to connect to friends, family, followers, fans, and subscribers in all corners of the world at any hour of the day. With all these conversations fighting for our attention, we must feel a connection to something before we're inspired to engage, and the best way to do this is to show a human side of your brand and demonstrate what's *really* going on behind the scenes.

We talk about courting the social customer in Chapter 4. Once you've established a connection, how are you going to maintain a mutually beneficial relationship with your customers? In order to successfully position your brand in social media, you have to be willing to look at your customer relationships in human terms, with consideration for issues like trust, emotional connection, respect, and so on. If your brand doesn't show willingness to evolve and change, it may get brushed to the side by consumers looking to have a personal connection with companies today. You have to stay relevant, and you can do that by humanizing your brand.

Showing your company's human side

Humanizing your brand is more than a new marketing ploy or effort. It falls in line with the major cultural changes we talk about throughout this book. Humanization is a deep, evolving characteristic necessary to stay in the social media game.

Information on the web is overflowing. In order to make your brand stand out, you must drive your brand the way you do personal relationships in your own life. This means talking the way your customers do, admitting mistakes, and having fun with the content you post. For instance, IKEA, a large furniture and home store, made its brand more human by taking its signature blue shopping bags and creating a fashion show around them, where the clothes were made entirely out of these bags. They then posted the photos on their Facebook page and asked fans to upload their own and vote for their favorite.

Community building inside and outside of the organization will help you keep moving forward in the new social business model. First, it's an inside job that starts with employees. Enable your human capital (your people, employees, coworkers) to tell the story of your brand to outside audiences such as customers, vendors, investors, partners, and so on.

A newer trend that might make traditional marketing professionals cringe — and for which consumers seem to have a growing affinity — is to share your brand's flaws. In order to be trustworthy, you have to be humble enough to let people know that you make mistakes (you're fallible). When appropriate, use humor when allowing your customers to see your weaker side. If the error is of a more serious nature, let your more empathetic side show and become helpful and resourceful.

A great example of this comes from The American Red Cross. An administrator of its Twitter account accidentally tweeted this from @RedCross instead of her personal account: "Ryan found two more 4 bottle packs of Dogfish Head's Midas Touch beer . . . when we drink we do it right #gettingslizzerd." The Red Cross quickly deleted the tweet and owned up to the mistake, tweeting this response: "We've deleted the rogue tweet but rest assured the Red Cross is sober and we've confiscated the keys." They went on to partner with Dogfish Head to drive donations.

People use social media platforms to call out their own flaws every day. A mom who found her toddler painting the walls with nail polish and a new college student who showed up the wrong class may quickly craft a post or tweet to poke fun at themselves. They broadcast their flaws and in turn are expecting your brand to the same. After all, "To err is human."

Just be careful you don't overdo it. Companies have been known to post pictures of their entire staff attending, for instance, a group picnic, only to receive angry posts from customers saying they can't get anyone on the phone because the whole company is out partying. So make clear to your social media representatives that after hours fun shouldn't get in the way of providing customer service.

Here are some tips to start building a culture-rich internal community that humanizes your brand:

- ✔ **Leverage the influence of your employees' personal networks.** Each one of your employees shares stories about your company to their friends, family, and social sphere of influence. Encourage this brand ambassadorship.

- ✔ **Listen to the stories being shared about your brand.** Through social media and social media monitoring tools like HootSuite and TweetDeck, you can track conversations about and mentions of your brand. Respond and engage in kind. Join the conversation.

✔ **Share your brand's stories across different channels.** Repurpose stories gathered from one channel or audience to a different channel or audience for integrated branding.

Discovering personalization

One of the most powerful ways a brand can connect with its customers is by allowing customers to play with the brand and make it their own. Here are some good examples:

✔ Coca-Cola shares fan stories on its Facebook Page, as do countless other brands.

✔ Lilly Pulitzer, a fashion brand, created an app where users could design a bedroom and enter to win all the products in the room.

✔ Paint company Benjamin Moore took this idea a step further, allowing customers to upload their own photos and then use Benjamin Moore's room builder tool to change paint colors and rearrange furniture in their own space.

Moving from digital to the real world, Starbucks may be the most successful case study of all case studies for just about any topic in marketing and business. Personalization is no exception. On the customer side, you approach a knowledgeable, friendly barista at Starbucks and get to hyper-customize your beverage. When your beverage is ready, a barista calls you by name and hands you the drink, reiterating your customized choices. That's personalization!

Your company can discover personalization opportunities without being a mega-brand. You have to go beyond just humanizing your brand and get in the same mindset as your customers to discover personalization opportunities. Consider hosting a focus group of customers, or start closer to home and ask employees to contribute ideas. Put aside the fact that you work for your organization for a moment, and think about what you, as a consumer, would want from a personalized experience with the company.

Measuring the Impact of the New Model

Anyone who takes on a new business venture or investment wants to know how to measure success. We talk a lot about how social CRM requires patience, with a focus on long-term goals and benefits. We hope that you can see the many benefits to be realized within the social business model — more deeply engaged customers, brand ambassadors, a wider understanding of customers and their motivators, and so on.

For actual measurement, you turn to the abundance of information and data that accompanies the swiftly growing and ever-changing technologies integrated into our daily lives. Knowledge-sharing through a multitude of social networking platforms increases our customers' impact on our business practices. Measuring the success of all this data and knowledge collection can prove challenging for any business, especially if the organization still holds onto the idea of old metrics for success. Social CRM success metrics need to be examined under a different lens, not the lens of CRM 1.0. Conversely, limiting social measurements only to information sharing or anecdotal engagement may miss the mark as well.

CRM 2.0 is just another way of saying social CRM. It's what CRM has evolved into with the proliferation of customer-driven social channels. The technology piece of social CRM focuses on centralizing all the extensive data generated in social media and turning it into efficient solutions to be used across your entire organization.

When your business implements a new social business model supported by social CRM software, you first determine the business-critical goals. These goals will guide the internal roles and infrastructure necessary to launch the cultural shift.

Take some time to determine what you want out of social CRM, generally, and how you can translate those desires into measurable goals, as we outline in these examples:

- ✔ **Improve customer service.** You might accomplish this by shortening your response time to within a certain number of hours.

- ✔ **Improve social reach.** Consider setting a goal of adding a certain percentage of fans to your social networks within a specific time period.

- ✔ **Gain brand awareness.** Tweak your content and strategy to reach a goal of receiving a set number of shares of your content within a month.

- ✔ **Grow sales.** Set up a system that can track sales associated with social media, and establish a goal to reach a certain percentage of those types of sales each month.

Track and measure your success and work toward your goals. Social CRM monitoring platforms can tell you how long your current response time is, as well as track the growth of your accounts and your reach. To track sales or leads, create dedicated e-mail addresses or landing pages for social media, as well as tracking clicks.

Engaging in Co-creation

Brand value isn't defined only by marketing people. Its value is *co-created* by many individuals, including consumers, employees, partners, and so on. The communities surrounding these individuals and varying stakeholders play a key part in co-creation of experience and ultimately value. Truly social businesses encourage social collaboration in every fabric of the business, especially amongst their employees.

Co-creative initiatives can start anywhere within your organization, including customer service, IT, HR, web development, and marketing. Each of these areas (and more) present experiences internally and externally. Tapping into different stakeholders through collaborative interactions can innovate new products, operational processes, and business strategies.

Starting with internal co-creation

Build a co-creation team, taking into account the strengths and weaknesses of your company's different departments, as illustrated in Table 5-1. Let the co-creation start with internal collaboration.

Table 5-1	Building a Co-Creation Team	
Role	*Positive Influence*	*Possible Hindrances*
Information technology	This department is often the frontline of change, through new software and application development. These team members are also accustomed to collaboration.	Some team members may be more familiar with technical experience and less in touch with the actual human experience.
Marketing and communications	Typically, this is the department closest to the customer experience.	Some of these team members may be less likely to co-collaborate with other departments because they're already the experts in customer experience.
Research and development	These folks are already very familiar with crowdsourcing for product and service innovations.	R&D looks outward for innovation and sometimes stumbles with collaborating internally.

If you have an internal customer service team, start the internal co-creation discussions with them. They'll have a wealth of knowledge on what customers do, like, and ask about. Then move to the marketing team, who will be full of creative ideas and suggestions they've wanted to try. But don't ignore other departments — you never know where a great idea will strike.

Aggregating information

Market research turns into an ever-evolving creative process with co-creation, which generates open dialog with customers that goes beyond simple demographic data. But it must also set clear expectations and limitations to access. Your organization has to offer transparency in these interactions with your customers. True co-creation requires trust, from both the organization and the customer.

After you establish trust with your customers, information can begin flowing. Aggregate this information in a central place and gather as much as you can. You want to collect not only customer basics, such as age and location, but open-form content like ideas, complaints, and compliments. Information aggregation refers to the collection of relevant information from multiple sources. But in order for this information to do any good, you've got to keep it flowing.

Co-creation is a great way to keep relevant information feeding into your system. With its emphasis on consumer content and opinion, co-creation is a natural funnel for information.

Dell's IdeaStorm (www.ideastorm.com) raises the bar on aggregation of information for co-creation. Dell launched this community-focused site in 2007 to foster interactions and ideas from its customers. IdeaStorm invites users to post ideas on how to improve Dell's product offerings and services. Other users in the community vote on the ideas. Five years later, Dell had implemented over 500 community-created ideas into product enhancements. With an abundance of ideas flowing into the community site, Dell assigned 16 employees with the title "idea partners" to foster, track, manage, and engage the community's storm of ideas.

Customizing the overall experience

Co-creation and collaboration with your customers can be a true test of your company's ability to evolve with the times. It requires you to loosen the reigns of your brand a bit, but not entirely. You still get to

✔ Build the community for your customers.

✔ Design the infrastructure to support them.

✔ Implement the technologies to drive ideas.

The following steps walk you through the big-picture process of creating a custom experience for your customers that enables them to co-create with your business:

1. **Determine your business's goals for co-creation**

   For co-creation to be successful, you need to know what you want to achieve with it. Some look to co-creation simply for content, but the best campaigns actually utilize the information captured to their advantage.

   My Starbucks Idea is one example of this, where they asked customers to tell them anything and everything about how to make the Starbucks experience better. Then, instead of putting that information in a drawer, they used it to improve the drinks, service and layout of their stores—all while telling their customers exactly how and why they made these changes.

2. **Choose technology to support co-creation**

   After you know the goal of co-creation for your company, determine where it will take place. Facebook and Twitter are easy to use, existing systems, but they are owned by someone else.

   Explore the idea of building your own application or web platform to collect the information you receive through co-creation, as both Starbucks and Dell did.

3. **Respond to feedback from the co-creation forum.**

   Think about what you are going to do with this information. Answering the following questions can help you develop a well-rounded response:

   • Will you be allowing users to post in real-time, or will you be moderating their contributions?

   • Will you reply to them immediately, or wait until you have reached the end of your campaign?

   • After you have the information you need, how will you implement it and communicate these changes both to your co-creators and customers (who may be unaware that other customers assisted you)?

If you discover a divergence of audiences within your community, you can develop new outlets that cater to different segments. You can give your customers more choices on how they engage, further customizing their own experience and probably enhancing the environment of each community.

Birds of a feather flock together, and we all like to engage with people who "get us." Focus not only on the experience of one customer but his or her entire community.

United Kingdom–based mobile network giffgaff (`http://giffgaff.com`) employs no customer service agents or representatives, only community managers. The online community empowers customers to provide answers to fellow customer questions or concerns, as shown in Figure 5-2. Community managers stay engaged to keep the brand on track and step in where the community can't provide answers, for example on billing issues.

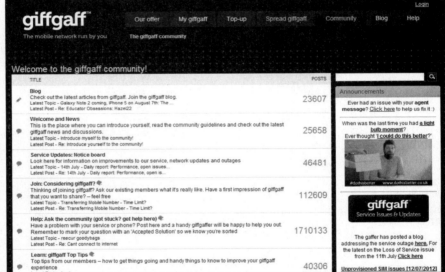

Figure 5-2: giffgaff's online community fields a variety of customer ideas and concerns.

Blurring between the producer and consumer

The customer experience is everything today. With the negative economic factors of the last several years, a highly competitive landscape has emerged. Giving your customers more than they ever expected when experiencing your brand is the way to the top. You have to find ways for your product or service to pull away from the very congested pack.

Value lies in the experience you're able to provide customers. Sure, you have a brilliant product or service that should really sell itself, but how are you going to generate referrals and word-of-mouth business?

Within the ecosystem of co-creation, it becomes more difficult to discern user-generated content from brand-driven content. Customer-created content, like blogs, videos, and photos hosted on a customer's own site or shared with the brand, (some people call this *DIY content*) weave into enterprise-generated content. Many TV shows have found success with this type of co-creation by taking user-generated content (with permission) and reposting on their own sites. Travel companies often hire outside bloggers to report back on their trips. This engages customers on a deeper level because it creates a deeper relationship with the brand.

Chapter 6

Refreshing Marketing 2.0 for Social CRM

In This Chapter

▶ Treating attention like a commodity

▶ Focusing on customers in every marketing message

*T*his is the Marketing 2.0 model: In all communications, companies need to engage and address the needs and interests of the consumer or risk losing credibility and quickly becoming irrelevant. Marketing is less about generating one-to-many discussions and more about creating an ongoing dialogue with customers. This allows companies to stay on top of customer preferences and concerns.

New marketing looks at customers' actions — clicks, shares, e-mail opens, shopping cart surrenders — to generate a truly targeted conversation. Old marketing took demographic information about customers and put them into silos or segments. Marketers would craft messaging to reach specific groups of demographics, but the truth is, a demographic isn't enough information to provide a true picture of your customer. For example, a 22-year-old consumer may conduct online research before sending her parents to an over-50s resort, or a grandmother may look to contribute funds to a younger person's college education. In these situations, the target audience isn't necessarily the typical target audience. Old marketing would have us crafting incorrect messaging to these customers based on blanket assumptions. New marketing allows us to start considering specific actions of individuals and connect with our customers in a more personalized way.

Knowing how our customers behave online can help us to better catch their attention. The Internet throws a lot of information at us, but our brains can divvy up our attention to only so many places at once. In this chapter, we dig more into the idea of an attention economy and allowing marketing to evolve from old ways to the new day Marketing 2.0.

Attracting Attention in an Attention Economy

In the 1970s, psychologist Herbert A. Simon coined the term *attention economy,* the idea that human attention is a scarce commodity in a world overflowing with information. In the early 21st century, the term has become popular because information available on the web is only increasing. Thus, web users have much more to choose from. Many technologies and software developments strive to identify factors that may lose a user's attention. Here are some identifying factors:

- ✔ Time spent on a site
- ✔ Ease of navigation
- ✔ Time to navigate the site
- ✔ Application download times

Information needs to be easy for users to find. Users move on to the next resource available to them if they can't locate information quickly and easily through any given application or platform. More importantly, once users find the information, it needs to be relevant. Plenty of other resources stand ready, willing, and able to capture users' attention.

The more information that flows into cyberspace, the harder it is to grab anyone's attention. In a day, we each make many more decisions about where we'll direct our attention than we do regarding where we'll spend money. Attention economy seeks to address issues that surround getting a piece of the attention pie. These issues don't just affect enterprise-level businesses but also news sources, government sites, retailers, medical professionals, basically anyone who has a message to share.

Discovering the past marketing economy

Grabbing customer's attention isn't a new concept to marketing and advertising. However, the way you actually capture attention has evolved greatly. In the past, billboard ads were enough to earn consumers' attention. Marketing 1.0 (the old way of marketing) was comprised of push techniques: push outbound messages, and then push some more.

The Golden Age of Advertising of the 1960s gave life to biased advertisements that were carefully crafted to tell consumers what they wanted. The cable network hit show *Mad Men* gives us attractive images and a glimpse back to times when men (and a couple of women) sat around a boardroom table and determined how to lure consumers to a brand. A witty and clever message was enough to market a product or service. And advertisers pushed and pushed that message out to the masses.

Redefining attention in the new economy

As mentioned earlier in this chapter, in the new economy, attention is a commodity. Nearly anywhere you go online, advertisements greet and follow you. Newsfeeds, search engines, and e-mail providers sell advertising space. All these ads are competing for your customer's attention amidst personal messages, business-critical searches, and newsworthy posts.

Users, in many instances, must give brands permission to connect with them digitally. Chances are people don't want to be immediately sold once they've given that permission. You've got to earn their trust, and their continued attention. By keeping their attention with useful and relevant information, you'll also earn the right to ask them for a sale or transaction.

As your business proceeds gradually into social engagement and data collection, be cautious about how your business interprets that data. Consumers' online behaviors — clicking, bookmarking, and so on — is of great value to marketers. However, the information that's collected can be interpreted in different ways. For example, any personal Gmail account is riddled with advertisements, many of which users never click through. One of this book's authors noticed that skid steer attachment advertisements appeared every day in her account as she was e-mailing back and forth with a client regarding skid steer attachments. Whereas she discussed these attachments via e-mail, she wasn't in the market for a grapple or snow blower. However, it's easy to see how a marketer could make that assumption. It's a logical leap, and one that's fine-tuned every day to ensure more targeted, relevant ads are delivered to the right audience online.

To refine the way your business competes for attention, remember that your approach must offer the customer relevancy, permission, and trust to gain any engagement, not just visibility. The following list explains each component of capturing consumers' attention:

- ✔ **Relevancy:** Your messages have to be delivered to the right audience, in the right context. You may have an awesome new product to share, but it won't matter to a significant portion of audiences. You have to imagine consumers asking, "What's this have to do with me?" Through community-building and conversations with your customers, you start to learn how to deliver relevant messages to the right people. Consider the many facets of your customers — such as consumer, professional, mother, father, book lover, race car fan, and so on. Dig into the layers to find out what really motivates them.

✔ **Permission:** No one wants to feel locked into a brand, especially if they're just starting to explore it and haven't truly engaged with it yet. Be clear about what type of relationship potential customers are getting into with you. Asking for permission to share your messaging leads to the next key element: trust.

✔ **Trust:** Users want to know how their attention will be used. Be transparent and upfront with them. People want to be able to change their minds on how they give their attention. Give them options and the flexibility to change their preferences.

Battling Between Old and New Marketing

Business operations have surely evolved over time. Often, the evolution progresses with advances in technology. When you start looking at new business philosophies, progress isn't as apparent. Certain aspects of marketing are so deeply ingrained in business culture and the individuals who are a part of that culture that it's extremely challenging to implement the big ideas of new marketing, including social CRM strategies. To implement social CRM, your business needs to catch up with the progress of technology, because today, technology is woven into nearly everything that we do.

The cost to place and disseminate advertising is significantly lower today than in the days of Marketing 1.0. Advertisers can produce clever, crafty, and effective advertisements on a low budget. With the power of targeting and segmentation, low-budget messages can compete with the mega-ads to deliver relevant messaging to the right audiences.

In advertising, what worked in 1959 didn't necessarily work in 1987. Similarly, messaging of the 1990s and early 2000s doesn't necessarily resonate in today's social business atmosphere. In the next sections, you learn about differences between old and new ideas about marketing.

Defining product-centric marketing

Content has been a main focus of advertising for decades, if not longer. We hear *content marketing* thrown around like a new term, but ads have always focused on content for the better part of a century. Product-centric market-ing emphasized content in its messaging, and that content was simply centered around the product itself, making *product-centric marketing* a more apt term.

Many ad campaigns around new products have been designed with the expectation that consumers want to buy said products, so advertisers create content to sell the product, sell features, sell benefits, and sell a value state-ment. Table 6-1 shows how product-centric messages are crafted.

Table 6-1	Key Components of Product-Centric Marketing Content	
Component	*Description*	*Example*
Feature	The advertising industry has spent millions of dollars to develop for-mulas for TV, radio, and print. One formula is that an ad must men-tion a particular feature a certain number of times for the consumer to digest the message.	"Check out this hose attachment that we've added to your vacuum."
Benefit	Marketing messages with an emphasis on benefits can reach a targeted audience but can alienate many others.	"This hose will allow you to take your vacuum places you never dreamed!"
Value	Building messages around a value (or perceived value) makes the assumption that the marketer knows what the customer wants or needs from the product feature.	"What this means to you, dear customer, is that you will have the clean-est couch on the block and can kiss that plastic couch cover good-bye."

Features, benefits, and value are tried-and-true approaches to marketing and sales, but that doesn't mean they're the only — or even the best — approach. Too often, companies don't invest the necessary time to tap into the actual needs of their customers before they develop and build a product. *They* think the product will sell, but they have no idea what the intended audience thinks.

The value piece is a crucial element that must remain as you move deeper into social business. With steep competition amongst similar products, your business must increase the perceived value of your brand to increase market share. You have to accept and embrace the fact that your product isn't the only option for consumers.

Meeting the embattled company-centric marketing

Do you put your customers first? Nearly everyone in business will answer with a resounding, "Yes!" And they mean it with every fiber of their being, but how many of us actually focus on our customers in every aspect of our business? Many have the best intentions, and a good portion of businesses involve consumers in product research, focus groups, customer service lines, and so on. But many others follow the company-centric marketing philosophy, where the desired results are whatever is best for business.

In these cases, the accomplishments of the company, such as a new product launch, a new website, or a signed contract on a large order, are revered more than customer praise or success. These accomplishments are really just tasks to be completed. Where is customer-centricity in that?

And where are the results in that? We are by no means saying that a company shouldn't celebrate hard work and milestones. However, if you want your business to fully join social business, you must move beyond tasks and start building goals that emphasize your customers and community.

When business leaders are busy thinking about their business, they often edge out customer consideration. For instance, a company that's rolling out a new product or process can hyperfocus on staff training, generating sales collateral, and getting the team on board. In social business, the real accomplishments happen when customers start championing your brand to the masses. Customer loyalty and customer engagement is the responsibility of the brand — not consumers.

Welcoming customer-centric marketing

You've likely heard or experienced for yourself that it costs far more to generate new customers than to keep the ones you already have. Thus, your business, especially your marketers, should make a common practice of listening and learning from your existing customer base, right?

When you really start focusing on customers in every aspect of your business, you begin to embark on customer-centric marketing. Because customers are driving brands today, make sure that your brand messaging disseminates with some consistency. Stay in touch with your customers every step of the way.

Consider the following to see where your organization stands with customer-centric marketing:

✔ **Hearing consumers:** Are you listening to consumers everywhere that they're talking? Are you tapped into the channels where they prefer to communicate about your brand? Customer-centric marketing requires understanding our customers' perceptions about our brand. For instance, what are they really saying about your brand when they're talking to their friends, family, and peers on social networking sites? Their messages may be very different from what they share directly with your organization.

Take a look at your monitoring software and see what sites have a lot of mentions for your brand. Then do a quick search online for your industry and see if you might have missed some niche sites. And always monitor keywords outside of your exact brand name, taking into consideration that customers may misspell or use abbreviations when talking about you.

✔ **Providing solutions:** After you hear what's really going on with your brand and consumers, you can offer real solutions. A customer-centric organization wants to help consumers — really and truly. Marketing 2.0 breaks down walls with customers. In order to engage consumers in social channels where they're surrounded by their personal networks, brands must approach them as their friends would. When a friend struggles with something, we want to rush to help him, to the best of our ability. That's the mentality needed for social CRM.

✔ **Adding value:** People want more for their money and attention today. The marketplace is flooded with options. Social businesses must really determine how they can offer value to consumers to set their brand apart. When you're listening and hearing your customers, you can unveil the value sweet spot.

✔ **Building advocates:** You get the opportunity to wow your customers when they feel heard and understood. In this world of customer-run business, consumers determine and demand a lot of what happens. However, it doesn't always mean they really expect that all of their demands will be met or even heard. So when you see a real opportunity to provide a solution and add value, you increase your chance at brand advocacy. Consumers are connected to people with similar interests and needs on social channels. If, for instance, a customer found a solution with your brand, it's likely that someone in his network needs a similar solution. Be top of mind for the instances!

Also, take the time to thank your brand advocates. Make them feel an even deeper connection to your brand. You may want to brainstorm low-cost ways to make them feel special, such as upgrading their membership status, offering them lifetime free shipping, or sending them a personalized gift.

✓ **Retaining loyalty:** Continue to strive for what we mention in this chapter, and your customers are naturally going to keep coming back.

✓ **Measuring relationships:** Customer-centric marketing has relationship goals in place, not transactional goals. Social business aims to have conversations and engagement with consumers. From these conversations, businesses can yield new customers and deeper insight into the ever-changing needs and interests of their audience.

Current and repeat customers are a gold mine of information and data, but it's what you do with all of that data that sets your business apart from the competition. Gathering data is one thing; understanding the data is a whole other piece to the CRM puzzle.

Chapter 7

Using the Social Media in Social CRM

*T*here's a conversation going on. A majority of your customers are engaged in a discussion about brands they like, the service they don't, and just about everything in between. If you're not part of it, you're missing out on an opportunity to learn what your customer really wants. The customer is ready to tell you.

But you need to listen in a way that is meaningful for your customers and your business. Auto magnate Henry Ford was quoted as saying, "If I asked my customers what they wanted, they would've said a faster horse." Developing a relationship with your customer is a careful blend of understanding and vision. But make no mistake; social CRM is also big business. Forrester Research predicts that software to run corporate social networks will be a $6.4 billion business by 2016.

In this chapter, we show you the implications that social media have for every aspect of your business. We examine the rules for creating valuable content and the need to collect and track behavior.

Understanding the Role of Social Media

Social media has impacted many facets of our lives. When you consider that social media is a relatively recent phenomenon, you can see just how big an impact it has made. Everyone seems to be online and using social media.

According to the Nielsen Social Media Report from the third quarter of 2011, the average social media user is

- ✓ **Gender:** Female
- ✓ **Age:** 18–34
- ✓ **Ethnicity:** Asian or Pacific Islander
- ✓ **Location:** New England
- ✓ **Education:** Bachelor's degree or higher
- ✓ **Household income:** Less than $50,000 per year

That's how Nielsen describes the average user, but what about your customer? Do you know who he or she is? Your customers might not look anything like the average user. Knowing who you're speaking to is the key to a successful online business. Speaking to your audience through social media is the way to have the most impact.

Social media can be viewed as a two-sided coin used to establish relationships. It is both an experience and technique. From your customer's point of view, it's an experience. From your point of view as a businessperson, it's a technique. If you don't understand both sides, you won't develop the kind of full relationship you hope to achieve with your customers.

The following are ways to think about each side of the coin:

- ✓ **An experience:** Your customers interact online with their family, friends, and followers. They can exchange opinions, recommend products, or just share daily updates. They experience social media as a vehicle to interact with others around the world.

- ✓ **A technique:** For your business, the tools are available to develop a relationship with your customers. Not only do you interact, but you sell, provide information, and drive traffic to your channels.

If you think of managing social platforms as only a technique and not also an experience, you miss out on the richness of the relationships that can be formed. You need to see the potential of both to build your social CRM. Creating experiences for your customers and analyzing their reaction will help you get to know and understand them.

You want fudge with that?

Sometimes your relationship can be super-seded by the unpredictable buying habits of your customers. In the spring 2012 issue of *Marketing Matters* from the University of Minnesota, Professor Joseph Redden points out a very strange buying habit. He reports that, "Branded products are not always consumed in isolation. Some products are experienced in concert with other products such as ice cream and hot fudge, televisions and surround-sound speakers, razors and shaving creams, designer shirts and slacks, shampoo and conditioner, even makeup. Consumers enjoy matching brands because they infer these items were specifically designed to go together." So even though you may make the best-tasting hot fudge, unless you make the preferred ice cream to go with it, in some cases, you just won't make that sale. This shows that additional psychological factors may override social media influence.

Changing CRM with social media

To illustrate how social media has transformed CRM into social CRM, Get Satisfaction created an infographic called The Evolution of Social CRM. You can find the original infographic at Get Satisfaction's blog, at this address:

```
http://blog.getsatisfaction.com/2010/12/17/the-evolution-
          of-crm-v2/?view=socialstudies.
```

The analysis illustrates what makes social CRM so different from the business functions of previous years. The critical points in the Get Satisfaction info-graphic, in terms of how social CRM has changed, include the following:

- ✔ Instead of specific departments handling CRM, everyone in the company is involved in CRM.

- ✔ CRM processes used to be company centric, but social CRM is customer centric.

- ✔ Channels used to be defined, but now channels are dynamic, in that no one department can own a social media channel.

- ✔ CRM happens on the customers' time frame, not the set hours a company establishes.

- ✔ The purpose of CRM has transformed from transactions to interactions with customers.

- ✔ Whereas businesses used to handle CRM by sending messages from within the business to customers, messages now come from customers to the business using a social CRM model.

It's easy to see that social CRM requires a whole new paradigm. The customer is the center of all the action. Effective tools haven't completely caught up with the requirements. For this reason, social media tools are layered on top of typical CRM systems to gather all the needed data.

Dipping into real-time analytics

Understanding how customers respond to your material is key to producing more of the best content. To do this, you need to spend some time monitoring your campaigns, website, and other channels to see what works and what doesn't. For this reason, you should consider using one of the following real-time monitoring tools:

- ✔ **Google Analytics:** Because it's created by Google and has lots of free built-in features, including keyword suggestions, Google Analytics (at `http://google.com/analytics`) is the *de facto* standard for free web analytics. It's easy to set up and use. When you add a blog or other channel, you can hook it into your account.

- ✔ **Adobe Insight:** Many of the big-name brands use Adobe Insight, which has a variety of tools that help companies analyze their business. Find out more about pricing and features at `www.adobe.com/products/insight.html`.

- ✔ **Clicky:** Clicky provides real-time analytics data that most other applications do not (at `http://getclicky.com`). The real-time capability is helpful if you want to monitor a specific campaign as it's happening. It's available in a free version with reduced features and a fee version that's $5 per month if you pay the annual rate.

Building the Content Pillars

Without solid content, you'll have a difficult time attracting and holding an audience of any kind. There are several ways to look at what content means to your business. One way is to think of content as the foundation upon which you build a successful business. For this reason, some have used the term *pillar content* to refer to the content that you need to have to support your business. Pillar content includes the basic information that you believe your customers should know.

For example, if you run a gardening site, your pillar content would include everything you think hobbyists should know about planting and caring for a garden. As shown in Figure 7-1, Garden Guides (`www.gardenguides.com`) is a membership site, run by Demand Media, that provides extensive content on gardening. You can see what Garden Guides considers pillar content by looking at the main menu items. They include such topics as plants, gardening design, and organic gardening.

Figure 7-1:
Garden
Guides.

Creating and using content

The key to understanding the type of content that you'll create is knowing who your audience is. Are you speaking to a shareholder audience? Does your content need to convey a serious tone for potential investors?

One of the mistakes that content creators make is to use the same tone for all their content. Your social media channels are read by a multitude of audiences. You want to sing a coherent song, but you need to use more than one note.

You can find lots of paradigms used to present the ideal content process. We think that if you boil it all down, there are three key components to creating great content. You want to

- ✔ **Write or curate content.**
- ✔ **Use the content.**
- ✔ **Share the content.**

The following sections explore each of these ideas and identify tools to help manage your content.

Write or curate content

As anyone tasked with writing content knows, it can be challenging. You'll find books filled with advice about the many facets of developing good content. To start, you should think about the "why." You need to ask yourself why you're writing it. What's the goal? Do you want to sell something, educate, or entertain? Probably a mix of all three would be ideal. As we discussed, when you know the tone of the piece and the intended audience, you're ready to write.

Before you starting writing a piece, assemble all your material: images, links, and anything else that must be included. (See the upcoming section, "Writing your brand post" for more on the process for developing content.)

Curating content means that you find great content on the web and share it with your constituency. As we know, the web has unlimited content. Much of it is good, but there's a lot of junk, too.

Curating content adds real value because a person with expertise is involved in selection instead of a search engine. You take the time to read and select what you consider to be the most informative material.

The following tools can assist you in content curation:

- ✔ **Scoop.it:** This tool (available at www.scoop.it) enables you to pick topics you want to curate and display those topics on a page for others to see, as shown in Figure 7-2. In turn, other people can rescoop the content you've shared. You can also find topics that other people are curating and follow them. You can scoop with both free and paid versions of the tool.

- ✔ **Storify:** This is a different type of curation tool (available at http://storify.com). It allows you to pull together your own social media content into a story. For example, if you were launching a product, you could pull together your content from your social platforms, Instagram, Flickr, YouTube, and other URLs to tell the product story. Storify is free.

- ✔ **The Tweeted Times:** This tool (at http://tweetedtimes.com) gathers all your tweets and turns them into your own newspaper. It's free to use and displays your tweets in an easy-to-read way by categorizing them and displaying them on one page rather than in a stream.

- ✔ **Curation Traffic:** This full-featured tool curates content and has a plug-in version and a standalone version. This means you can curate directly from your WordPress blog or a new blog you create for this content. There is a fee. Curation Traffic (at http://curationtraffic.com) has lots of sharing features built in to grow your traffic.

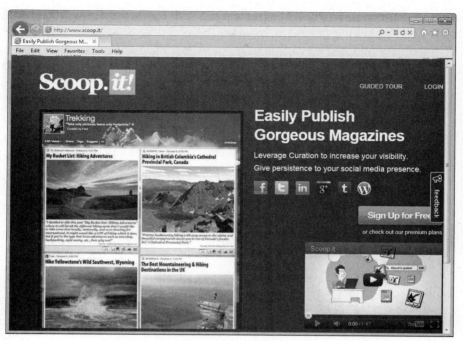

Figure 7-2:
Scoop.it.

Use content

When you're writing a specific blog post or a sales letter, you know where your content will be seen. If you're writing more general content, make sure that content is used immediately for some purpose. The reason for this is simple: The content monster must be fed. You have a hungry crowd that constantly wants to consume new material. People are attracted by what's novel to them. If you don't supply fresh content, they won't seek you out.

If you're not sure about all the ways your content can be used, you can always repurpose it (use it in different ways, such as turning a post into a video script) at a later date. You'll learn something about what your customer wants whenever you publish content, so keep working. You should consider everything you post as an experiment.

As the Greek philosopher Heraclitus is quoted to have said, "You can't step in the same river twice." That's a great mindset to have when you're doing anything online. A river is always flowing and changing; so too is the web. You're speaking to different people all the time. Popular culture is also shifting so that what works for you today may not work tomorrow.

If you've written something that gets a great response, you'll know you need more on that topic. If no one reads it or comments, you'll know that writing more about it will be less valuable. Make the time you or your team works on content as productive as possible.

Share it

When it comes to social media, sharing is what it's all about. A customer using your content to learn about your products is valuable, and that customer becomes even more valuable when she recommends that product to her network. Then she becomes part of your sales force.

Following are some free tools that you can use to share content:

- ✔ **AddThis:** This tool allows you to put share buttons on all your channel content. *Channels* include social media platforms like Facebook and your blog. It also includes (at www.addthis.com) analytics so that you can see how your content is shared. These types of analytics include user statistics such as how many people clicked a link, shared content, and so on.

- ✔ **ShareThis:** This application, shown in Figure 7-3, enables your customers to share any content they like on blogs, websites, Tumblr, and other channels. ShareThis is available at http://sharethis.com.

Figure 7-3:
Sharing content with ShareThis.

Discovering storytelling principles

Storytelling has become a hot topic for marketers and other content developers. Information overload causes customers to skip the long boring text passages that marketers carefully place on a website. From this realization, the phrase *customer engagement* was born. Managers began to understand that they were going to have to work a little harder to capture someone's attention. As marketing guru Seth Godin famously declared, "interruption marketing" is dead.

Customers want to consume their marketing content using games, videos, funny tweets, and so on. What they don't want is the dry, dull corporate-speak that populated the web in the early days. The competition is fierce, so all eyes turned to Hollywood. Content creators realized they had more in common with the storytelling of Walt Disney than the dull documents of Dow Jones.

I'm sure you struggle with making your content engaging. Almost everyone does. Creating interesting prose had previously been the domain of novelists and script writers. Now it's your job to tell the stories. But how? Collecting and making sense of customers' comments, data logs, and marketing campaigns was never easy. Now you're inundated with data from all sides.

To make your content memorable, you can construct your stories in the following ways:

- **Specific users:** You can seek out stories about how customers or others are using your products or interacting with your brand in some way. (See examples later in this section.) You can then cite these customers in your stories to illustrate your point. Most big companies have gotten the hang of telling stories about their products because PR companies have been helping them do this offline for years.

- **Trends:** Look at your data and see what it's telling you. Then you can tell your customers about themselves based on ratings or percentages. For example, imagine you're mining your data and find that a particular industry extensively uses your products. That could be an interesting story.

- **Company or product:** You can tell a company or product story. In addition to stories about your customers, you'll want to tell stories about how you created your product or how the brand got started.

One way to get a handle on creating engaging content is to understand what makes a great story. Well-known screenwriter Robert McKee has said that a story "unites an idea with an emotion."

A story isn't memorable if it doesn't evoke some emotion in the person hearing it. When you've heard about great tragedies during your lifetime, you always remember where you were when you heard the news. That's because it evoked such a strong emotion that you took note of everything happening at that moment.

The following are some ways you can approach your business content from a storytelling perspective:

- ✔ **Get people's attention.** To do this, screenwriters use what they call a *hook,* which is something that catches the audience by the coat tails and won't let them go. Think about the last PowerPoint slide show you sat through. Was there anything that grabbed your attention? Probably not. You want to open your business story with something meaningful.

- ✔ **Identify the hero of the story.** The hero of your business story can be the product, the storyteller, or the object of the story. For example, when you watch a commercial about a cleaning product, the product is usually the hero — the product saves the dinner party from unwanted odors. But when you talk about your company's effort to get people to volunteer, the hero is the audience. You want potential volunteers to see themselves as people who can make a difference. Be clear about the hero and make his journey an interesting one.

- ✔ **Give the story some emotional content.** As we say earlier, make sure that what you're presenting evokes feelings. Historically, business content was written to be as unemotional as possible. Use words that evoke emotions. If the hero is in danger of losing his business or damaging his product, make the emotion sing out.

- ✔ **Be clear about the desired outcome.** When you tell your business story, make it clear what needs to happen to effect a positive outcome. Spell it out. It may be crystal clear to you, but your audience may have very different ideas. Never leave it up to the audience to guess what constitutes success or failure.

- ✔ **Include a call to action.** If you don't make it clear to your audience what you want them to do, they won't do anything. No matter where you put the story, it should tell the reader or viewer what to do after they read it.

Look at two examples that perfectly illustrate how great stories constructed for the web make a difference. In 2011, Google started a project called Project Re: Brief. The purpose was to demonstrate that the iconic advertisements of the past could be reimagined for the web using stories. They contacted the creators of several of the iconic advertisements and asked them to update those ads for today's web audience. Here's how they recreated two of those advertisements:

✔ **Volvo's "Drive like you hate it" commercial:** The gist of the original commercial, written by Amil Gargano, was that Volvo was such a substantial and rugged car that you could drive it like you hated it. No matter how tough the driving course was, it would still perform brilliantly. Google and Gargano got together and updated the story.

They decided to tell the story of Volvo owner Irv Gordon, as shown in Figure 7-4. Gordon loved his Volvo and had driven it for many years. After hundreds of thousands of miles, he reluctantly sold it. Although it was gone, he remembered it fondly. As a present to him, his sons decided to track it down and bring it back to him. Gargano and team filmed the emotional event for the commercial. By telling a true story about how important his car was to him over a lifetime, they were able to make an emotional impact and drive home the point that Volvos survive.

Here's the link to the finished commercial `www.projectrebrief.com/volvo`.

✔ **Alka-Seltzer's "I can't believe I ate the whole thing" commercial:** In 1972, Alka-Seltzer, a stomach relief product, ran a commercial written by Howie Cohen and Bob Pasqualina. In it, its main character and overeater Ralph laments over and over that, "I can't believe I ate the whole thing." This saying became iconic.

Figure 7-4:
Volvo's "Drive it like you hate it" commercial reimagined.

To update the story, as shown in Figure 7-5, Cohen, Pasqualina, and the Google team decided that the new version should follow Ralph throughout the fateful day when he eats "the whole thing." In this case it's a large birthday cake. Since they were using Ralph, the same character from 1972, they designed the commercial to look like a 1970's sitcom. We watch Ralph as he tries and fails not to eat the big cake nestled in the refrigerator for the birthday party.

What makes the updated version (you can see the finished commercial at `www.projectrebrief.com/alka-seltzer`) unique was that it showed a complete backstory and utilizes many of the web tools Google has to offer. They provided custom coupons and links, including a link to Google+ to put Ralph in your circles.

You can see how much more appealing the information is because these old commercials are bundled as stories that take advantage of tools not available to the creators at the time like video and custom links.

To make your social media content even more powerful, consider going back through your website and other content and reworking it to either tell a story or include stories about customers.

Figure 7-5:
Alka-Seltzer's "I can't believe I ate the whole thing" commercial reimagined.

Sometimes, if you haven't thought the story through, a story strategy can backfire. Social customers can be unpredictable. They don't always do what you want them to. After a 2012 incident when a Twitter hashtag (see more about hashtags in the upcoming section on Twitter) unintentionally invited unwanted Twitter comments, Rick Wion, director of social media for McDonald's U.S.A. commented, "You don't control things. You can only hope to steer things in certain directions."

Following is a brief description of the incident that caused McDonald's to quickly pull their social media campaign:

McDonald's wanted to showcase the farmers they work with to emphasize their interest in quality. They created a hashtag called #meetthefarmers to support the campaign. Concerned that they weren't being specific enough about what the hashtag represented, they quickly changed it to #McDStories.

But instead of getting the stories they anticipated about how fresh their ingredients are, they got a torrent of negative stories about the quality of their food. Even when they took the hashtags down, the stories continued. It was clearly a PR disaster.

This exemplifies the fact that a company vision of itself and its products may not match everyone's opinion. Whether the negative comments represented the actual customers, they were enough to stop the campaign dead in its tracks.

Should McDonald's have anticipated this response? Probably. But clearly they were thinking that they understood the social customer. They forgot that everyone with an opinion can use the hashtag, not just their loyal customers.

Did McDonald's learn a lesson? Apparently so. In May of 2012, McDonald's purchased a promoted trend with the hashtag #bluberryoatmeal to herald their new breakfast offering. This time, things went better. It seems that blueberries and oatmeal are less controversial.

Taking a trip with the customer

Sometimes the easiest way to understand your customer is to "walk a mile with his mouse." Ok, we know that's not really how the proverb goes, but when you need to determine where your customer gets lost, can't buy, or loses interest on your website, you need to create a content trip to investigate the problem.

A *content trip* describes the path a customer makes to complete an action on your channel (such as a website or blog). If you take the path as though you were a customer, you can begin to understand what can be improved. If you pair that with data and feedback, you can craft a solution.

Here are some key items to consider when creating customer paths:

- ✔ **Navigation:** It may seem very clear when you start at the home page where you can go next, but once you get down a few layers, the organization of the content may need an overhaul.

- ✔ **Shopping cart:** Cart abandonment is still an issue for most online vendors. When customers get frustrated, they'll just leave their purchase sitting in the cart. That's revenue you could've had if you had taken a content trip to solve that problem.

- ✔ **Returns:** Don't stop at looking at the return information posted on your website. Actually order a product and attempt to return it. This can be a real eye-opener. At first, it may appear that the information you've posted is complete, but when you actually return something, you may find that the essential information is either hidden or unclear.

Keeping a content inventory

Whether you're in an enterprise or a small business, your inventory of content is likely scattered and unmanageable. Don't assume that big companies manage their content any better than small businesses. Most businesses are just too busy to organize their content.

Even if you have a web team that manages such areas as press releases or the videos collected from conference interviews, that content isn't integrated with everything else. Only companies that dedicate resources to their knowledge base will know what they really have in the way of information assets.

You can task different groups in your company to round up content so that the job doesn't seem so massive. If one group creates most of the videos, then have that group contribute an inventory of videos. Breaking down the creation of a content inventory into small chunks is the only way you'll be able to get a handle on such a big task. Use a spreadsheet if you have to, but identify what content you have throughout your organization so that you can repurpose it.

Incorporating Blogging

Blogs have been around long enough that some experts have already pronounced them dead, but they are alive and well and a great source of customer traffic. They also play an important role in your social CRM. They are part of the conversation that you need to integrate into your system to ensure that you're interacting with your customers.

When blogs started in the 1990s, people used blogs like diaries or journals. They wrote mostly about their day or their interests. The blog form slowly gained favor, and businesspeople began to use blogs to talk about their brands and business. Thought leaders and others found them to be a useful way to share their expertise and build a following.

According to the Nielsen Wire blog post, "Buzz in the Blogosphere: Millions More Bloggers and Blog Readers," more than 173 million blogs were tracked by NM Incite in 2011. Who are these bloggers? According to Technorati's report, "The State of the Blogosphere 2011" hobby blogs make up around 60 percent of the population, and business blogs make up approximately 40 percent. The Technorati report indicates the following about the business blogs:

- ✔ **Corporate bloggers:** 8 percent
- ✔ **Entrepreneurs:** 13 percent
- ✔ **Professional (part-time and full-time):** 18 percent

Defining a brand blog

Because of the large number of blogs, you may assume that most companies have one. Not so among the Fortune 500 companies. According to Go-Gulf.com, only 23 percent of Fortune 500 companies have public-facing corporate blogs. This indicates that many corporate managers may be reluctant to undertake an endeavor that requires a public risk.

Most successful business blogs are a fine mix of conversation, information, links, and products and/or service information. When you create a brand blog, you're usually speaking to an audience of customers, vendors, investors, and other interested parties. Because anyone could drop by, carefully consider your brand blog before taking it live.

One of the most effective ways to ensure that your company has a cohesive voice is to create a guide for your employees. (See more about employee guidelines in Chapter 13.) A guide for bloggers is akin to the type of guide you create for your brand look and feel. For example, Pepsi's ad creators (as well as ad creators for any major brand) are required to follow certain guidelines that dictate the size of the logo, the fonts, and so on. Create a guide that applies to all of your social media channels and helps everyone understand how to maintain the look and feel of the brand.

If a blog is written by the owner of a small business who has sole responsibility for everything, guest posters will be the only ones who need guidelines. If your company has financial restrictions or many bloggers, then you'll need more comprehensive guidelines. Don't regard the guidelines as restrictive. If you don't establish clear rules, you could end up in a PR mess.

Here are some questions that brand managers need to ask when creating a brand blog:

- **Who will be the voice of the blog?** The voice refers to the persona that the blog represents. It could be the leader of the company, an employee, a group of employees, or an outside writer. Obviously, a blog written by management will have a different style of voice than one written by a team.

  Some leaders want to be visible on the web, like Scott Monty, head of social media for Ford Motors. Most avoid it. The best mix for your company depends on how you plan to leverage your blog.

- **Who will have the final say before a post is published?** State whether the post writer must obtain approvals before hitting the publish button. Some companies must ensure they're working within legal restrictions.

- **Are you publishing copyrighted media in a post?** Companies need to be careful about publishing something with a copyright held by someone else. Make sure you have the rights to publish content that's posted on your company blog.

- **Can bloggers respond freely to comments or are there some restrictions?** The last thing you want to do is create controversy with a reaction to a post. If comments have a negative tone, decide who must evaluate them and frame the response.

- **Can bloggers recommend products (not your own) in a post?** If the employee likes a product and thinks it's worth mentioning, can she do so or does she need approval? And does the blogger have to reveal whether she received a free product for review? The web is full of recommendations, opinions, and suggestions. How will your blog handle them?

If you're looking for some ideas, you can examine the social media guidelines that IBM has created for its employees, at (www.ibm.com/blogs/zz/en/guidelines.html).

Searching the blogosphere

When you're planning your company blog, you want to make sure you get an idea of what others — especially your competitors — are doing. Make a point of looking at several blogs and taking notes about their pros and cons. Understanding how your competitors' customers respond to their content will help you craft your own. In addition, make sure to look at blogs that are popular regardless of topic. Looking at the best content will help you ensure that your blog has integrity.

The following resources can help you find your competitors and their blogs:

- ✔ **Technorati:** This site (at `http://technorati.com`)is the largest directory of blogs on the web. You can search blogs by topic and the content of posts.

- ✔ **Alltop:** Former Apple evangelist Guy Kawasaki created this site (at `http://alltop.com`). It's a curated collection of the best blogs on a variety of topics. This is a great place to start when you're unfamiliar with the blogs written on a particular topic.

- ✔ **Google Blogs search:** From this Google search box (at `http://blog search.google.com`), as shown in Figure 7-6, you can search all the blogs that Google has indexed, which is to say most of them.

Figure 7-6: Google Blogs search.

Planning your posts

One of the hardest parts of sustaining an active blog is to constantly feed it with new posts. To help with this process, create an editorial calendar. Most magazines and other publications maintain a calendar so that their content is created in advance. The last thing a publication needs is a big hole in its content.

A blogging schedule will help you manage blog content, whether you're working with a team or alone. If you're working with a team, you can assign posts in an orderly fashion and ensure that all your bloggers have something productive to do. If you're working alone, you need to prepare for the times when the unexpected happens and you don't have time to create a post. The key is to have something ready to go when your schedule dictates it's time to publish.

Following are some decisions you need to make to create your calendar:

- ✔ **How often will you post?** The best way to organize your calendar is first to decide how often you want to post. You should work at least three months in advance; some bloggers set up their schedule at the beginning of the year and try to finish the majority of their posts in the first several months.

   Don't think that just because you have all your posts planned you can't add in something timely right on the spot. The value of having posts in reserve is that you're never without a quality post to publish. You'll want to also create posts that relate to current topics and events to show your readers that you're present and interested in what's happening.

- ✔ **What themes will you select?** Another facet of your editorial calendar is your themes. By establishing a theme for each month, you assure readers that you're providing ample content on all the subjects that relate to your business. You want to ensure that you have both evergreen content that you can use at any time and specific content that dives deeper into specific subjects. If you have a financial blog, for instance, one month your theme could be investing techniques, and another month it could be saving for retirement.

- ✔ **What style of post will you create?** A variety of well-known formats can help a blogger write more quickly and with greater variety. See the next section for a list of these format examples.

If you want to use an editorial calendar that plugs right into your WordPress blog, try the plug-in that's available here:

```
http://wordpress.org/extend/plugins/editorial-calendar/
                  screenshots
```

With this tool, you can easily drag and drop posts into a calendar. This visual method is much easier than having to type in the information line by line.

Writing your brand post

Brand posts should engage the customer and make her feel like you're interested in what she has to say. Like any good social media content, you want to develop a dialogue with your readers.

It's hard to stare at a blank screen and hope inspiration will strike, especially when your job might depend on how well your blog posts are received. Management rarely buys the excuse that you just weren't inspired. If you send out posts to be written by team members or outsourced writers, give them specific instructions about the post you want. The instructions are important because you want all the posts to be consistent and use the same terms and tone. Then, when visitors read several blog posts in a row, they aren't confused by different styles.

As you write posts on your own or direct writers in the content you want, consider the following blog post formats

- ✔ **Questions and answers:** Your customer service department is aware of the questions, problems, and needs of the customer and can serve as a solid pipeline of content. Ask your customer service department to suggest topics for the blog. This will encourage department members to participate and take ownership of the social media discussion.

- ✔ **Embedded video or podcast:** Your blog should have all kinds of multimedia formats on it. If you have a podcast that was created by one of your salespeople, or a video taken at a conference, make sure you create blog posts with the content embedded right in the post.

- ✔ **Several posts that constitute a series:** Two of the most interesting words that any blog post can use are *part one*. These words indicate that more is to come. The words also set an expectation that the reader will return to learn what part two has to say. If you don't have any series posts available, try breaking a longer post into two parts.

- ✔ **Product recommendations:** The web thrives on recommendations. If you know of a product that you suspect your customers will like, by all means create a post about it. Also, remember to share your recommendation with the product owner. You may establish a new connection.

- ✔ **Top ten lists:** Everyone likes top ten lists. (Check out Chapters 16–20 of this book.) Lists are easy to understand and provide a wealth of information in a compact form.

✔ **Tips about productivity tools:** Can you advise your customers about how to do something better, faster, or cheaper? Increasing productivity is everyone's goal. These posts will be appreciated.

✔ **Behind the scenes:** People are always curious about what goes on behind the scenes. When you talk about your employees or describe an event you put on, you help to draw the audience in. Customers see that your company is populated with real people. When your customers feel a connection with the people who make up your business, this connection goes a long way toward developing customer relationships.

Fitting SEO into blog content

Search engine optimization (SEO) is a topic that many businesses would like to ignore. SEO is frustrating because it's a moving target, and there's no one right way to do everything. But you can't ignore SEO because search-engine friendly content enables people to find your blog content when they need it. As we explain in earlier chapters, showing up on social media channels when and where customers have a need is critical to a social CRM strategy.

In SEO, the greatest concern is the keywords you place in each post. For example, Google will help users find your posts if the keywords correspond to searches that your potential customers run. Google will also penalize you if you try to stuff your posts with keywords; repeating the same keywords over and over beyond their usefulness is just as bad as not using them at all. The key is to find the correct balance between including the keywords that are needed for SEO versus making the post seem overstuffed with the same words.

Your company probably has a defined list of major keywords that everyone uses. However, when you're writing a blog post, you will also want to add keywords that are specific to that post to encourage traffic. For example, if your post mentions specific industry leaders or company products, include them as keywords for that particular post. That way, people who search for those specific names will find you through that post.

Following are some tools to help you find the right keywords while you're writing your content:

✔ **Scribe:** This tool (at `http://scribeseo.com`) is for writers of content of any kind. For a fee, it evaluates keywords, analyzes your titles and text, and helps you build backlinks, which are links that others place on their blogs that link back to your post.

✔ **InboundWriter:** This tool, shown in Figure 7-7, uses web research to help post creators write their content. It's available at `www.inboundwriter.com`, in both a free and fee-based version. Among the great InboundWriter features is a tool that grades your content as you write it. You can see if you have the right balance of keywords and a title that will work for SEO.

Figure 7-7:
Inbound-
Writer.

One keyword trick that some bloggers use to attract readers is to tie a post to a celebrity's name or major event. It's come to be known as *newsjacking*. For example, if Lady Gaga is in the news, a blogger might create a post entitled, "What you can learn about marketing from Lady Gaga" and include her name as one of the keywords. When someone searches for her name, that post may come up. The problem with this trick is that you will also be seen by lots of people who have no interest in your post, but it's a way to get immediate traffic.

Encouraging readers to leave comments

On your blog, comments on each post help create community and build relationships. However, the value of the comments section is often overlooked. One reason may be that comments aren't easy to come by. Some blogs have a wealth of comments, but most have just a few. Social customers are more likely to comment within a social media platform like Facebook than on a specific blog.

The kinds of comments you want on your blog are the ones that invite discussion by a larger group. To encourage readers to leave comments, especially comments that generate discussion, help your readers frame their responses. For example, in a blog post, ask readers specific questions that they can reply to. Replying to a question is an easy way for your readers to interact with you. You could also describe an experience that happened to you and ask readers to share a similar experience. Broad questions aren't as likely to generate comments. When you ask readers to simply "Let me know how you feel," you're inviting a blank comment box.

Looking at the available blogging tools

Blogging tools are relatively easy to use. They're structured so that you use a template to fill in all the required information that helps search engines find you. This information includes the title, text, keywords, images, and links.

The following two tools are especially popular among business bloggers:

- ✔ **WordPress.org:** This tool — shown in Figure 7-8 and available at `http://wordpress.org` — is the most widely used platform to create websites and blogs. To create a relatively inexpensive yet professional-looking site, purchase predesigned themes. A host of plug-ins extend WordPress.org functionality. To avoid confusion, be aware of the tool called WordPress.com that hosts WordPress sites. Wordpress.org sites are hosted on your own site.

- ✔ **Typepad:** With Typepad (at `http://typepad.com`), you create and host a blog on the Typepad site. You can customize your design, and the fee you pay includes technical support.

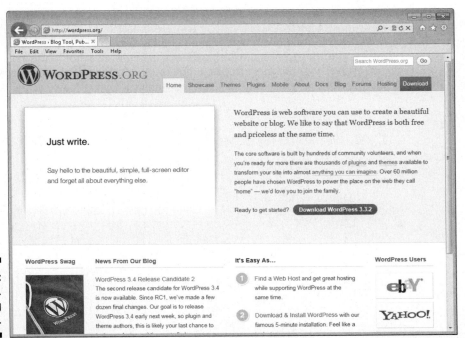

Figure 7-8: WordPress.org download.

Discovering the Podcast

No company using social media should overlook podcasts. A *podcast* is an audio file that listeners can either directly download to their computer (or mobile device) or *stream* (play) online. It's most likely formatted as an MP3 file. (In this definition and the research that follows, songs are excluded.) Podcasts allow companies to vary the content format.

When podcasts were first introduced early in the 21st century, the technology wasn't perfect, and downloading was difficult. As the technology improved (including the introduction of the iPod), podcasts became more popular.

Now, most companies understand that podcasts have value, but they don't always use them to the extent that they could. The problem isn't hard-to-use technology, but finding people who are willing to speak at length in a nonrehearsed way. Just like any public speaking, discussing a topic in a podcast requires the willingness to try.

Defining the value of podcasting

To understand who podcast listeners are and what social media they consume, a survey, *The Current State of Podcasting 2010,* by Edison Research, found that the average podcast listener is

- Male: Fifty-three percent are men.
- Neither young nor old: Twenty-two percent fall into the 35–44 age range.

The percentages of people on social networks who listen to podcasts are as follows:

- 66 percent of Facebook users
- 19 percent of LinkedIn users
- 15 percent of Twitter users

Apply the preceding statistics to your company's podcasting strategy. For example, because a high percentage of Facebook users listen to podcasts, if your audience is on Facebook, consider linking to a podcast via your company's Facebook page. Is your audience in the 35–44 age range? Then podcasts could be your medium.

As you develop your podcasting strategy, don't go by these statistics alone. Do testing on your own by tracking them in Google analytics or other analytics package. This way, you will know if your assumptions about your audience are borne out by real-world tests.

Benefitting from podcasts

Are podcasts of interest to you? Here are some ways that creating podcasts could benefit your company:

- **Listeners can hear a podcast anytime.** No one has to listen to a podcast as it's being recorded. They can listen at a time that's most convenient for them. This makes it more likely that your podcast will be heard.

- **Listeners can multitask.** With a mobile device, customers can use your podcast to entertain or educate themselves while they're out and about, running errands or commuting. In this way, you remind customers about your business even when they aren't at their desk.

- **Podcasts are easy to forward.** Podcasts are digital, and fans can easily forward links to them on blogs, social media sites, or through e-mail.

- **Your customers can easily subscribe to a podcast series.** Several tools, such as iTunes, make subscriptions easy. If you have an ongoing series, make sure your customer doesn't have to search for it. Post all podcasts in a series in one place and clearly label them.

- **Your company can create its own talk show with very little effort.** Talk shows used to be the domain of major radio stations. Now you can hear talk shows about almost any topic.

- **You can create products that include podcasts and generate revenue.** Podcasts are perceived as more valuable than text. If you're creating an information product, for example, consider bundling several podcasts in it.

- **You can record meetings with customers and send the recording as a follow-up.** If you're consulting or providing custom training, a recording of the conversation would be appreciated. It could be viewed as a premium service.

- **Professionals who hear your podcast may call you for speaking engagements or other deals with your company.** You never know who might take an interest in your podcast. Journalists, conference organizers, and business owners are all listening.

- **When your company launches a new product or service, you could interview the product manager to explain its value to consumers.** You can use your podcast as a marketing vehicle to get your message out to potential customers.

Look over your inventory of content and see if something your company has already created would make a good podcast. Put a catchy title on it to help capture attention.

Planning your podcast

Recording a great podcast can be challenging if you don't plan what you're going to do ahead of time. The first step in planning is to gather inspiration by listening to popular podcasts. The following podcasts were among the nominees for the Podcast Connection's 7th Annual Podcast Awards:

- ✔ **Planet Money from NPR:** Check out the contest winner at `www.npr.org/templates/archives/archive.php?thingId=127413729`, as shown in Figure 7-9.

- ✔ **Market Foolery by Motley Fool:** At `http://wiki.fool.com/Market Foolery`, you can listen to brothers Tom and David Gardner discuss the latest business and investment topics with a fresh approach.

Because these podcasts represent one of the final nominees and the winner , the standards are high. Don't be intimidated by the quality and content. Just try to see what makes them so interesting.

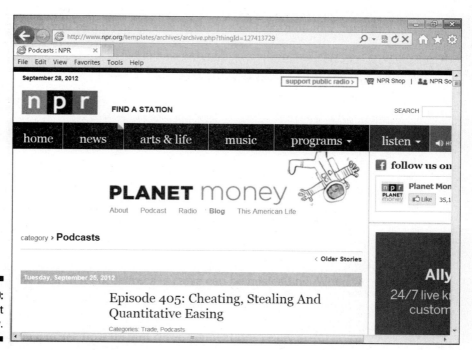

Figure 7-9:
Planet
Money.

When you're gathering your team or planning a podcast on your own, consider these tips:

- ✓ **Make sure you're comfortable with the technology.** If you find it difficult to run the equipment and host the podcast at the same time, get someone to help with the technical duties — not the least of which is to hit the record button. Having someone to turn to can be a real lifesaver when something goes technically wrong in the middle of a great interview.

- ✓ **If you're interviewing, speak to the guests ahead of time.** Ensure that they know what the show is about and what's expected of them. Even though this sounds like common sense, we've all heard podcasts that include confused guests.

- ✓ **Clarify your call to action.** You want to let your audience know where they can go for further information. If you're pointing listeners to a website, check the URL ahead of time to ensure it's correct, and write down the link so you're sure to repeat it accurately during your podcast. You don't want to issue corrections along with the podcast. During your podcast, repeat the web address frequently. If your call to action is a limited-time offer, note the date it expires. You don't want to disappoint potential customers.

Choosing podcasting tools

To create podcasts, you can choose from several types of tools. Your choice will depend on such things as the following:

- ✓ Where do you want to store and retrieve files?
- ✓ How many files do you want to create?
- ✓ What will your file size be?
- ✓ Are you working alone or with a team?

The different types of tools are as follows:

- ✓ **Record and store in the cloud.** You could use a service that stores your files *in the cloud* (on someone else's computers).

- ✓ **Record and store on your company's computers.** If you have an IT team to manage files, you may want to store your files on your company's equipment.

- ✓ **Broadcast over the Internet and store in the cloud.** Tools like these enable you to create your own talk show. Blog Talk Radio, an example of this type of tool, is shown in Figure 7-10.

In Table 7-1, you find an example of each type of podcasting tool.

Table 7-1		Examples of Podcasting Tools		
Tool	*Type*	*Description*	*Cost*	*Web Address*
Audio-Acrobat	Record and store in the cloud.	Configure files in different styles.	$19.95–$49.95 per month	www.audio acrobat.com
Audacity	Record and store on your company's computers.	This popular, free tool has lots of helpful features.	Free	http://audacity.source forge.net
Blog Talk Radio	Broadcast over the Internet and store in the cloud.	Provides call-in lines and lines for guests.	Free and Premium versions (with multiple pricing packages)	www.blog talk radio.com

If you have a WordPress blog, you can use a free tool called Audio Player to create your MP3 podcasting files. The colors of your player are configurable so that you can match your site. You can find Audio Player at this address:

```
http://wordpress.org/extend/plugins/audio-player/download
```

Getting your podcast heard

After you've created a podcast, the next step is to spread the word to potential listeners. If you're creating podcasts for an internal audience, your distribution is clear. If you want to attract traffic to your website, attention to your product, or credibility as a thought leader, you'll need to find wider distribution.

One good way to figure out where to distribute your podcast is to look at how people find podcasts. The Edison Research's 2010 report on the state of podcasting (mentioned earlier in this chapter) asked its respondents the following question: "How do you typically find out about the podcasts you listen to?" Their responses were as follows:

- ✔ 32 percent said iTunes
- ✔ 20 percent said recommendations on social networks
- ✔ 13 percent said search engines
- ✔ 7 percent said recommendations on blogs
- ✔ 29 percent said other (these could include newsletters, e-mails, and so on)

We recommend using all these channels and any others that relate specifically to your audience.

Including Video in Your Mix

Video has become a very important content format for social media users in the last few years. Its impact on the web is enormous. In February 2011, comScore Video Metrix released the following data about online video viewing:

- ✔ 82.5 percent of the U.S. Internet audience viewed a video online.
- ✔ U.S. viewers watched online video for an average of 13.6 hours per viewer in February 2011.
- ✔ The average video was 5.1 minutes.

Most people like the idea of using videos. The problem arises when you have to shoot videos. You have to figure out answers to all sorts of questions. What should I shoot? How should I do it? Unless you outsource videos or work in a company with a video studio, you're going to learn more about taking video than you ever expected. The following sections help you create a plan for your online video.

Knowing how to use videos

Before the bandwidth and technology for online video became available, businesspeople and users alike eagerly anticipated online video. Now that it's here, everyone is hoping to launch the next viral video (as long as it goes viral for a good reason, not because it's a PR disaster).

Your customers can view your videos in two main ways:

- **From a link:** If you want to link to a video, you must first upload the video file to a hosting site or your own site. Then, you can link to a video in almost any e-mail, blog post, tweet, or other social media message box. The link points to the video's Internet address. When the viewer clicks the link, he watches the video on the site to which you uploaded the video file.

- **Embedded:** The other way your fans can view your video is directly from your website, as David Siteman Garland does in his blog The Rise to the Top (www.therisetothetop.com), shown in Figure 7-11.

  You can also embed the link from YouTube and send it via e-mail or other source to be viewed. You still need to upload your video file to a hosting site or your own site before you can embed the video. But instead of clicking a link, your viewer clicks a Play button to see the video, or the video can play automatically as soon as a visitor lands on the web page that contains the video.

You can create videos to serve a variety of business purposes. Consider the following:

- Marketing current products
- New product announcements
- Advertising
- Interviews
- Customer service
- Training
- Conference activity

Figure 7-11:
Embedded
video on
The Rise to
the Top.

After you decide what to create, you need to figure out how to proceed. Depending on what you're shooting, you can use a relatively inexpensive video recorder or even a smartphone. When you want to grab an interview with someone on the fly, these devices will suffice. Obviously, if you're recording a more formal event such as a speaker at a conference, you'll need a more professional rig that includes a good microphone.

Understanding video-hosting requirements

Video hosting is an important consideration. If you don't want to host videos on your site, you need to pick a host that will serve your needs. When you're reviewing sites, consider the following:

- ✔ **How well can you customize the player?** You want to make sure that if you're paying for site hosting, you can create a professional-looking player.

- ✔ **What kind of limits can you put on privacy?** You want the ability to control who can see your videos and under what circumstances. Check whether you can you can password-protect the video or prevent others from e-mailing the link. Privacy is a consideration if you want to limit viewing to a select audience, such as a training class.

✔ **What kind of analytics does the host provide?** Reviewing your analytics will help you make better videos. You want to see data such as how many times a video was viewed and for how long.

Following are some possible video-hosting sites (see the upcoming section on YouTube) to consider for your business:

✔ **Vimeo:** Shown in Figure 7-12, this popular site has both a free and fee-based option. Vimeo (at `http://vimeo.com`) does a good job of helping you share your video on social networks.

✔ **Screencast:** This service (at `www.screencast.com`) is inexpensive or free. The same company that provides this service, TechSmith, also makes Camtasia, the video-recording software.

✔ **Wistia:** When you pay for video hosting at Wistia (`http://wistia.com`), you also get helpful analytics and built-in way to create a call to action within your video.

✔ **Viddler:** This option (available at `http://viddler.com`) is designed specifically for business videos and can handle most video file formats.

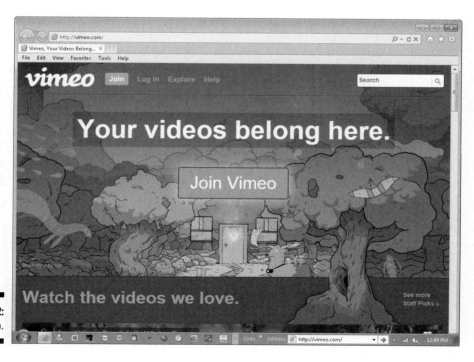

Figure 7-12:
Vimeo.

Considering YouTube for video hosting and distribution

When you are evaluating how to distribute and host your videos, you may want to consider YouTube where you can do both at the same time. Its built-in features make it worth considering. You can host a video in a variety of places that don't have distribution. What makes YouTube valuable is that they have a huge waiting audience to which you can distribute videos.

The benefits of using YouTube for video distribution include the following:

- ✓ **There aren't many restrictions on topic.** After you register for a subscription, the site accepts videos on almost any subject. That's great news for businesses whose videos may not be about exciting topics.

- ✓ **Signing up is free.** You don't pay a fee, but your videos are public.

- ✓ **You can create your own channel.** You can brand your own channel with your colors and logos. Check out what Orabrush has done in Figure 7-13.

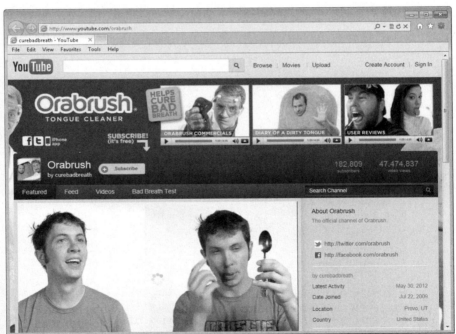

Figure 7-13: Orabrush on YouTube.

✔ **You save storage costs.** You can send customers to view your videos on YouTube instead of incurring the cost of storing videos on your own site.

✔ **Your customers can subscribe to all your videos or select one and add it to their Favorites list.** Your customers can sign up to receive notices about new videos so that you can keep them updated.

✔ **Built-in analytics are available.** If you post a product video or a video on another topic that you want to track, you can see how many people watched and accessed other measures of your video's success by using YouTube's built-in tools.

✔ **The site offers a huge audience.** You may find new customers when people search the site for your topic; YouTube is one of the top websites.

Of course, using a no-fee public service like YouTube to host your videos has downsides. For example, if you assign an employee to manage the YouTube site, you need to make sure you have the password as well, or that you can get in if the employee is unavailable.

Tweeting with the Microblog Twitter

People either love or hate Twitter. The ones who hate it say they just can't pack enough meaning into 140 characters. The ones who love it say that they can establish relationships with people they could never reach any other way. Twitter lovers have an important case to make for anyone involved in social CRM. Because Twitter is such a powerful tool for reaching out to people, you can't ignore it. According to statistics compiled by Cara Pring at The Social Skinny,

✔ There are over 465 million Twitter accounts.

✔ Twitter is growing at a rate of 11 accounts per second.

✔ 30 percent of Twitter users have an income over $100,000.

Twitter creates the opportunity for the pint-sized post that packs a wallop. In this section, we look at the true value of making Twitter part of your social CRM ecosystem.

When you create a Twitter account, you're required to pick a name for your profile. Think about the name carefully before you choose it. If it's a company name, consider whether you intend to use the account for a specific department or purpose, such as customer service, and choose a name that reflects that purpose. You can always add another account, but you risk diluting the main one if you do. Start by concentrating your efforts.

If you're just getting started on Twitter, you may want to follow an account like TweetSmarter (https://twitter.com/#!/tweetsmarter). What makes this account unique is that it's run by two people (Dave and Sarah Larson) who directly answer your questions and try to help you better understand Twitter.

Understanding the microblog (Twitter)

Just like the hours in the day, you get the same amount of Twitter characters as everyone else: 140 characters, including spaces. If you use them wisely, you can reach a large audience. Twitter allows you to easily connect with your niche. No matter what your interest or business specialty, you can find like-minded followers on Twitter.

However, you need to be aware that when you create a Twitter account for your business, you're committing to actively responding to customer thoughts and opinions. By having the account, you raise customer expectations that you're listening.

But are you? According to a 2011 study by Maritz Research, only 30 percent of the people surveyed received a company response to their tweet. This unresponsiveness defeats the purpose of having a Twitter account as part of your social CRM. Not only do you want to show customers that you care about what they have to say, you also want to capture data about your loyal followers. You won't be encouraging them if you don't engage.

From a big-picture perspective, tweets serve two basic functions:

- ✓ **Tweets send out content within the tweet itself.** Within 140 characters, you are free to say pretty much anything. Comments can include quotes, opinions, and responses to others, and you can attempt to reach out to someone new.

- ✓ **Tweets provide links to other content.** You can include in your tweet a URL that takes your audience to another place on the web. These tweets have additional value because they can drive traffic to your channels, promote a product for sale, or alert followers to additional information you want to share.

Tweets allow you to communicate with others in real time. If you monitor your Twitter stream throughout the day, you'll see brand mentions and developing news right in your stream and in trending topics.

Reviewing Twitter basics

To participate in the tweet stream, it's useful to know something about the elements that make up Twitter. Following are some of the key parts:

- **Tweet:** This is the basic unit. When you create a Twitter account, you start by typing in the box that says Compose New Tweet. The tweet is then posted in the stream and people who follow you can see it.

- **Direct Message (DM):** A direct message is one that is sent directly to a Twitter address and doesn't go into the stream. It's a private communication between you and another user.

- **Followers:** This is what Twitter calls the people who choose to read your tweets.

- **Retweet:** When you like what someone has tweeted, you can click the Retweet button to send it back out into your stream. You can type **RT** and the person's handle, to identify who wrote the original. It looks like this: RT @person.

- **Hashtag:** This is a search tool that people create by placing a hashtag symbol (#) in front of a keyword so that people can follow a specific topic. For example, if you're holding a conference, you might want to create a hashtag for that event so that people can see all the tweets related to it.

- **Promoted tweets and trends:** Twitter sells advertisers the ability to tie a tweet to a particular search term. If the search term is used, the tweet shows up at the top of the results list. Advertisers can also select a mobile platform (such as Android, Blackberry, iOS, and so on) where the tweet will show up.

  A promoted tweet lets advertisers pay for a tweet to show up at the top of the trend list. The promoted tweet is tied to a keyword related to upcoming events or holidays. For example, if an advertiser's product is related to Thanksgiving, the advertiser should tie the tweet to that search term.

 Twitter allows you to create a custom background for your profile. If you create one, make sure it matches your company branding. You don't want to confuse your followers.

Looking at some specialized Twitter tools

A whole industry of tools has grown up around Twitter. People have figured out ways to make it easier to follow and use. For example, here's a quick introduction to tools that can help you with the following tasks:

✔ **Grade your account.** You may want to analyze how well your Twitter account performs compared to others in the Twitterverse. If your manager wants to know where your company stands, use these tools.

Twitalyzer is shown in Figure 7-14. The free account (you can sign up at `http://twitalyzer.com`) shows you analytics, including what percentile you rank among all Twitter users and the average age and gender of your followers. For example, if you have a rank of 80percent, that means that 80 percent of Twitter users rank lower than you do on a scale of 1–100 percent.

Tweet Grader (`http://tweet.grader.com`) is also a free tool. You are assigned a grade based on such things as number of followers and length of time you've been on Twitter.

✔ **Find the best time to tweet.** You want to tweet when the most eyeballs are available. These tools help you figure out when you'll get the largest audience viewing your tweets. Whether your followers want to retweet your content is still based on the value of the tweet itself.

TweetStats is a free service (at `http://tweetstats.com`) that analyzes the best time for you to tweet and shows it to you in a graph.

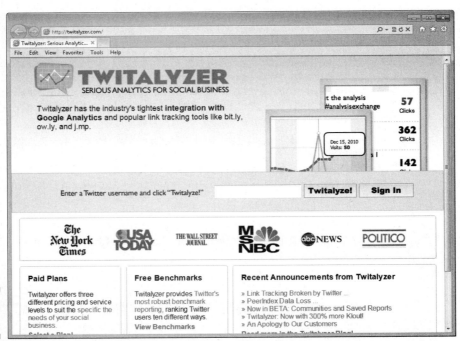

Figure 7-14:
Twitalyzer.

Tweriod, shown in Figure 7-15, is also free (go to http://tweriod. com). Tweriod sends the analysis to your e-mail or DM on Twitter.

✔ **Find tweets on a particular topic and display them on their own page.** If your followers are interested in a particular topic, you can create a page that displays tweets on only that subject.

Tweetwally enables you to do just that (at http://tweetwally.com). You can provide a link to your Tweetwally topic from your blog or other channel. For example, author Stephanie created a Tweetwally on visual thinking, as shown in Figure 7-16.

✔ **Provide analytics for your Twitter account.** You want to know more about your Twitter account than just number of subscribers. You want to know about their demographics.

SocialBro (www.socialbro.com) provides statistics through Google's Chrome browser, or you can download the SocialBro app to run from your desktop. This service provides an interesting mix of analytics and management. You can see your community mapped out via location or find out who your newbie followers are.

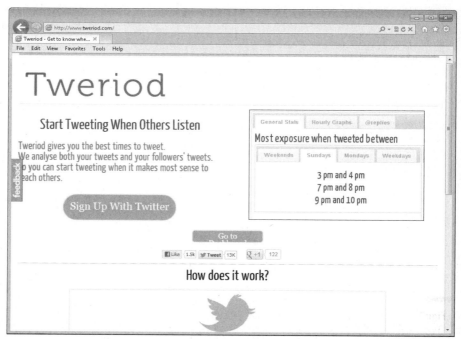

Figure 7-15:
Tweriod.

Figure 7-16:
Tweetwally.

🗸 **Schedule your tweets to be sent out over a period of time.** These tools are handy for timing your tweets based on feedback you get from tools like Tweetstats or Tweriod, mentioned earlier in this list. Scheduling tweets is also useful when you need to disconnect from the Internet but still provide content via Twitter. (Still, make sure someone is minding your company's Twitter account for feedback from your customers, even when the main person needs to step away.)

Buffer provides free and fee-based services (at `http://bufferapp.com`). The application stores your tweets and sends them out on a schedule of your choosing. It also has built-in analytics.

Timely (`http://timely.is`) is another free and fee-based tool that allows you to time your tweets, as shown in Figure 7-17. Timely is easy to use: You type your tweets into the application and choose how often you want them to be sent to Twitter. You can also see the performance of the tweets and learn which tweets get the most attention.

Even though social media is gaining a huge foothold, most businesses still use e-mail as their main way to communicate. Don't forget to consider e-mail when you're developing your campaigns. According to a 2011 presentation by Jeff Hardy at SmarterTools, Facebook hosts 60 million updates per day and Twitter hosts about 140 million tweets per day, but people send a billion e-mail messages per day.

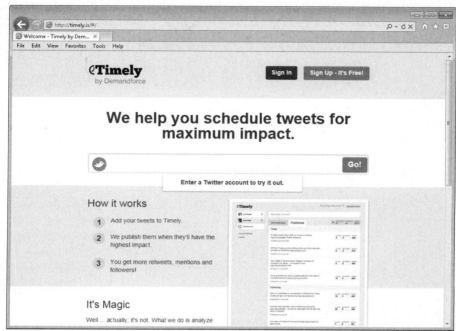

Figure 7-17:
Timely.

Facing the Valuable Facebook

Facebook is the 800-pound gorilla. In March 2012, it had over 900 million monthly active users. If you know anything about social media, you know that Facebook is considered *the* platform to be on. Its sheer size makes everyone pay attention. But just like any site or tool, you have to make Facebook work for your specific business.

Understanding the importance of Facebook

In 2012, Facebook is facing some challenges. Its IPO was investigated by the Securities and Exchange Commission, and General Motors pulled all its advertising. Like any other publicly traded company, Facebook is open to a higher level of scrutiny, but no one expects a mass exodus of users in the near future. According to comScore, one out of every seven minutes spent online is spent on Facebook. That's a hard habit to break.

Discovering Facebook features

A study by CMB Consumer Pulse and iModerate Research Technologies reports that of those who click a brand's Like button on Facebook, 60 percent of them are more likely to recommend that brand. That gives most brands a reason to be on Facebook.

To maximize your use of Facebook for your brand, following are some of the most popular features for you to consider:

- ✔ **Timeline:** At the end of 2011, Facebook released a new feature called Timeline. In his introduction of Timeline, Mark Zuckerberg said that its purpose is to keep a visual record of your life. As you look back through the months and years, the Timeline shows your posts, activity log, photos, and so on. This sounded like a great concept to many.

  When the Timeline feature was rolled out, users realized that there were some things they didn't want prominently displayed there. Perhaps some photos, events, comments were best left hidden. For this reason, Facebook allowed users a good deal of time to remove any items they didn't want displayed. For businesses, Timeline helps them keep their content visible and circulating.

- ✔ **Cover photo:** One of Timeline's features is a large photo at the top of the page. This photo, Facebook says, should demonstrate your individuality. Brands like Pepsi have made good use of this feature, as shown in Figure 7-18.

- ✔ **Followers:** This is Facebook's term for people who choose to follow your brand's News Feed. When visitors are on Facebook, brands believe there is prestige in having a high number of followers because it shows that many people are engaged and interested.

- ✔ **The What's on Your Mind box:** This is where you post your content, including links to your other channels, thus driving traffic.

- ✔ **The Like button:** When you click the Like button, you're signifying that you like or appreciate the content or the brand. This allows Facebook to include the brand's content in your News Feed. There is some debate about whether likes translate to revenue, but no brand wants to turn away likes.

- ✔ **Facebook advertising:** Facebook has an audience who is massively engaged with its content. The reason for this is that the content they see is from friends, colleagues, and family. In this age of information overload, recommendations by people you know are highly valued. It may be for this reason that the value of advertising on Facebook is hotly debated.

Figure 7-18:
Pepsi's
cover photo.

As mentioned earlier, General Motors pulled its $10 million ad campaign from Facebook. Contrast this with Ford, who said its ad buys are doing just fine. Every advertiser has to be able to convince themselves that their investment is providing a real return. A May 2012 poll by the Associated Press (AP) and CNBC found that in the U.S., 83 percent of Facebook users said they "hardly ever or never" clicked online ads or sponsored content. This is a developing story.

Adding Specialized Social Platforms

In most of this chapter, we discuss the major platforms that most companies who use social media choose first, but other specialized sites might be just right for your business. If you have a niche that's clearly defined, you might find another network that's perfect for your business.

Considering social network alternatives

If you think that being on the major sites assures that your customer will find you, think again. Is there something unique about your product or service that lends itself to one of the less traveled social networks? They include the following:

- **Google+:** As this book goes to press, the success of Google+ (at `https://plus.google.com`) is still an open question. Because of its late entry into the social network scene, users have been reluctant to add yet another social network to their to-do list. At the end of 2011, Google+ was reported to have 62 million users, whereas Facebook, as of April 2012, had a reported 900 million active users. When you compare the two, the number of people on Google+ makes it seem like a start-up.

  But don't ignore Google+ as a potential social network for your business. One of the important things to remember about Google+ is that it's tied to the Google ecosystem. As we all know, it takes effort to get on another social network, so Google+ users are there because they want to be. It's not a me-too proposition.

  Social media thought leader Chris Brogan, President of Human Business Works, abandoned Facebook at one time to operate from Google+. He also wrote a book called *Google+ for Business: How Google+ Changes Everything,* so clearly he's a fan.

  What does Brogan say about Google+? He's quoted in a 2012 article at online news source InTheCapital saying, "Go on Google+ looking to establish a place where you can share information that might help with customer acquisition and community nurturing." He recognizes the value.

  One of the unique features on Google+ is that you can segment followers into circles, as shown in Figure 7-19. After you've established a circle on a specific topic, you can read and post to that circle directly. The circles feature gives you the opportunity to send the right message to the right group.

- **LinkedIn:** If you work for a B2B company, you may want to consider using LinkedIn (`www.linkedin.com`) as one of your social platforms. (See Chapter 8 for more on this.) In March 2012, a HubSpot survey called the State of Inbound Marketing found that 62 percent of the respondents said they acquired a customer from LinkedIn.

  LinkedIn has over 100 million users who have uploaded all sorts of business information about themselves. In addition, LinkedIn has all sorts of special-interest groups that you can join to meet like-minded people. Everyone on LinkedIn is interested in networking with other business people, so LinkedIn is fertile ground for prospecting and developing customer relationships.

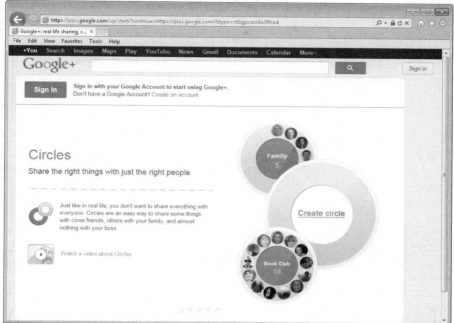

Figure 7-19:
Google+
circles.

Using visual platforms

Some popular social networking sites that emphasize visuals have been cropping up of late. The following two make sharing graphics and photos very easy:

- **Pinterest:** Launched in 2009, in its short life, Pinterest (`https://pinterest.com`) has become the darling of social media. According to comScore, Pinterest hit 10 million users faster than any other site. It has also been demonstrated that Pinterest's referral rate is higher than that of Facebook. *Referral rate* refers to the rate at which Pinterest users refer their pins to others.

  Pinterest is a visual site. The majority of users are female. When someone pins (shares) a photo of interest to their board, another interested pinner can pin it on their board. In this way, the photos can create traffic to the pin's original site.

  Pinterest allows you to add prices to your pins and places them in the upper-left corner. (See the Gifts navigational tool at the top of the Pinterest home page for pins with pricing info.) If you have great-looking graphics or photos of your products or services and your demographic skews female, you may want to consider Pinterest.

Figure 7-20:
Tumblr.

✔ **Tumblr:** Some consider the microblog Tumblr (www.tumblr.com), shown in Figure 7-20, to be a more visual version of Twitter. Tumblr is very customizable and allows almost any content format: photos, quotes, links, music, and videos. According to Tumblr's own site, as of February 2012, Tumblr has over 46.2 million blogs. Tumblr's growth has been very rapid. Between 2010 and 2011, it increased 218 percent. This made the social media community take notice.

On average, Tumblr users are young. comScore reports that half of the users are under age 25. If this is your demographic, consider creating a Tumblr blog.

Presenting as a Social Campaign Tool

When considering content creation, some companies don't realize that presenting is a powerful social tool, because they don't realize that any content they create can be repurposed and shown elsewhere on the web. We discuss some ways to repurpose content in the following sections.

Hosting webinars

More and more companies are jumping on the webinar bandwagon. The word *webinar* — a mash-up of the words *web* and *seminar* — refers to any online meeting where information is exchanged.

Webinar content can be sent to prospective customers, used in training, and edited further for audio podcasts. Links to the content can be sent through all the major social networks.

Early webinars were clunky, but that's not the case today. In the formative years of the webinar, the technology would cut you off, fail to record, or incorporate strange noises that rendered it unintelligible. Today, the technology has improved to the point that most webinars are enjoyable to attend.

When you're choosing a webinar host, consider the following:

- ✔ **Support:** Does the host offer tech support to help you with any problems you might run into?

- ✔ **Toll-free access:** Does the host provide a toll-free phone number for access to the webinar, or do participants have to pay local charges for the call?

- ✔ **Registration:** Does the service provide a registration mechanism for participants, or do you have to arrange for that separately?

- ✔ **Number of participants:** Can the host handle the number of participants you expect to have on the call?

If you're selecting a webinar host, consider the following services:

- ✔ **GoToWebinar:** This service, run by Citrix, has been around a long time with different offerings, including GoToMeeting and GoToTraining. Over the years, GoToWebinar (at `www.gotomeeting.com/fec/webinar`) has beefed up its features with tools such as whiteboards and polls.

- ✔ **WebEx:** This service, now owned by Cisco, has two-way video (at `http://webex.com`). The cost can be pricey if you want to have more than 25 attendees. Consider limiting participation unless you have a large budget.

- ✔ **Instant Teleseminar:** Created by former Microsoft employee Rick Raddatz, this service (at `http://instantteleseminar.com`), as shown in Figure 7-21, focuses on the needs of marketers by providing a one-stop shop to promote, record, and distribute webinars.

Figure 7-21:
Instant
Teleseminar.

✔ **Free Conference:** This is a free service, available at `www.free conference.com`. One disadvantage of this service is that it doesn't offer a toll-free number for callers. If you think this will be a big issue for your callers, don't consider using services without a toll-free access number. For business audiences, this may not be an issue.

Extending your reach with slide shows

We've all experienced what some people refer to as death by PowerPoint, but have you considered the value of sharing your presentations on a slide sharing site? Sharing your presentations gives them a second chance at a life. If they don't contain proprietary information or reveal some great competitive truth, you'll find a larger audience by sharing your presentation.

Some say the presentations increase in value because they can be watched at the viewer's convenience and don't have the droning voice of the presenter attached to them. If you're doing research or looking for new ideas, a presentation site may be just what you're looking for.

Sharing your slide presentations includes the following benefits:

- ✔ **Thought leader status:** If your contact information is included, you can demonstrate that you are a thought leader or that your company produces quality content.

- ✔ **Embedded links:** Uploading your slides to a sharing site means you have a link to your slides. Send that link to potential customers so that they can learn more about your work before a meeting.

- ✔ **Analytics:** Most presentation sites have analytics that tell you how often your presentation has been viewed. You can see what's popular and do more of it.

- ✔ **Social sharing buttons:** Presentation sites have social media buttons built in to help you multiply your sales force with loyal customers.

- ✔ **Leads:** You never know who might view your presentation. It could lead to a new customer.

If you'd like to upload your presentation to a site that houses slide shows, consider the following options:

- ✔ **SlideShare:** Shown in Figure 7-22, this is the most popular (and free) site for presentations of all kinds. Through the interface, you can easily display slides, PDFs, video, or content in another format. People can comment and connect with other SlideShare users. If you don't want everyone to be able to see your content, you can create a private presentation. You can find SlideShare at www.slideshare.net.

- ✔ **SlideRocket:** With this service (at www.sliderocket.com), you can create and display presentations. You can also collaborate with others to work on presentations. The basic service is free, but those who want to get more out of it can pay for a subscription.

- ✔ **Prezi:** This is another site, shown in Figure 7-23, that you may want to try, but it isn't slide based; it uses a proprietary application that creates digital stories. Its zooming techniques are a break from the slide paradigm. You can find Prezi at http://prezi.com.

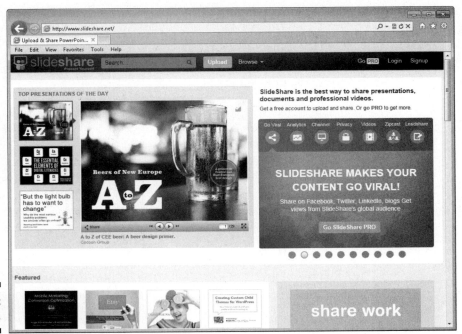

Figure 7-22:
SlideShare.

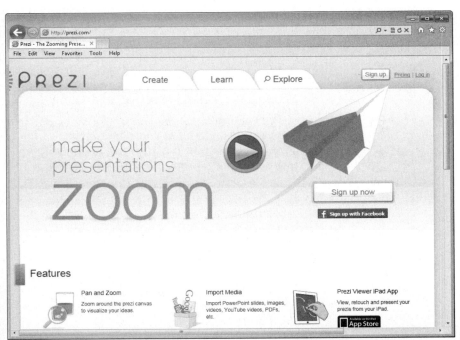

Figure 7-23:
Prezi.

Sharing e-books

It seems like everyone is reading e-books. It's a convenient way to package up your brand's information and share it. Don't be limited by the notion that an e-book has to mimic a physical book. You can create e-books that include your product information, recommendations, and anything else that interests your customers.

For example, Seth Godin's *Tales of the Revolution* (Domino Project), promoted in Figure 7-24, tells the stories that happened as a result of the Domino Project publishing *Poke the Box.* The key idea here is that now that we can publish digital book content so inexpensively, we can make an e-book from almost any ideas. In contrast, when a physical book was the only option, many ideas weren't published because of the high cost of publishing a physical book.

Another great example of using both digital and physical books to spread ideas is the book, *End Malaria,* by Michael Bungay Stanier (Domino Project). This book (its accompanying website is shown in Figure 7-25) is available in hardcover and e-book formats. By partnering with sponsors who were committed to spreading the word, the book raised over three hundred thousand dollars to fight malaria.

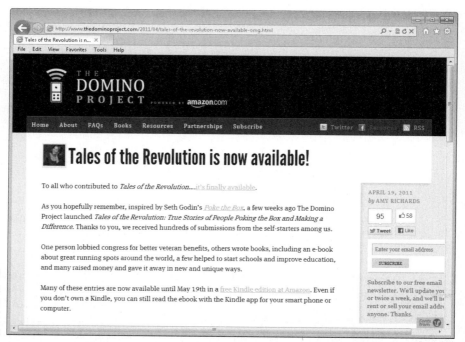

Figure 7-24:
Tales of the Revolution.

Figure 7-25:
End Malaria.

Rethinking what constitutes a book is a great way to make your own business content go viral.

Amazon allows you to publish an e-book for distribution in the Kindle Store. If you think your e-book would have wide interest, consider submitting it to Amazon for consideration. Amazon must approve it before you list it. Also, the Kindle Store allows you to promote your book for free for a limited time to boost interest. Take advantage of that if possible.

Mining the backchannel

Have you heard of the backchannel? If it sounds mysterious, it's not. The term *backchannel* refers to the stream of real-time comments on social platforms like Twitter when someone is giving a presentation. This can be another source of content from a presentation.

A few short years ago, the backchannel didn't exist. People sitting in the audience might comment to one another, but there was no widespread sharing of opinions on the spot. The backchannel allows anyone on a social platform to publicly share their opinions, make a nasty comment, or praise the speaker.

Some companies, aware of the power of the backchannel, establish a Twitter hashtag for a presentation before a conference or event begins. Companies know they can't control what's being said, but they can at least watch the comments along with everyone else. This is a good idea for your company. When you're aware of what the audience is saying, you may have the opportunity to modify what you're saying or respond to the comments.

At some conferences and other presentations, the backchannel comments are projected right on a big screen beside the presenters. When the comments appear on stage, the presenter can use those comments to further the discussion and extend the presentation's content.

One example of this is Pivot Conference (`http://2012.pivotcon.com`), as shown in Figure 7-26, a social media conference run by Brian Solis. Not only were the backchannel comments projected on the screen during the conference, but after the conference concluded, the conference presenters continued to capture tweets relating to the content. This is a great way to keep people engaged.

Figure 7-26:
Pivot
Conference.

Having Influence

Influence is a topic that every online business wants to know more about. Robert Cialdini, a psychologist, has written a classic book on the topic called *Influence: Science and Practice*. In it, he outlines several ways that people are persuaded. They include things like reciprocity (you give something and get something in return) and social proof (other people have purchased a product before you and were satisfied).

Influence has taken on new importance for social media users because people who write blogs and communicate to large groups online now wield influence. Several tools measure influence, but it's hardly an exact science. There has been much debate about whether these tools really measure influence or just social media activity. Following are some free tools you may want to use to check your company's (or your own) influence score:

- **Klout:** This was the first of the influence ranking tools, launched in 2009. It's available at `http://klout.com`, and it measures your activity and influence across social media platforms including Twitter, Facebook, and Google+.

- **Kred:** This company's tagline is, "We all have kred somewhere." With this as a starting point, this tool (available at `http://kred.com`) shows you your kred score (the highest is 1,000) and your outreach level (the highest is 12) based on your activity on Twitter.

- **PeerIndex:** This tool (available at `www.peerindex.com`) gives you a visual display of your areas of influence that it calls *topic footprints*. It also gives you a score that can be compared to others on the site.

Chapter 8

Aligning Sales in Social CRM

· ·

· ·

*W*hen implementing social CRM, your company needs to help salespeople adapt to the social media style of customer engagement. This requires salespeople to manage significant change. However, salespeople can transition to social CRM more smoothly by adopting the following attributes:

✓ **Collaborative in the way they approach the sales process:** Salespeople need to collaborate both within the company and with customers. With social CRM, data about customers isn't nestled only within the sales team, so departments need to share information and work together more. Similarly, sales doesn't own the key data about a product anymore. Customers are finding the data themselves and looking to sales for support in resolving specific questions or issues. In other words, customers are looking for more collaboration, too. You explore the importance of collaboration in the section "Valuing the collaborative Sales Model."

✓ **Open to forming close relationships with customers:** Social CRM expands sales representatives' access to the customer. To get the most value from this type of access, sales listens to what social customers are saying and who those customers are. Through listening, sales can form relationships with existing customers and reach out to potential new customers, too. We explain how sales can effectively build relationships in the sections "Interacting with the New Social Customer" and "Leading the New Lead Generation."

✔ **Transparent about what they know and how that impacts the customer:** Whereas sales used to have exclusive access to product information, today, customers can often find detailed data about a product online via their social networks, blogs, and review sites. When a company provides data to customers upfront, the company builds trust with customers that can help the company close the sale. Find out what transparency means in today's world of social CRM in the section "Leading the New Lead Generation."

✔ **Authentic in their motivation and dealings with the customer:** In a social CRM model, customers are looking for a salesperson to be a trusted advisor. It's important that salespeople connect authenticity to closing the sale. We explain how salespeople can demonstrate a sincere desire to help customers via social media in the section "Becoming the Trusted Advisor."

Salespeople need to put customers at the center of their world and work outward from there. If they're used to old-school sales techniques, that can be a tall order.

In the following sections, you find out how social CRM changes the sales cycle and learn strategies that will help your sales team adapt.

Challenging the New Social Salesperson

The new social salesperson is called upon to place special emphasis on customer relationships more directly than ever before. The ability to reach a customer directly is an advantage to the salesperson who likes relationship-based selling. If the salesperson is used to focusing on the product, she'll have a much harder time in this environment. In the sections that follow, you find out what characteristics can help your salespeople support you company's transition to social CRM. We also offer tips for persuading your sales team to use the new social CRM technology and sales methods.

Identifying your sales team's strengths

For their book, *The New Power Base Selling*, Jim Holden and Ryan Kubacki interviewed more than 28,000 business-to-business sellers in 35 countries during the years 1998–2011. The researchers measured the salespeople and their skills in the following seven core competencies that a successful salesperson has. They list the first three competencies that follow as the most important ones:

- ✔ **Value creation:** This is the ability to articulate the value that the salesperson's solution brings. Those who are successful in this category can pull the focus away from features and benefits and talk directly about how their solution brings a range of improvements — both immediately and over time.

- ✔ **Political advantage:** The salesperson with a political advantage can size up the political situation in the company and exploit it to his own advantage. Every organization has its own set of politics, so being able to work within those constraints is the mark of a true sales professional.

- ✔ **Competitive differentiation:** This skill allows salespeople to communicate how their company is both different and better than the competition.

- ✔ **Business acumen:** These salespeople can leverage the existing climate with emerging trends to develop solutions.

- ✔ **Relationship adeptness:** This refers to a salesperson's ability to form relationships with all the people involved in the process, including support people and members of other departments.

- ✔ **Executive bonding:** Salespeople who excel at executive bonding have the knack of forming a relationship with the executives who make the decision, even if they aren't working directly with them.

- ✔ **Resource optimization:** Those salespeople who optimize their resources need to understand how their company's products can be a good fit with the customer's assets.

To help your sales staff cultivate these characteristics, offer training and reading lists. You need to make it as easy as possible for salespeople to make the transition to social CRM.

Encouraging compliance with social CRM

Aside from the challenges to the salesperson, we've identified several challenges in this chapter when businesses try to integrate social CRM and sales. The issue of *compliance* among their sales force is often mentioned. Compliance refers to the fact that some salespeople don't use the social CRM tools and systems available to them and fail to comply with new policies for a company's social CRM initiative.

It's critical that businesses convince their sales force to use these systems so that businesses can meet the following challenges:

- Understand the new social sales ecosystem and find better ways for their employees to collaborate.
- Listen to customers in the new ways available to them.
- Change the way they look at lead generation and real-time marketing.
- Integrate their customer information with other intelligence.
- Discover the new social buying path and its implications for content creation.
- Assist salespeople in creating a sales persona for their social networks and becoming skilled with tools like LinkedIn and Twitter.
- Learn how to use the tools to follow conversations and mine data.
- Analyze the social data to make it useful throughout the enterprise.

If your sales team struggles to see social media as an added value, they'll need proof that social media will make a difference to their bottom line. So what are some of the benefits that can accrue to salespeople who adopt social media and use social CRM tools? They include the following:

- Building better customer relationships based on trust
- Connecting faster to the people who make the decisions
- Getting referrals from current customers
- Finding new cross-sells or upsells when appropriate
- Gaining recognition as thought leaders
- Following the interests and activities of current customers so that they can find ways to personally engage them

Those benefits sound great, don't they? You may wonder what stands in the way of adopting these methods. The main impediment is that it requires a lot of training and extra effort. That would stop any busy employees in their tracks.

The salesperson has to become well-versed in the tools, set up and learn new procedures, and spend time doing new things. Any businessperson faced with that challenge would be reluctant to meet it without a lot of proof that it will close more sales and increase commissions. Another issue is the amount of collaboration required by almost the entire enterprise to make social CRM a reality. The details in later sections in this chapter help you make the case to your sales team.

Building Sales Intelligence

Today, sales intelligence means getting vast stores of information into the hands of employees. However, advances in computing power generate more data than your sales team could ever use.

The development of dashboards has been a welcome addition for managers who were drowning in data they couldn't utilize. The abundance of this data has come to be known as *big data,* a term that refers to data that is so numerous that the usual databases are inadequate.

When you add social media data to the typical CRM system, the integration is problematic.

The mix of real-time external data and internal data adds a layer of complexity. *Internal data* is data that is produced inside the company — for instance, data regarding sales and expenses. *External data* is the data that's produced outside the company and pulled from such places as social media, news, and competitors.

At this point, it's helpful to look at the kind of data you expect to have in a social CRM system designated by source — either external or internal — so that you can understand the complexity. This list is by no means an exhaustive one.

Here are some categories and examples of data sourced internally:

- ✔ **Customer history:** Customer purchasing behavior and support tickets

- ✔ **Financial information:** Equipment costs and salaries

- ✔ **Licenses and copyrighted material:** Patents, photos, and collateral

- ✔ **Specific employee sales data:** Data generated by the salesperson to support her own efforts — e-mails, contacts, appointment calendar info, and deal documents

Here are some categories and examples of data sourced externally:

- ✔ **Industry news and breaking stories:** This includes any real-time information that impacts your industry generally or breaking news that directly impacts your company.

- ✔ **Competitors and partners:** Data that changes the way you'll conduct business. Remember that your competitors are also educating your customers. They'll use all the same types of content and distribution channels to reach them. Make sure you review this data so that you know what may be in your customers' minds.

- ✔ **Government documents:** Regulations about how to conduct business and handle employees.

- ✔ **Technical information:** Data to support mobile systems.

- ✔ **Social media platforms:** Data collected from customers' comments and reviews, bookmarking sites, photo sites, forums and community groups, and blogs.

External data can come from current customers, industry influencers, self-identified loyalists, active social media commenters, and the news media. Obviously, tying this all together requires finely tuned systems, which is why the enterprise is grappling with it.

The Satmetrix *Worldwide Social Media for Business Study* in 2012 found that in the U.S., 31 percent of the companies surveyed didn't track or follow up with social media. It's one thing to collect the data and quite another to use it.

One of the major problems businesses face is using the data they collect. Both managers and salespeople alike have more data than they can use. What companies need to do is to take the raw data and package it up in a way that makes it accessible to everyone.

Valuing the Collaborative Sales Model

The use of new technology makes collaboration much easier. Today, teams can work across time zones and share whiteboards that are in the cloud. Video conferencing can bring everyone face to face across a virtual table.

But issues still arise about the best way for sales teams to collaborate across the enterprise. The pace is usually frantic as groups struggle to meet deadlines and complete projects. It can be hard for teams to assimilate the new technology available to them. It can also be hard to reach across to other business functions.

Regardless of the business function involved, most enterprises deal with the issues brought on by a *silo mentality* — a term that refers to the mindset that each business function operates independently of the others. They don't share information or work and play well with other departments. In this section, we look at some new ways that sales teams are collaborating within their organization and how innovation and productivity tips can help.

Categorizing the social sales ecosystem

Previously, sales departments often ran their own fiefdoms. They dictated the type of data they needed and controlled the information necessary to make sales. Now, groups can't work in isolation. To have a well-functioning social CRM system, several groups need to be intimately involved in the sales process.

Aside from the sales function itself, each group in the ecosystem has a major contribution to make to the new social sales environment. Without collaboration, each group couldn't function. The social sales ecosystem is as follows:

- **Marketing:** They run the social media promotions and campaigns that create leads for the sales team. The PR department is often included here.

- **Customer support:** Customer service needs to monitor what's being said on social networks and other channels.

- **Information technology:** Sales teams need the CRM data and technology so they can work unassisted in the field.

- **Customers:** In this new sales ecosystem, customers play a different role than they did in the past. In a nutshell, their role (previously) was to buy the product — period. But now, customers contribute feedback about everything. They critique the products, praise or vent about the support they receive, and recommend products to their friends. The customer, in some cases, can also guide product development.

- **Partners:** They provide potential customers, investors, or new ways to reach your audience.

- **Vendors and suppliers:** They provide the materials in a timely fashion so that products can be made and shipped.

Collaboration becomes the key that will help the entire organization realize its business goals and make social CRM a reality.

And the winner is . . .

In the *Harvard Business Review*, an article called "Which Kind Of Collaboration Is Right for You? " by Gary Pisano and Roberto Verganti, discusses four different models that could work to help the enterprise collaborate and innovate more effectively. No one model is better than another. It depends on how it fits with your needs. The four types are listed in the following table.

You can use these models in a variety of ways and apply them to internal or external groups.

One example of the Innovation Mall is IdeaScale (`http://ideascale.com`), which provides a place where companies (including Intel and Subaru) can sign up to receive suggestions from their customers. Other customers can vote for their favorite ideas. If customers don't vote for the idea, it doesn't rise to the top. The winning suggestions are selected by the company. (*Note:* It isn't strictly an Innovation Mall because ultimately the company decides whether the highest voted choices can be implemented.)

Using new technology to *crowdsource* (get input from people online) allows you to do two things:

- ✔ Offer the problem to the largest number of potential problem solvers.

- ✔ Pay for only the solution instead of employing a full-time group who may not solve the problem.

Mode of Collaboration	Problem to Solve	Employee or External Source	Solution
Elite Circle	The company defines the problem. company.	Employees are hand-selected.	The company chooses the winning solution.
Innovation Mall	The company defines the problem.	Anyone can offer a solution.	The company chooses the winning solution.
Innovation Community	Anyone can pose a problem.	Anyone can offer a solution.	Anyone can pick the winning solution.
Consortium	The group offers a problem to solve.	The group offers the solution.	The group chooses the winning solution.

Embracing the cloud

Who ever thought that big business could be driven by something as ethereal as a cloud? But that's what happened. *Cloud-based computing* refers to the use of software that you access and use online (metaphorically in the cloud). Previously, companies housed all enterprise software on its internal computers or at big data centers full of equipment.

Big companies had the advantage because they could afford more and faster equipment. Small businesses suffered in comparison. They weren't considered for major assignments because they just didn't have the computing power to execute on large projects. Enter the cloud! The playing field starts to level.

With the advent of new cloud-based applications, any company can have access to the data that its employees need to get the job done. Cloud computing levels the playing field because small businesses don't need special equipment. It makes it easy for everyone to access the same data and collaborate with their team members. Previously, teams couldn't be sure if they were all using the same data. Now with cloud computing, everyone can have the latest, best data.

Some benefits of cloud-based applications are as follows:

- ✔ **Security:** The vendor, not the user, is responsible for ensuring that all its customers are safe from data breeches and theft.

- ✔ **Backups:** The vendor backs up the data and makes it available to the users 24/7.

- ✔ **Current or real-time data:** Because the data is synced, it's current. No salesperson should get old pricing or out-of-date documents.

- ✔ **Scalability:** The vendor can supply more power or less as necessary so that companies don't have to worry about purchasing more computing power or scaling up on their own.

- ✔ **Communication:** Many of these applications allow employees to communicate in real time with other employees on deals and projects.

One of the most well-known cloud-based applications that serves salespeople is Salesforce.com (`http://salesforce.com`), as shown in Figure 8-1. The company works toward making its system one of the best social CRM systems available. Find out more about Salesforce.com and similar systems in Chapter 16.

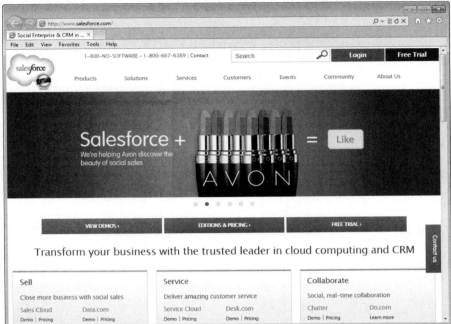

Figure 8-1:
Salesforce.
com.

Checking out collaboration tools

If an organization doesn't have a social CRM system, employees can still find online tools that will help them collaborate effectively. There are hundreds of new collaboration tools available that can help salespeople work effectively as a team. We list several here to get you started:

✔ **Meetings:**

Google+ Hangouts: This is Google's free entry (at `https://plus.google.com/hangouts`) into the online meeting market, and it's directly tied to your Google+ circles.

Any Meeting: This company has free and fee-based solutions (at `www.anymeeting.com`) for all types of meetings, including video.

✔ **Scheduling:**

Genbook: This is a fee-based application (at `www.genbook.com`) that assists with business scheduling.

Doodle: This company provides scheduling services, as shown in Figure 8-2. Find out more at `www.doodle.com`.

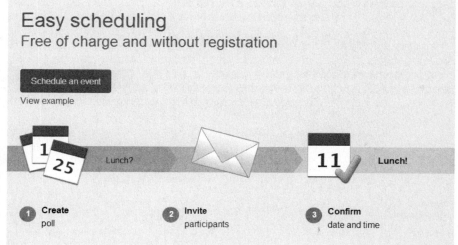

Figure 8-2:
Doodle
offers a
scheduling
service.

✓ **Document sharing:**

Dropbox: This very popular free application (at `http://dropbox.com`) allows you to store and share documents.

ShowDocument: This service offers both free and fee-based products (at `www.showdocument.com`) that allow you to share your documents and hold a variety of different meeting types to review them as a team.

✓ **Project management:**

GanttProject: This free application (available at `www.ganttproject.biz`) allows you to plan projects using a Gantt-style chart, helps you show how each item on the chart relates to the others and what must be done to complete each phase before moving to the next.

Freedcamp: Several major enterprises use this free project management application (available at `https://freedcamp.com`) because of its robust features at no cost. Figure 8-3 shows the Freedcamp company's home page.

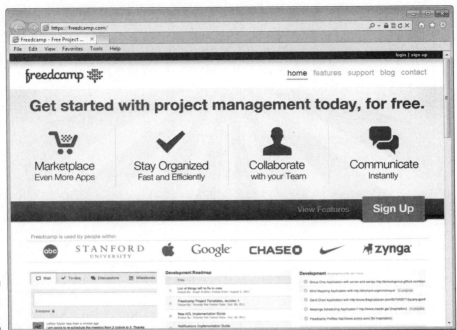

Figure 8-3:
Freedcamp.

✔ **Brainstorming:**

Wridea: With this free application (find out more at `http://wridea.com`), you can expand your ideas and share them in several different ways.

MindMeister: You can create mind maps and share them with others with this free mind-mapping application (available at `www.mindmeister.com`). A *mind map* is a brainstorming tool that helps you develop your ideas without having to work in a linear fashion like an outline. You can put your ideas down as they occur to you. Then you can see what patterns emerge. The resulting map shows you both the details and the big picture all on the same screen.

✔ **Whiteboarding and design collaboration:**

ConceptShare: This tool (find out more at `www.conceptshare.com`) allows teams to get together to mark up their graphics in real time.

Twiddla: With this free, fun tool (at `www.twiddla.com`), you and your team can surf together and mark up graphics as needed. You can see Twiddla's home page in Figure 8-4.

Figure 8-4:
Twiddla.

Interacting with the New Social Customer

Most businesses understand that they need to focus on the fact that their customers are talking back in record numbers. The part they often overlook is the establishment of effective plans to listen to their customers. Listening effectively requires staff and resources dedicated to the effort.

Once they have the resources in place, the data then needs to be analyzed to provide real value to the entire organization. The question, then, becomes what to monitor. It's easy to follow a Twitter stream or look at daily Facebook comments, but brands have to go much deeper to get any real meaning from these comments. They need to understand trends and be able to predict what comes next.

Listening to the customer

With the advent of big data, listening to the customer becomes one of the most valuable ways companies can figure out what customers want. It also can be problematic because there is so much of it. You need to figure out how you will analyze and use it. In his book *CRM at the Speed of Light* (McGraw-Hill Osborne Media), Paul Greenberg cites a Price Waterhouse study from 2008 called *How Consumer Conversation Will Transform Business*.

In the study, Price Waterhouse identified these four ways to monitor the customer conversation in a meaningful way:

- ✔ **Volume:** This refers to the amount of conversation about your brand. Obviously, spikes in conversation should be closely monitored by the social media team, and appropriate information should be passed on to the salespeople. Does a lack of volume indicate disinterest or satisfaction? One way to determine this is to ask your readers to tell you stories about how your product has helped them. Offer the respondents a free report for participating. If they don't respond, it could indicate lack of interest more than satisfaction.

- ✔ **Tone:** Is the conversation favorable? If it's not, it's important to determine if it's a trend and to what extent it relates to a specific issue. Major PR disasters can arise if no one is listening. If it is, you might amplify that by engaging with the writers.

- ✔ **Coverage:** How large is the conversation? Do you have a host of voices, or is most of the conversation generated by a small number of people? This is an important measure. If you're trying to expand your reach, you'll want to study why that small group is engaged and figure out how to find others who fit that profile.

- ✔ **Authoritativeness:** Are industry influentials and high-ranking business-people discussing your brand? If so, have you established a dialogue with them? If not, why not? You need someone to take the initiative to contact influentials and find out how you can grow your relationship with them without seeming self-serving.

When the data is categorized in these four ways, all functions in the organization can use these categories to make better decisions. For example, you can see how customer service would want to be aware of data about the tone, and the marketing department would want to know about authoritativeness. The sales team would also want to know about authoritativeness to determine if any of their accounts were part of a larger discussion about the brand.

The key is to make sure everyone gets this data. That's the big challenge in making social CRM a reality.

Selling to the buying brain

As research becomes more sophisticated in its knowledge of the inner workings of the brain, marketing and sales groups try to formulate newer, more effective ways to sell to us. They appeal to our emotions. They realize that although we think we're rational when we make buying decisions, we buy on emotion.

In his book, *The Buying Brain* (John Wiley & Sons, Inc.), A.K. Pradeep explores how we feel about brands and their relationship to us as people. He found that if we relate any of the following benefits to the use of a certain brand, we're likely to buy:

- Promoting physical beauty
- Representing intellectual accomplishment
- Being in the know technically and intellectually
- Achieving career and financial success
- Providing access to power and resources
- Being exclusive and elite
- Supporting uniqueness of personality

You can see that features and benefits are important, but they don't really get to the heart of why people buy. For instance, a particular car may get low gas mileage, but if the buyer believes he appears financially successful when he drives it, we know he may buy it anyway.

We're all guilty of buying for less than rational reasons. In addition, studies show that we provide ourselves with rational reasons to hide the emotional ones. Add this subconscious motivation to the recommendations, critiques, and opinions of social media users and you've got a complicated stew of buying motivations.

For customers to connect emotionally to your product, you need to provide multisensory experiences, whether those experiences are in a store or online. In a store, you may sell products by encouraging customers to interact with a product. A store can structure these interactions so they're informative and entertaining. Research has shown that buyers who pick up physical items are more likely to buy them than those who just look at them. Think about this the next time you go into a store saying that you're just going to look. If you pick the item up, you may be standing in the checkout line sooner than you intended.

Because buying online is a different experience, how can your sales team translate the multisensory experience that customers find in a store into an online environment? Here are a few ways you can translate the power of multisensory experiences to a website or other online channel where you conduct sales:

- ✔ **On your website, make sure you include content in a variety of formats.** You should have video, audio, and anything else that stimulates the buyer's curiosity for novel things. Of course, you can't engage all the same senses online and off, but you can make sure to vary the applicable ones.

- ✔ **Your sales approach should always set out to educate and entertain.** No one sets out to bore the customer, but a majority of sales pitches can be mind-numbing. That's one reason why gamification is gaining favor online. (More about this in Chapter 9.) Buyers' expectations are raised by their online experiences. They know that they enjoy themselves online and they want the brand to show them the same kind of experience no matter what type of product it is. Humor is used in business ads as often as it is in movie trailers.

- ✔ **Offer customers ways to pick up or experience your product.** You can create a user experience for the customer if it's software or app driven. You can let them have a trial of the product. If it's a hard good, you could send a sample or let the customer use a coupon to sample it from a local store.

Leading the New Lead Generation

When you peruse information about selling to the social customer, you'll find two concepts virtually absent from the discussion — cold calling and purchasing leads. Social media has changed the way buyers let you interact with them.

You may still get a phone call from someone selling a service, but the approach seems like an anachronism. It's more likely that you'll get an e-mail from a brand representative following up on a white paper you downloaded or a comment you made on a social platform. As sales guru Jeffrey Gitomer has said, "Social media is the new cold call."

Customers don't want to be picked seemingly at random to receive a sales pitch. Everyone is overwhelmed, with little time to spare. The idea that they would have the time to take calls that don't interest them is laughable. Customers believe that they will spend some of their time identifying the products and services they want and then they will let the salesperson educate them.

Technology has facilitated the change in the way customers are contacted. The definition of *spam* is an e-mail that is sent to someone without a prior business relationship or permission to send additional marketing e-mail. For this reason, brands are loathe to send to e-mail addresses from a purchased list. In addition, the CAN-SPAM act has alerted brands that you don't want to hear from them unless you grant them permission.

Connecting ROI with social media

A key to understanding how managers move from an old sales paradigm to a new social one is the issue of return on investment (ROI). Companies often have a hard time quantifying the return they get from participating in social media.

For example, how does a business manager calculate ROI for the amount of time a salesperson spends on Facebook? If she sees no direct sale as a result, does that mean the time was wasted?

Managers are used to tying revenue to campaigns, so it stands to reason that they would want to do the same with social media campaigns. Managers want to be able to look at statistics like "20 percent increase in Likes on Facebook" and attach a revenue number to it. The problem is that it's hard to quantify the value of a recommendation or a positive comment. Clearly that's not possible in the same way sales data is quantified.

An infographic called The ROI of Social Media (created by MDG Advertising) is published here:

```
www.mdgadvertising.com/blog/infographic-the-roi-of-
          social-media-2
```

According to the infographic, managers are looking beyond the usual sales metrics to measurements like:

- ✔ **Increased ability to close business**
- ✔ **Establishment of new partnerships**
- ✔ **A drop in marketing costs**
- ✔ **Improvement in search engine ranking**

When you look at the social media data that way, it becomes a tangible way to value the activity. So the question becomes tying social media to lead generation by looking at how the social media buyers determines what they will buy. In the next section, you see how at every step in the buyer's decision-making process, social media plays a role.

Following the path of the new social buyer

Some salespeople still need to be convinced that social media adds value to their efforts. Previously, salespeople conducted B2B sales in the same way as the generations that came before them. The introduction of social media into the sales process changed everything, but old habits die hard.

A salesperson who's used to getting results from a certain set of techniques needs to be convinced to try something different. One of the best ways for salespeople to convince themselves that social media matters is to take a look at customers' online buying path.

A 2011 study by GroupM and comScore called *The Virtuous Circle: The Role of Search and Social Media in the Purchase Pathway* found that 48 percent of those who eventually purchased used both search and social media to make a decision. This finding has a tremendous impact on how salespeople can best generate leads with social CRM.

To understand how customers' buying decisions play out, the researchers documented the customer journey. We use the example of searching for a new toaster and follow the path to see how the conversion evolves. The consumer starts with search and follows through to the purchase taking the following path:

1. **Searching for brands:** The consumer begins her journey by learning which brands make the type of product she wants. It's a general search that helps her narrow the search to specific brands. Here are some examples of searches: *toasters best, toasters four slice,* and *toasters stainless steel.*

   A Google search of possible toaster brands includes brand names like Black & Decker, T-Fal, and Cuisinart. Search terms could include the brand name with the word toasters, such as *T-Fal toasters.*

2. **Searching for blogs with product information and reviews:** Next in her investigation is a look at blogs that contain information about toasters. You can do this easily by using the Blog option on Google Search and typing in *toasters.*

   For example, a search on toaster blogs yields results that include Consumer Reports (`www.consumerreports.org/cro/toasters.htm`) and HouseKool (`www.housekool.com/shopping/?okw=toasters`).

3. **Visiting competitors' websites:** After the consumer determines who the competitors are and gets a feel (via product reviews on blogs) for the issues she should consider, she looks at the actual competitive sites. For

example, she goes to Cuisinart's toaster page (www.cuisinart.com/products/toasters.html) and that of other competitors to compare specific models.

4. **Searching review sites for the industry or product:** Next, she looks at review sites that discuss competitive advantages of and prices for specific toasters. For example, Epinions (www.epinions.com/toasters?sb=1), shown in Figure 8-5, provides tools that help consumers compare toasters and price by brand, size, price range, features, and stores.

Recommendations, reviews, and critiques from customers drive today's sales process. A wealth of data and opinions about products is just a click away. Customers who want to get the best value for their money can't help but investigate the information available to them. For B2B (business-to-business) buyers, the information is so plentiful that they have to actively work to separate fact from fiction. That's where other businesspeople's opinions really matter. They want to know if products really deliver on their promise and won't settle for the salesperson's word. Previously, the only way a customer or buyer could research a salesperson's claim was to belong to a business group or call his colleagues. In contrast, today's customer can roam the world to get the opinions of others.

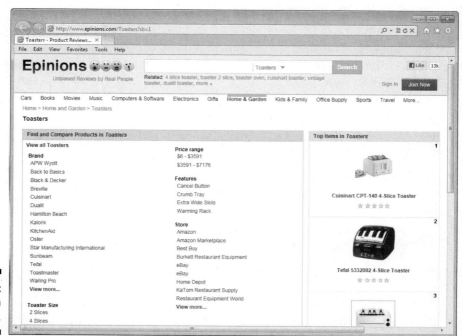

Figure 8-5:
Epinions on toasters.

5. **Searching for deals or discounts:** The consumer follows links to specific advertising, looking for deals or discounts.

6. **Buying a product (conversion):** The consumer makes her purchase decision and most likely follows the brand on Twitter or clicks the brand's Like button on Facebook.

In this example, we used a consumer product. Notice how often social media and search figured into the investigation.

If the consumer instead undertook a B2B search, the path wouldn't look that different. The key to understanding the B2B path is to analyze the type of information the buyer looks at prior to making a decision. We cover that in the upcoming section, "Creating content for buying."

Recognizing the new social media persona

When you're targeting customers, it can be helpful to develop personas. This tactic has been used for several years and has proven to aid salespeople in better understanding the customer. A persona is a representative of one of your company's target customers. You can create as many as you need, but if you don't create any, you won't be able to focus on selling with the kind of precision that personas allow.

When creating personas, you should give each one an actual name, gender, and a face (stock photo) to help make the persona real. When your whole team focuses on selling to a prototypical customer, it's easier to stay on the same page.

Besides a name and picture, a typical persona includes

- ✔ **Demographics:** This includes age, gender, and the like.

- ✔ **Sociographics:** Data in this category includes what the customer believes and what he thinks about things related to your product.

- ✔ **Occupation:** Decide how your persona supports himself.

- ✔ **Places where he consumes his media:** You want to know where he goes online to find information, consume news, and network with friends so that you can reach him.

- ✔ **Tech tools he uses:** Obviously, this helps you know on which devices to optimize your information. Does he use a smartphone or other gadgets?

Who's got the power?

When you think about powerful buying groups on the web, do moms come to mind? They should. They're big social media users. Performics and ROI Research released a study in April 2012 that revealed that moms are more likely to make a purchase decision based on social media recommendations versus non-moms (those women who don't have children living in the household). 50 percent of them own a smartphone, as compared to 32 percent for non-moms.

Moms also make big purchases as a result of social media — things like automobiles, travel, telecom, entertainment, and apparel, and they also love contests and sweepstakes. 53 percent of them have already participated in company and brand contests, as opposed to 44 percent of non-moms. Don't overlook this very important group when you're looking for the new social customer.

It's also interesting to note that in 2012, BlogHer (a media company and community of women bloggers; www.blogher.com) did a study of its audience of women versus the total U.S. population and found that both audiences trusted information from blogs the most in relation to Facebook, Twitter, and Pinterest. The general population said that they trusted blogs and Pinterest (a tie). If you think social media isn't playing a large part in your audience's choices, think again.

✔ **Household:** Establish who resides with your persona and how those people may influence his purchases.

✔ **Pets:** Does he have animals in the home who require care? Will he be buying pet food and accessories?

✔ **Hobbies:** You want to know if the persona spends money on specific interests, which also impact where he goes online.

Personas help the team focus on all they ways they can develop relationships with customers.

A study by Aimia called *Staring at the Sun: Identifying, Understanding and Influencing Social Media Users* identified six social media personas, shown in Table 8-1, that can help you begin to think through your own company's target customers. Look at them and see if you see your customer profile there. You can find the study here:

```
http://aimia.com/files/doc_downloads/aimia_socialmedia_
          whitepaper.pdf
```

Table 8-1		Aimia Social Media Personas			
Name	**Percent of U.S. Population**	**Income**	**Age**	**Description**	**Favorite Social Platforms**
No shows	41%	$30K	65	Doesn't participate.	None
New-comers	15%	$75K	39	Mainly observes.	Facebook and YouTube
On-lookers	16%	$85K	36	Consumes but doesn't contribute.	Facebook and YouTube
Cliquers	6%	$95K	47	Engages with family and friends.	Facebook and YouTube
Mix-n-minglers	19%	$95K	29	Engages with a wide group.	Facebook, Twitter, and LinkedIn
Spark	3%	$80K	24	Uses social media daily and creates content.	Facebook, Twitter, and blogs

Don't assume that the personas discussed here relate only to B2C or B2B buyers. If a consumer is comfortable with social media, that will translate into her use of social media for business purposes. People don't switch off their social media skills when they enter the office.

You can use the previous information about social media personas to help you create your company personas. For example, you could look at the age groups of the social media personas and see how closely that matches your audience. The age range they cover is approximately 20–50. If your audience fits somewhere in there, see if you can narrow it down by income.

Creating content for buying

It's important to be aware of how much information the buyer has before he gets on your radar screen. Some say approximately 75 percent of customers research a product before buying. If you ignore the quality or type of information available to your customer, your sale could be dead before you're even aware of the customer's interest.

If you work for a large enterprise, the quality and quantity of the information created is usually controlled by a central group. The likelihood that you have to create your own collateral increases as the size of the organization decreases.

Here are some types of content the social media customer wants before ever speaking to a sales rep:

- ✔ Downloadable product comparisons
- ✔ Webinars
- ✔ Podcasts
- ✔ Video training
- ✔ Case studies
- ✔ Video product demos
- ✔ Community forums

Today's social customers spend time reading reviews, looking at product descriptions, and comparing prices before they ever consider making a purchase. Therefore, your goal should be to provide all the content your prospects need along the sales cycle.

As a salesperson, you need to make sure that you are aware of online content that your customers are finding and using. The content your company provides about your products keeps the customer on your site. This is very important. If your customer frequently comes back and spends time on your site, you're more likely to make a sale.

Closing the social sales cycle

The most important thing about your content is that the buyer can access it online and never have to speak to a salesperson until she's ready. This changes the sales dynamic. The new social customer is usually well-informed about products and pricing.

The role of the social salesperson is to add value to the information that potential customers already have and become a trusted advisor, with an understanding of what the buyer needs. A salesperson who only recites the product or service's features and benefits won't usually get the sale; she needs to go the extra mile. Following are some technical things she can do to close the sale:

✔ Point potential customers to the answers to complex questions using social media.

✔ Host a custom pricing meeting using an electronic whiteboard.

✔ Video-conference the sales and customer teams together to hold a kick-off meeting to begin to explore solutions.

✔ Use an electronic tablet at customer locations to access and sign the most current documents.

Becoming the Trusted Advisor

A change in mindset is required for salespeople who want to utilize social media in their sales efforts. They need to think of themselves as both independent entities and as parts of the enterprise team.

If you work in a small company or are the sole salesperson, it's easy to see how stepping out and building your own sales profile will get you sales momentum. Most likely, you will be encouraged to take an active role.

If you work for a larger company, you need to create a fine balance between representing your company as a whole and getting publicity for yourself. When salespeople didn't have access to the tools to speak directly to potential customers, there was no conflict. Today, salespeople need to understand the complexity of gaining popularity under their own name as well as representing the enterprise.

In this chapter, we suggest many of the ways you can network on social media to get recognition and close sales, but remember that you have to be clear about your company's policy for each network. This is still uncharted territory for many companies. If you're unclear, ask first. In some cases, legal issues may be involved. (Chapter 13 explains what to consider in your company's social media policy.) Needless to say, you also shouldn't mix your personal profile with your business profile, ever!

So which social networks are most effective for salespeople? According to the infographic Social Media Facts & Figures for B2B Sales created by InsideView (www.insideview.com/social-media-facts.html), the most popular social media sites for generating B2B traffic in 2011 are

✔ LinkedIn

✔ Reddit

✔ Wikipedia

✔ Twitter

✔ Facebook

✔ StumbleUpon (shown in Figure 8-6)

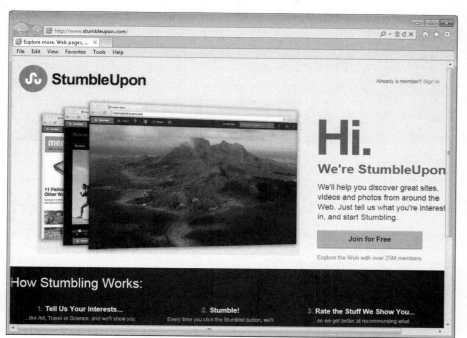

Figure 8-6:
Stumble-
Upon.

These are all social media networks that require a variety of activity from the salesperson — posting articles, talking about products, and alerting customers to new promotions. The key to unlocking value for your enterprise is to find out how your company wants sales to engage on these channels.

For example, if you establish a profile on LinkedIn, can you send out articles of interest to your audience or must you use only approved company content? (See the next section.) You could ask the same question regarding all the previously mentioned channels.

Establishing a sales profile with content

A salesperson is most often required to use the collateral her company provides. Usually, she can use product sheets, white papers, and all sorts of other material that support the sales effort. If the company has a website, it's likely that customers can find a great deal of information there.

But what about content that the salesperson wants to create to support her own efforts? Usually, the company grants permission for staff to create their own custom sales presentations and other written material to support a specific sales effort.

In this social media environment, salespeople also find the need to create content to communicate with a wider audience. If they want to be seen as experts, the quality of the content they create is critical. This puts pressure on them to develop content that supports the specific needs of the customer. So what's the criteria for creating that type of content? According to Marketo (www.marketo.com) in their white paper *Creating Content that Sells,* these six rules of effective content marketing should guide salespeople:

✔ **Be nonpromotional.** This is a tricky one to pull off. Obviously, you want to talk about how your product solves a problem, but readers don't want to spend their time reading one-sided promotional material disguised as objective information. When you create a blog post or other content, make sure to include information that potential customers actually need to make good decisions. They will respect you for educating them.

✔ **Be relevant to your reader.** Help potential customers focus on the key issues. As the expert, you know which issues really count when making a buying decision. Present those as directly as you can and cut down on superfluous information.

✔ **Close a gap for your reader.** "Closing a gap" refers to the idea that your customers have questions that need answers, and closing that gap can help them make good decisions.

✔ **Provide well-written content.** Your writing should be clear, not fancy. Your readers are seeking information, and the more succinctly you present it, the more likely they will want to work with you. Don't fret about your lack of writing skill. Simply provide potential customers with the answers that you have.

✔ **Be relevant to your company.** The customer knows you're representing your company. Don't be coy about what you offer and how it can help. Just make sure that you're focusing on solving the right problem.

✔ **Give proof.** *Proof* in this context refers to testimonials and other evidence that people have used your products and are satisfied. Provide customer comments, pictures of actual customers if possible, and quotes from industry influentials. Display them prominently. Don't assume your customer knows about your company's awards or other notable achievements.

Once you've written your content, decide where to distribute it. You want to make sure you get the most eyeballs. Following are some suggested venues and tactics for distributing your content:

✔ **Communicate in forums and industry-wide communities.** You don't have to search very far to find online forums and communities related to your industry. You can use a tool like BoardReader (`http://board reader.com`; shown in Figure 8-7) to find them. You can also find groups on LinkedIn related to your industry and join several of them.

✔ **Capture multimedia coverage of your activities.** Use videos, audio from conferences and speeches, and any other representations of your interaction with your customers. You can also publicize your multimedia activities on YouTube.

✔ **Create webinars and teleseminars.** If permitted, create your own webinar or teleseminar instead of only using the ones created by your company. You'll learn about your customers, see who shows up, and get potential leads from people who specifically respond to you and your content. Make sure that you publicize these events on sites like Google+ Hangouts and LinkedIn.

✔ **Create your own account on LinkedIn, Twitter, and other networks.** Having your own account on the major social networks can provide a place for you to step into the spotlight. If your company permits, make the effort to get comfortable publicizing your activities on social platforms.

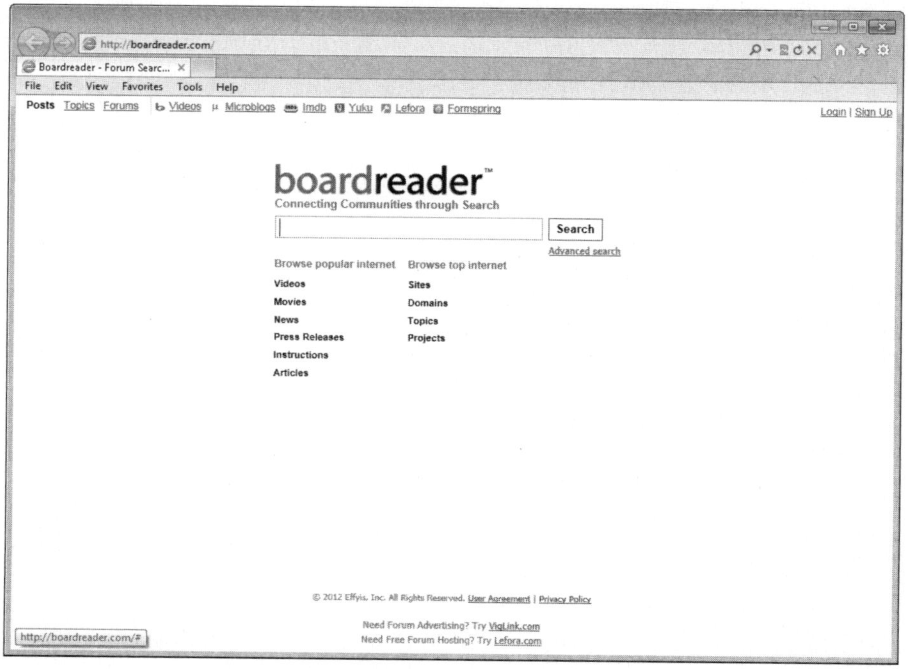

Figure 8-7: Board-Reader.

Use your Twitter account to publicize your activities on Twitter with hashtags. (In Chapter 7, you can find more info about tweeting and creating hashtags.)

✔ **Write articles for industry publications and blogs.** Create articles and blog posts. Remember that the goal is to supply great information, not write like a famous novelist. Make sure to include the company's keywords as well as your own name in the articles and blog posts. You want the search engines to find them when someone Googles your name.

Distribute your content on the most popular B2B traffic sites: LinkedIn, reddit, Wikipedia, Twitter, Facebook, and StumbleUpon. That way, your content will get wide distribution.

Creating relationships on LinkedIn

According to most surveys, LinkedIn (www.linkedin.com) — the signup page is shown in Figure 8-8 — is the social media platform that salespeople prefer for networking, for these reasons:

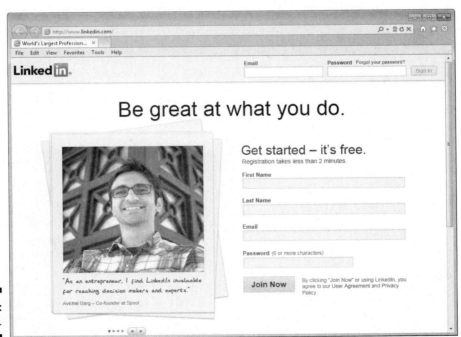

Figure 8-8:
LinkedIn.

- ✔ **It's a business site.** People are on LinkedIn specifically to network and talk about business topics. No one is talking about personal issues.

- ✔ **It's a job-hunting site.** It's a very popular network for finding jobs, so most salespeople record their activities on the site. They feel this will help them network with their peers.

- ✔ **Company structures are transparent.** Salespeople can identify the decision makers in a company by looking at who is part of a company group and networking with them.

- ✔ **You can establish your reputation as an expert.** Salespeople can establish themselves as experts in their field by answering questions and giving advice.

- ✔ **The platform provides useful built-in features.** Salespeople can use the structure that's already in place to invite people to events and research information. There's no steep learning curve.

Consider the following best practices for salespeople using LinkedIn:

- ✔ **Connect.** Request a connection online after you've met a colleague at an event or meeting.

- ✔ **Recommend.** Ask for testimonials when appropriate and give them to others.

- ✔ **Join groups.** Pick several groups and network with others in your field.

- ✔ **Answer questions.** It helps people recognize your expertise and seek out your advice.

- ✔ **Share interesting content.** Pick content from around the web and share it with your network. (You can synch your Twitter account or blog posts if they're pertinent.)

- ✔ **Keep your account active.** Be present on a daily basis. Interact and be useful to others without expecting a *quid pro quo*.

Using a tablet to be more productive

Although there were skeptics who thought the iPad wouldn't be popular, it has sold more units in a two-year period than any other tech device. In fact, tablets as a category are doing quite well. Staples predicts that by 2015 there will be 82.1 million tablet users in the United States. Tablets are lightweight, have multiple apps, and can do lots of things your laptop can do. The only drawback that people perceive is its lack of a keyboard and mouse.

For some salespeople, tablets have become invaluable because they are easy to carry, less expensive than a computer, and can keep documents up to date while you're on the go. They let salespeople more easily interface with a company's social CRM system when they're out in the field.

Some benefits include

- ✔ **Save money and time.** Apps work from the cloud and can always provide you with the latest information. Tablets are less expensive than laptops.

- ✔ **Show that you're using the latest tech tools.** Working with a tablet at a customer location differentiates the salesperson and can leave the impression that his company is tech savvy.

- ✔ **Close more sales with visuals.** An tablet display can be very inviting and help your customer remember your content.

Several companies have picked up on the fact that presenting a sales pitch on a tablet can be very appealing. The images look great, and the ability to link to online content on the fly gives a presentation more depth. Here's some interesting technology that's available to create presentations on tablets:

- ✔ **Brainshark:** This is a cloud-based application (available at `www.brainshark.com`) that lets you show your own sales presentation (which may be in PowerPoint or another native format) on your tablet.

- ✔ **Mediafly:** This company offers a variety of tools (at `www.mediafly.com`) that allow the enterprise to create sales presentations for a variety of devices including tablets.

- ✔ **PresentiaFX:** This app (available at `www.presentiafx.com`) has a dedicated tablet presenter and is very easy to set up and use.

- ✔ **StoryDesk:** This proprietary technology lets you build your own sales presentation and display it using the best visual components (iPad only). You can find out more at `http://storydesk.com`, shown in Figure 8-9.

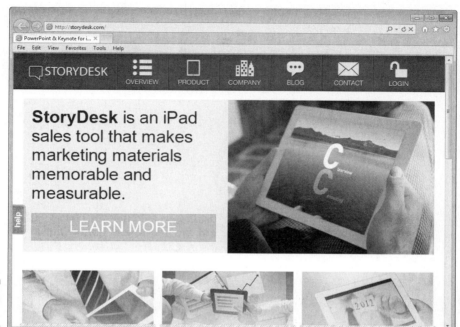

Figure 8-9:
StoryDesk.

Chapter 9

Building a Customer Loyalty and Advocacy Program

Customer loyalty has always been a key factor in the health of any business. Without loyal customers, business owners would constantly be reinventing and changing their products to find ones that generate steady revenue.

If you think loyalty programs are old school, you might be envisioning programs like the trading stamps or S&H Green Stamps programs that started in the late 1890s and became very popular in the 1950s and '60s. These programs issued stamps with each purchase and a stamp book to paste them in.

When you filled up your book, you would take a trip to the local redemption center to pick out your prizes — mostly things like small appliances and toys for the kids. Families would enjoy these outings and come home with a small reward. This motivated them to keep coming back for more. For a while, this worked really well.

A variety of different programs gained and fell out of favor in the years that followed, but if you think loyalty programs aren't in favor now, consider this report from Jupiter Research: "Approximately 75 percent of consumers have at least one loyalty card and the number of people with two or more is estimated to be one-third of the shopping population."

The nature of customer loyalty itself has changed with the advent of social networks. In the context of social CRM, loyalty programs are based not on products, but on relationships. Businesses need to recognize that loyalty is a two-way street, and pay attention to their customers in new ways. Customers want to be assured that their favorite businesses are listening to them and treating them with respect. This is quite a change from the advertising practices of the 1950s (highlighted in the popular *Mad Men* TV series) when all the messages were directed outward.

In the following sections, you learn why customer loyalty programs are valuable and how you can incorporate them into your social CRM.

Understanding Customer Loyalty

Customer loyalty programs are big business. The 2011 Colloquy Loyalty Census is available at

```
www.colloquy.com/new-2wps-ma-0418811.htm
```

According to that report, Americans accumulate approximately $48 billion in rewards points and miles annually. However, one-third of those points are never redeemed. More people are participating in loyalty programs and getting less value from them than ever before.

With this in mind, part of understanding your customers is understanding the value they place on your loyalty program's rewards.

Evolving loyalty programs

To understand how to cultivate today's social customer, look at several of the factors that changed the face of loyalty programs in the 21st century. These factors include the following:

- **Newer technologies help you engage your tech-savvy customers.** Audience members (especially younger ones) want their loyalty programs to include the use of social media platforms and new technology like QR (Quick Response) codes. A QR code is a visual symbol that is embedded with link information. When a customer scans it with his smartphone reader, he's sent to the link. The link can contain advertising info, a coupon, or anything the marketer wants to show the user.

  Think about how you can reward your tech-savvy customers who use smartphones and their increasingly advanced apps. You want to make sure that you speak to your customers where they hang out. Trying to create new customer behavior (such as asking customers to join a new network to get points) will never work. Try to provide a seamless experience. Some options include the following:

- *Quick Response Code (QR code):* QR codes can be a great way to engage customers. A QR code, such as the one shown in Figure 9-1, is a code that a smartphone user can scan with a reader installed on a smartphone or other mobile device. The smartphone then displays the web address associated with the code and gives users the option of opening that web address in their smartphone's web browser.

  The code can link the customer to different interactions with your brand. For example, a code can take customers to a place on your site that has more detailed information about your latest promotion.

  In addition to linking customers to information, you can link them to games or discounts, coupons, or other special promotions.

  When you use QR codes, remember that you have interested customers who want to engage with your brand, so treat them that way. Make sure to follow up through e-mail, direct mail, newsletters, mobile alerts, and social networks. Follow-ups like these prevent customers from drifting away after linking to you and demonstrate your commitment to earning customer loyalty. (For more information about QR codes, see *QR Codes For Dummies Portable Edition,* by Joe Waters.)

Figure 9-1: Scan the QR code with your smartphone's bar code reader.

- *Foursquare:* Another possibility is to link to online networks that directly deliver reward points. One example of this type of network is Foursquare (`https://foursquare.com`), shown in Figure 9-2. This geolocation app uses a mobile phone's GPS locator to display offers and information for nearby businesses.

  Foursquare is a social network that encourages your customers to visit your physical location. When they check in on Foursquare, they're rewarded with points or badges. They can also interact with other like-minded customers by checking the online Foursquare stream. In addition, Foursquare links to Facebook, so customers can interact with friends as well. For more on Foursquare and other social media platforms, see Social Media Marketing For Dummies," by Shiv Singh and Stephanie Diamond.

- *PunchTab:* Provides an established framework that allows your customers to participate in rewards programs, as mentioned in Figure 9-3. This can work well for smaller companies that can't afford to create a program from scratch. The data you collect here can be plugged back into your CRM. Go to `www.punchtab.com` for more information.

Figure 9-2:
Foursquare home page.

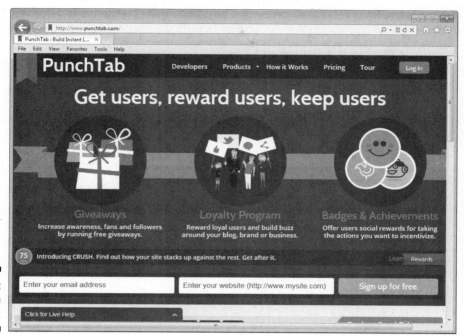

Figure 9-3:
PunchTab
home page.

✔ **Customers want companies to be socially responsible.** We all know that the Internet has dramatically changed the world. As author Thomas L. Friedman says in his book of the same name, "The world is flat." This means that people can instantly see what's happening around the world. Moreover, they can interact with the people to whom it's happening.

For example, it's widely believed that Twitter influenced the rise of the Arab Spring in 2010 by allowing protestors to tell and show the world what was happening. For reasons like this, the social customer wants to see companies pulling their weight in society.

According to the 2010 Consumer New Media Study by Cone Communications, 85 percent of respondents said they would switch brands, and 73 percent say they would try a new brand if a company demonstrates strong prosociety practices.

Burt's Bees, a beauty product maker headquartered in North Carolina, is a great example of a company that's benefitting from its strategy to give back. Burt's Bees employees teamed up with Habitat for Humanity to provide workers to help build ecofriendly homes.

This is only one of the programs in which they participate, as shown in Figure 9-4. This has proven a winning strategy for them. Burt's Bees was purchased by Clorox in 2007 for its GreenWorks line of products and their revenues continued to soar — in 2009, their revenue topped $250 million. Their generosity is widely known and appreciated by their customers, thus building loyalty.

✔ **CRM tools have evolved to provide valuable customer data that can impact customer loyalty.** CRM tools have dramatically improved as more sophisticated computing becomes available. Previously, contact management tools didn't provide the kind of data you really needed to impact your business. The computing capability just wasn't available. Now even a free tool like Google Analytics can help a business owner see her customer's online purchase profile.

A CRM system is valuable because it integrates different types of data about the customer from a variety of business functions. Last century, a business owner might have used a PC-based program like Microsoft Outlook to do contact management. He would diligently add names to the contact manager and try to personally collect information about each customer. His system was only as good as the time he put into it.

Once he graduated from this rudimentary software, he would've used something like PC-based GoldMine (a company previously owned by author Jon Ferrara). GoldMine was very advanced because it integrated sales data into the contact management system. Today's CRMs include data collected from all business functions.

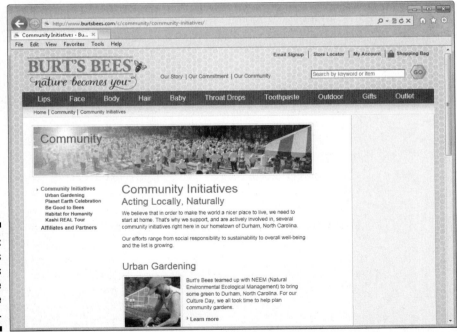

Figure 9-4:
Burt's Bees programs that give back to the community.

> ✔ **Customer kudos and complaints can reach thousands, even millions, of people at lightning speed.** The effect of the customer's advocacy is magnified. Online customer reviews are among the tools that have changed the balance of power between manufacturers and customers. In the past when customers were disgruntled with a product, they would tell their small circle of friends. That was bad for business, but the effects were hard to quantify. Now anyone with a computer can be heard loud and clear by submitting an online review of a product. (See the upcoming section "Hearing what customers are saying" for specific online sites where customers vent.)

Discovering why loyalty programs matter

Fred Reichheld — author of several seminal books on loyalty, including *The Ultimate Question 2.0: How Net Promoter Companies Thrive in a Customer-Driven World* — reports that "a 5 percent improvement in customer retention rates will yield between a 25 to 100 percent increase in profits." Wow, that's a statistic you can't afford to ignore! The key is to build a program that's highly relevant to the customers you serve.

Loyalty data is one of your company's best assets, no matter its size. By collecting data about your loyal customers, you can understand such things as the following:

✔ Customer trends in real time

✔ Promotions that impact your loyal customers most

✔ How to increase *conversion rates* (the rate at which a lead is turned into a customer) among new customers based on your experience with loyalty programs

How do companies view the value of loyalty programs today? According to a survey by SAS and Loyalty 360, here are the top goals of loyalty programs:

✔ To increase customer spending

✔ To reduce customer loss

✔ To turn customers into advocates

These are difficult goals to pull off. The ability to achieve them is enhanced by the fact that you can reach these customers directly on social media platforms. Your CRM can accumulate the data you need to make a connection with your customer meaningful.

After you're convinced your business needs a loyalty program, remember that your customer needs a reason to join and participate. You must create a reason for your customer to stay faithful. You want customers to value their incentives and engagement to the point that they wouldn't think of buying elsewhere.

You should also be aware that loyalty programs can have a negative effect. The stakes are higher. They raise customer expectations about the type and quality of the service you offer. If you anger a customer in a loyalty program, you're likely to lose that person forever.

The following two sections explore how you can enroll and retain customers in your loyalty program.

Introducing types of loyalty programs

You've probably heard the adage before: Finding a new customer costs more than selling to one you already have. Loyal customers are hard to find and hard to keep. Customers who strictly shop on price will go from company to company to find the best bargain. They will almost never become a loyal customer. If they can find the item cheaper somewhere else, they will grab it.

What characterizes loyal customers? They are the ones who are willing to pay a bit more or stay with you no matter what. Table 9-1 shows some potential ways to inspire customer loyalty with different types of loyalty programs. After customers join a loyalty program like those listed here, you can communicate with them via social media. For example, you could devote a Facebook page to loyalists in the program.

Table 9-1	Types of Loyalty Programs	
Type of Program	*Description*	*Example*
Fee-based	Each customer pays a fee for special experiences and benefits.	American Airlines Admiral's Club
Points	Customers are rewarded for purchases made.	Staples Rewards
Tiered rewards	Customers are rewarded for achieving milestones that increase the value of their points.	Hilton HHonors
Partnerships	Companies join forces to offer rewards to customers who use products from both companies.	American Express Membership Rewards
Games	A game layer is added to a rewards program.	Snooth

Making your most valuable customers feel loved

Everyone is vying for your customers' attention. Online ads, videos, points programs, and free samples are available everywhere. If you can think of ways to create a memorable experience for your customer, the rewards will be great. If you can do something extraordinary for a customer, you will cut through the clutter.

A great example of this is the experience Peter Shankman of HARO (Help a Reporter Out) www.helpareporter.com had with 'Morton's The Steakhouse in Hackensack, NJ. Shankman reports that in August 2011 he was on a business trip that would end back at his home airport at a late hour. He was a regular customer of 'Morton's across the country when he traveled. He hadn't eaten much that day, so while on his way home, food was on his mind.

As a joke, he tweeted, "Hey @Mortons – can you meet me at Newark airport with a porterhouse when I land in two hours? K, thanks. :)" Much to his amazement when he landed, a Morton's employee in a tuxedo was waiting for him with a bag that included a 24-ounce porterhouse steak. Needless to say, he experienced shock and amazement. He tweeted a picture of himself with the employee and expressed his uncontrolled joy. Even his dog was going to eat steak that night.

The great thing about this for Morton's was that not only did Shankman tweet his amazement, but his follower's on Twitter went wild with tweets about it. (He had over 100,000 Twitter followers at the time.) In addition, Morton's got free TV coverage and great PR. All for the price of a steak dinner and a trip to the Newark airport.

In retrospect, you can look at that experience and see how Morton's would benefit, but remember, they took quick action in real time. They didn't have time to plan and execute over several days. They had two hours.

What can you learn from this? Think about the following when you're trying to develop incredible experiences that create customers for life:

- ✔ **Follow your social networks in real time as often as possible.** Morton's had an employee watching its Twitter stream for mentions of their brand. If they didn't see the tweet right away, the opportunity would've been lost.

- ✔ **Take bold action to stand out.** The rewards are great if you're willing to break out of the "business as usual" category. A unique story often catches the eye of the media, as it did in this case.

✔ **Think about the visual potential of the experience.** Morton's sent an employee in a tuxedo to present the steak, as shown in Figure 9-5. When Shankman took the inevitable picture and put it on Twitter, it made a huge impression on customers (as well as potential customers).

Figure 9-5:
Peter Shankman receives his complimentary dinner from a Morton's employee in a tuxedo.

✔ **Give your employees the authority to make customers happy.** If your employees have to request permission for every unique experience they want to provide, the spontaneity will be lost. Let your employees know that you value their deep commitment to customers and reward them for it. If you don't walk the walk, they will be afraid to take the initiative.

As we can see from this example, there are many ways to reward loyal customers. The type of loyalty program you employ should depend on the types of rewards that customers find valuable. For example, in Table 9-1, loyalists are rewarded with perks that give them extra value. In the Twitter example, a loyalist is rewarded for mentioning a business on Twitter. The publicity of that tweet had great value to the company as well as the tweeter.

Understanding the Value of Loyal Advocates and Social Influencers

Today's customers demand to be heard. Listening to them and reacting to their requests can build loyalty not only among the respondents, but also among those who see that response. That's one of the true benefits of responding to your customers on a social platform. Others can see and appreciate your engagement.

The loyal advocate is the customer who will aggressively share your message with others. To understand the value a loyal advocate brings to a business, we need to analyze the difference between the social influencer and the true advocate.

Influencing the influencer

Social influencers play a key role in your ability to reach customers. A *social influencer* is a trusted person with a large faithful following. A social influencer's endorsement of your product or service can help your business acquire new customers. Your loyal advocate uses word of mouth to reach her circle of trusted friends and has the potential to reach a large number of people you might never reach. For more on influence, see Chapter 7.

To find the people who influence your customers, you can look in several places. Here are some data sources to consider monitoring to find influencers. If your CRM doesn't collect social platform data, you may need to integrate it into your data:

- ✔ **Traffic sources:** If you see that you're getting traffic from specific websites, you should investigate. Websites with high referrals to your website may already be mentioning your company or products.

- ✔ **Social media sites:** Use the search tools on Twitter, Facebook, Pinterest, LinkedIn, and Google+ to see who has major influence in your industry. Each of these platforms has a search function that allows you to hone in on your topic of interest. General feeds are useful, but you want to get directly to the people who are interested in you. To get started, try the search function on Twitter, which is in the upper-right corner of the home screen, as shown in Figure 9-6.

For example, if you provide financial consultation services, you might begin by searching broadly, with the term *financial information.* In the search results, you'll see the following:

- *Questions that people are asking*

- *Specific influencers who are providing information*

- *Links to sites that provide services*

Using that information, you can learn a lot about what customers want to know and who offers consultations.

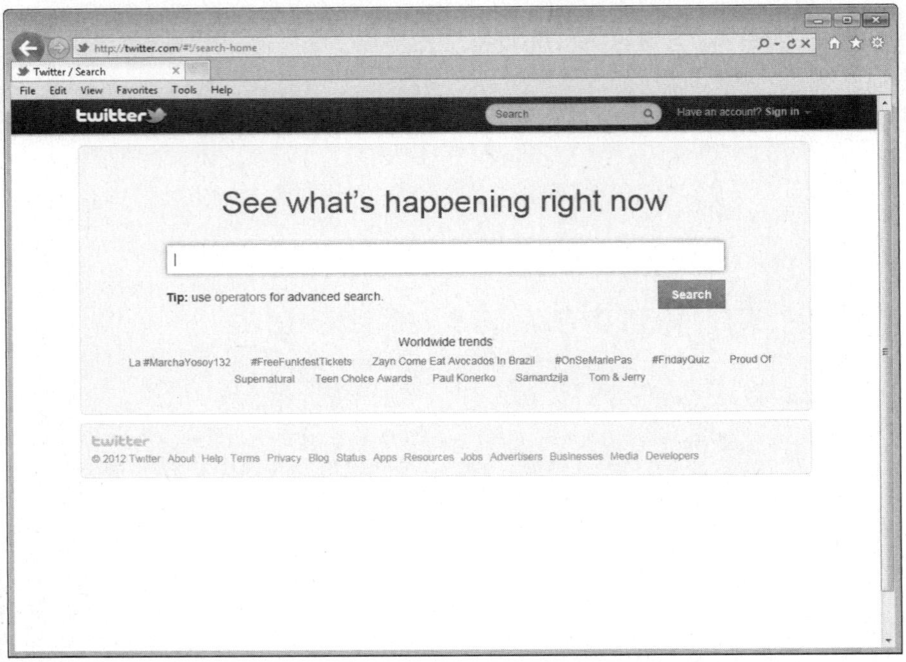

Figure 9-6:
Twitter
search
function.

✔ **Forums and blogs:** These tools provide a great way to find influencers. If you find forums on topics that relate to your business, you'll quickly be able to see who is leading the discussions. To get started, check out BoardReader (http://boardreader.com). BoardReader is an online search tool that allows you to search across forums and boards to find the ones that interest you, rather than having to individually search them. Begin to participate, and once people know you, they'll be interested in your message. Don't attempt any heavy sales pitch.

Understanding the needs of the loyal advocate

The true advocate is the customer who loves your brand and lets his family and friends know it. How can you spot a true advocate? Fred Reichheld, in his book *The Ultimate Question 2.0: How Net Promoter Companies Thrive in a Customer-Driven World*, thinks he knows. The ultimate question for him is, "How likely is it that you would recommend our company to a friend or colleague?" If your customer won't recommend your company to her trusted inner circle, she isn't a true advocate. (This kind of advocate is also commonly called a *customer evangelist.*)

To encourage and cultivate customer evangelists, examine what makes those customers respond to your brand in a way that others don't. Do they look to you to provide information about how to use products like yours? For example, if you sell wedding dresses, do potential customer evangelists look to you because you provide great information and advice about how to host a cost-effective wedding? When you solve customers' problems, do you make them feel special and valued by your company? With the downturn in the economy, customers are looking for more custom shopping experiences. One way to do this is to team up with like-minded companies who can make your sales experience unique.

A great example of this is the iOS app created by a company called SnapShop (www.snapshopinc.com), as shown in Figure 9-7. From an iPhone, iPad, or iPod touch, a furniture shopper can see how furniture (including such brands as IKEA, Pier 1 Imports, and Horchow) looks in his own room. Here's how it works: As the app user, you snap a photo of your room and place the virtual furniture in it. If it looks good, you can buy it on the site directly from the brand.

Think about how you can make the purchase of your products a unique experience that will keep your customer coming back.

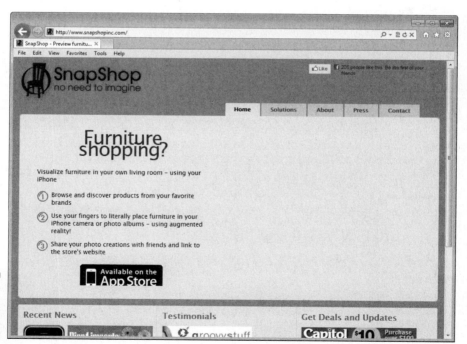

Figure 9-7:
SnapShop
home page.

Enhancing Customer Loyalty and Advocacy

To enhance customer loyalty and advocacy with social customers, you should attempt to provide a more personal experience. To do that, you should be right at the source of customer feedback, watching tweets as they fly by and providing quality customer service in real time whenever possible. (See more about customer service in Chapter 10.) For example, you can set up a Twitter account specifically to receive customer service questions, like United Parcel Service (UPS) does at `http://twitter.com/#!/upshelp`.

Utilizing customer touch points

To show customers that you're available to hear them, you want to be present at all your customer *touch points* — the channels where the brand interacts directly with customers. These touch points include e-mails, register checkouts, Twitter, Facebook, and so on. Major retailer Bloomingdale's recently created an innovative loyalty program at checkout called Loyallist, as shown in Figure 9-8, that makes excellent use of customer touch points.

Figure 9-8: The Loyallist program at Bloomingdale's.

Typically, high-end retail loyalty programs require customers to sign up for a store credit card. This confers exclusivity and benefits the retailer by having the customer pay the additional carrying charges. But Bloomingdale's cleverly sets aside this requirement. Their program allows all shoppers to participate by issuing them a Bloomingdale's loyalty card linked to their phone number.

If a shopper doesn't use a store credit card when he makes a purchase, he can simply offer his phone number or physical loyalty card at checkout. This is especially useful to Bloomingdale's because it allows the retailer to collect loyalty shopper data and issue rewards for all its shoppers, not just the ones who have a store credit card.

In addition, Bloomingdale's can utilize several of its touch points by allowing shoppers to accrue loyalty points whether they're shopping online, in a store, or at their outlets. Their loyalty slogan "Every shopper, every day" helps them get everyone into the program. In return, shoppers get one point for every dollar they spend and two points if they use their store credit card. A customer who accrues 5,000 points also receives a $25 reward card in addition to the rewards per point. Loyalists receive monthly e-mails that detail new products and discounts.

In your own business, think about how you can use your customer touch points to create a unique program that connects with your customers at more places than the point of purchase. Do away with any barriers that might be in place.

Hearing what customers are saying

Before the Internet, retailers never had to deal with was customers from across the globe sharing all manner of opinions with fellow customers in easy-to-access public forums with no permission required. For example, the web abounds with stories about restaurants that have treated their customers with disrespect or bad service. Pre-Internet, the complaints were only heard via word of mouth by local customers. Now customers get the benefit of hearing the opinion of customers they don't know personally.

The types of products and services you offer dictate where your products are reviewed. Here are some places where you'll find online reviews:

- ✔ **Epinions:** This is a mature site that hosts reviews on a variety of topics. Their tagline "Unbiased reviews from real people" ensures that reviewers are encouraged to give the unvarnished truth. (`http://epinions.com`)

- ✔ **Yelp:** This site hosts product and service reviews in various business categories at `http://yelp.com`, shown in Figure 9-9. Yelp has over 54 million unique page views per month and categorizes its data by location and type.

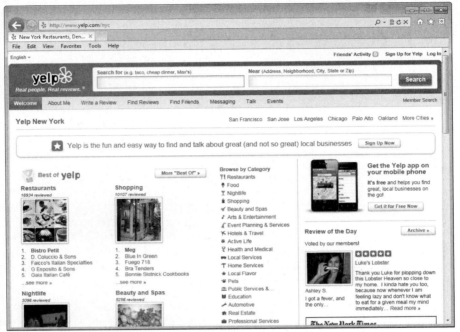

Figure 9-9:
Yelp's home
page.

- ✔ **Amazon.com:** This site's review database is actually the largest online opinion website because every product it sells has a space for reviews. Before purchasing, customers pour over what others have to say.

- ✔ **TripAdvisor:** This site provides extensive information and reviews about vacation spots, hotels, and restaurants. A great addition is the abundance of photos.

- ✔ **Urbanspoon:** This site is great if you're looking for menus and reviews for local restaurants. If you're in the restaurant industry, check here to find out what customers are saying about your business.

One general finding about customer reviews is that one or even a few negative reviews won't turn a customer off. Most people know that you can't please everyone and realize that some negative comments attached to a product listing simply means that real people are sharing their opinions.

Don't be afraid to let bad reviews stand, even when you've tried your best to resolve them. If potential customers sense that you're censoring your reviews, they'll leave quickly, never to return. Responding to negative reviews gives you the opportunity to demonstrate that you want to engage unhappy customers and fix things.

It's also a good idea to provide a link to these reviews from your site instead of trying to host the reviews yourself. You'll get more exposure on a site with multiple restaurants. In searching the database, someone may run across a review of your restaurant and be inspired to try it.

So how should you deal with feedback received in online reviews? Consider the following tips:

- ✓ **Stay positive when you react to negative reviews.** Don't get drawn into petty name-calling. It's a real turn-off to customers. Even if you are right, you need to maintain a respectful tone. Remember that you're speaking to the audience at large, not just one customer.

- ✓ **Look at the bigger picture.** Each review, whether positive or negative, is an opportunity for you to educate your audience about you. If you add tips, you'll have used the review as another social media channel. For example, if applicable, you could say something like, "Next time, try our deserts — the chocolate lava cake is very popular among chocoholics."

- ✓ **Be authentic.** Answer reviews like a real person would. If you use company-speak, you'll make reviewers feel like they aren't important.

Delivering relevant content

Key to the success of any loyalty program is the use of relevant content that provides real value to the customer. The term *relevant content* refers to such things as product suggestions and tips for using the products and discounts. This is where your CRM data becomes crucial. To understand how content impacts your loyalty programs, you need to consider the following two factors:

- ✓ **Internal data collected about your customers:** Data from your CRM system will obviously point the way for you to create relevant content. For example, by looking at historical data about your customers, you can see what types of articles are read most often on your website. Armed with this information, you can increase the number of those articles and tie that information back to promotions and discounts.

  For example, if you find that articles and blog posts with the best time-saving tips for using your product, for instance, are popular, you can make sure to include your promotion links in those specific articles and track their success. The key is to constantly monitor the data to see what kinds of changes occur over time. Consider each promotion an experiment that can be improved over time.

- ✓ **External data about the environment in which the customer lives:** It's easy to think that you really know your customer, based on the internal data you collect. You see your customers' shopping habits and draw conclusions, but it's also important to include data about such things as the economy, political issues, and popular culture memes.

As we know, the economy has been challenging for several years. Katherine Field Boccaccio of Drug Store News reported on a study released by MarketTools in April 2011. She found that grocery shopping habits had changed in the previous six months. It's unclear why specifically shoppers had shifted behavior at that time, but perhaps above all else, shoppers were seeking value.

According to the study, respondents reported the following:

- 80 percent buy with coupons.
- 62 percent buy store brands instead of name brands.
- 62 percent use store loyalty cards that offer discounts.
- 58 percent buy items only when they're on sale.
- 43 percent buy more large-sized products to save money on grocery bills.

Armed with information like this, you can create content that's highly relevant to your customers. Obviously things like loyalty cards and coupons might already be in your arsenal. But how about a promotion of store brands or bulk purchases?

This is just one possible example, but it gives you a direction upon which you can base small content experiments. The standard type of content that you create about products and services will always be in the pipeline. This type of specific data can help you impact your customer in real time.

Using gamification to encourage loyal customers

Gamification is a concept that's grabbing the interest of customers and loyalty program managers alike. It refers to the application of game dynamics to business functions to encourage customer engagement. According to a Gartner report, "by 2014, a gamified service for consumer goods marketing and customer retention will become as important as Facebook, eBay, or Amazon, and more than 70 percent of Global 2000 organizations will have at least one gamified application."

People are playing online games with others, buying virtual goods, and looking for the next hot game app in record numbers. Marketers are jumping on the bandwagon hoping that they can encourage loyalty by using this new-found interest in games.

The concept of using games behaviors in loyalty programs isn't really new. Some variation on the customer winning points has always been part of the process. What's new is the nature of social gaming. The technology goes far beyond old-style loyalty programs.

The benefit of applying gamification to business apps includes the following:

✔ A fully engaged and loyal customer

✔ The opportunity to solicit product ideas and feedback

✔ The potential for messaging associated with a game to go viral

✔ The opportunity to encourage employees to access training that isn't only fun, but educational

When you think of gamers, you may have some misconceptions about their profile and the value of social games for your business:

✔ **Misconception: The average gamer is young, male and always online.**

If your customer doesn't fit this profile, you've probably discarded the idea of using games in your CRM, but don't be misled. According to a study by the Information Services Group in 2011 and several corroborative studies, the average social gamer is a 43-year-old woman. Does this fit into your customer demographic? It's likely that your customers are interested in games that provide tangible rewards.

✔ **Misconception: Playing games online has no real value.**

Game designer Jane McGonigal has been pursuing the idea that social game behavior has value and should be used to help solve societal or personal problems. She created a game called SuperBetter (www.superbetter.com), shown in Figure 9-10, to help herself overcome the effects of a head injury, and now people around the world use this game to improve their own health.

From her studies, McGonigal found that when we play games we are

✔ Fiercely optimistic

✔ More resilient and prone to persevere

✔ Likely to build strong bonds with those we play games with

✔ More cooperative

✔ Prone to feel very productive

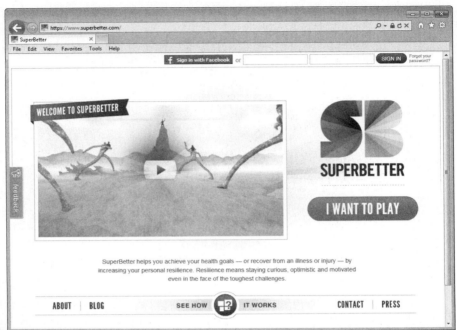

Figure 9-10:
SuperBetter.

Her goal is to marshal this behavior for good causes and to encourage others to do the same. With this in mind, think about the kinds of games you can create for your customers. There really is no limit to the type of business that could benefit from a loyalty game.

One fun example of a loyalty game is Snooth Wine Rack (`http://snooth.com/wine-rack`). Snooth is the world's largest wine site. Its mission is to simplify "how people select, learn about and purchase their favorite wines." The game lets you select wines and compete to become an expert. The home page is shown in Figure 9-11. As you learn about Snooth's selection, you can price wines and purchase them from vendors through the Snooth website.

This game is popular because it hits the mark in three important ways: It's entertaining, educational, and easy to use. Those are three criteria that most good games should have.

Figure 9-11:
Wine Rack
on the
Snooth
Home page.

Chapter 10

Creating Socially Relevant Customer Service

*W*ith the advent of the web, almost everyone who has surfed online has enjoyed watching an example of bad customer service on YouTube. (Oh, unless you're the company they're talking about.) Stories are legion — a Comcast rep falling asleep on a customer's couch, a bicyclist demonstrating that anyone with a Bic pen can pick a Kryptonite lock (which was touted as unbreakable). Some companies have survived, others haven't. Comcast has completely turned around its customer service as a result of this, but more about that later in this chapter.

We've laughed at the expense of many a company, both large and small, but as any company will tell you, customer service is no laughing matter. Especially now, with the power shift that allows customers to express themselves in real time and with a very broad audience about the latest customer service failures.

In this chapter, you look at the way the customer service function has evolved, from a controllable department into one that can damage a brand's reputation in a heartbeat. You also discover best practices and ways to avoid making the same mistakes other companies have made.

Defining Customer Service

Like every other business practice that has been redefined by social media, customer service has been turned on its head. Personalized customer service used to mean mostly that a call center operator would take a customer call in real time. The best measure of their level of service was how fast they answered the call. Today, that's a tiny fraction of what needs to happen to serve a customer.

Because social CRM is a nascent concept, it can be hard to get your arms around all the factors that affect customer service. To understand how social media has added a layer to CRM systems, we can look at it first from a micro level. For example, a traditional CRM has a data point about a customer purchase. Adding a social layer gives you a data point of that same customer's tweet about the product. This data is then integrated with other data to make decisions and serve the customer.

Now, take a look at social CRM from a 50,000-foot view. You can break the fundamentals of social CRM setup into a five-step process:

1. **Business data is collected.**

   CRM and other systems already in place collect company data. Information about financials, sales, and marketing are all part of the mix. For example, you can look up a customer's purchase history to see what he's bought and how long he's been a customer.

2. **The social web is monitored by employees and tools designed to pull data from social media accounts.**

   Employees look at the social web for customer comments, platform analytics (like those available through Facebook Insights), and anything related to the brand.

3. **Business data is integrated with social data.**

   This is where CRM becomes *social CRM.* Your company uses systems and/or manually mixes data of both types to obtain a fuller picture of the company's impact.

4. **Decision data is culled.**

   Your company uses the integrated data to make decisions about such things as marketing campaigns, advertising, up-sells, new products, and so on.

5. **The employee team behind an initiative receives feedback about the results of the initiative.**

   The feedback evaluates how well the initiative performed and what changes could be made to improve results.

When these processes are working effectively, you have a system that will help your company make smart decisions about the future.

Expanding the scope of social service

In this new social media environment, companies are expanding the traditional contact center to accommodate a focus on the customer, not the product offerings. The new social customer service function is very different.

In a study called *Campaigns to Capabilities: Social Media and Marketing 2011,* by Booz & Company and Buddy Media, respondents were asked how they used their top social media platforms. A resounding 75 percent said they used them to support their customer service function. They know that when customers look at a company's customer service offerings, their expectations are high. If a company isn't listening, it's likely its customers aren't buying.

We explain the following types of customer social sites in this chapter:

- ✔ **Self-serve knowledge portals from a website:** These are administered by companies and are usually part of their overall support system. They typically integrate with the CRM system. You would link to all your social media platforms from here. You may or may not house customer reviews directly on this site.

- ✔ **Community-based sites:** These sites are overseen by companies and have the support of dedicated users who answer questions and provide content. To run these sites, companies use platforms designed by outside vendors (listed later in the "Growing your community" section). Hopefully, you can integrate them with your CRM system.

- ✔ **External customer review sites:** These sites are run by independent companies that aggregate customer reviews and provide a place to vent frustrations and alert other customers to their opinions.

- ✔ **Voice of the customer platforms:** Companies engage platform vendors who help them quantify and effectively capture the voice of the customer, or they create their own. For example, Adobe created an in-house program called the Customer Immersion Program. The purpose of the program is to help their executives experience what Adobe customers experience. They do such things as listen in on customer calls and search for product information on their website. The executives report that this gives them an eye-opening look at customer needs.

Customers want to be able to communicate in the way that's most comfortable for them. For instance, if they prefer mobile customer ticket updates, they expect to get them. If they need real-time help, many times they want to use Twitter. This has created the demand for what is now known as the *multichannel support center.* It includes some of the following channels:

- ✔ **Twitter:** This is a great medium for getting real-time support. It allows customers to alert a company that they need immediate help. Their expectation is that the company will respond and, if necessary, send them to the appropriate representative to get that help. Most problems can't be resolved in 140 characters, but you can send the message that help is on the way.

- ✔ **Facebook:** Customer service on Facebook can get chaotic because the News Feed mixes all kinds of messages together in one place. Companies need to monitor their News Feed to cull out the service questions from the other comments. Customers use this method, but almost no brand relies on Facebook for the bulk of their customer service.

- ✔ **YouTube:** Some of the bigger brands pay to host a branded channel on YouTube. These branded channels pay more to be able to add superior graphic branding and features. Others make sure to post their training videos on the site with a link back to their website.

- ✔ **Mobile messages (SMS):** With some systems, companies can send responses to a help ticket directly to mobile devices. This is most useful in the case of emergencies with IT and other problems that affect critical business functions.

- ✔ **Blogs:** If customers aren't sure where to go, they may come to a company blog and leave a comment, but the best type of service a company can provide from their blog is links to all the support information available. They can also establish company experts from this venue.

- ✔ **Community-based help:** Companies establish platforms that support the interaction of interested users. This method is gaining favor as more tools become available.

- ✔ **E-mail:** The media keeps heralding the death of e-mail, saying it's old-fashioned and doesn't provide the kind of engagement other social media channels can offer. But in the customer service realm, e-mail serves an important function. You can e-mail customer service ticket resolutions and other communications directly to users.

Remember that not every customer is immersed in social media. You need to think about making sure you keep up with them using their preferred engagement method.

- ✔ **IVR (interactive voice response):** This is probably the customer's least-liked method of interaction. It's the one that uses voice-recorded messages like "Press one for customer service." Tales abound about customers getting into multiple loops that never end. Nevertheless, companies still rely on this as part of their customer service program. The use of this service will probably diminish as social media channels take over. Interactive voice response just isn't personal enough.

Adding social has its benefits

Companies have been slow to adopt social media as a customer service channel. Managers were reluctant to unleash the fury of the unserved customer for all to hear. But as it has turned out, not all of the managers' worst fears were confirmed, and many managers found some tangible benefits to the company, as well.

In 2012, consulting organization thinkJar conducted a survey on behalf of Sword Ciboodle, a top vendor of CRM solutions. Companies in the survey said the top five benefits of social customer service are as follows:

- ✓ **Increasing customer satisfaction.** Customers are happier when they have several ways to interact with the company and resolve problems.

- ✓ **Meeting customer expectations.** Customers appreciate the attempt by companies to meet their needs publicly, even if things aren't always resolved.

- ✓ **Providing intangible benefits.** Not all the benefits can be articulated, but customers simply feel more connected to companies that offer social service.

- ✓ **Increasing loyalty.** This most treasured of benefits is conferred upon companies that use social media to provide service.

- ✓ **Reducing the cost of customer support.** This one is music to the ears of any manager. Costs go down when people who take support calls can be available for more complex calls.

So how do you determine whether your social CRM initiatives are working? The difficulty with social CRM tracking is that you can measure lots of data, but sometimes it's hard to tell which measures are the ones that matter.

Here are some questions to ask yourself to determine your progress:

- ✓ **Traffic:** Do you find that your traffic from a particular source to your website is increasing? Does that lead to conversions? Can you determine what about that source is generating interest and repeat it?

- ✓ **Influencers:** Are people in your industry reporting about you and commenting on your products? Do these influencers give you opportunities to speak to their constituencies?

- ✓ **Social media activity:** Is your brand mentioned and discussed? Are the comments positive? Does your audience share and retweet your content?

 As managers expected, social customer service isn't all benefits. According to Gartner's research director Adam Sarner, as reported by CRM Idol 2012, "Only 50 percent of Fortune 1000 companies will see a worthwhile ROI from their social CRM initiatives."

Understanding the importance of social service

It stands to reason that if customer service is critical to the health of a company, social customer service is even more crucial. Some data supports that. The same Booz & Company and Buddy Media study cited previously found the following:

- 81 percent of respondents say that they use social media for customer insights.

- 54 percent say that investing in relationships with consumers is more important to their brands than mass reach.

From several of these statistics, you might conclude that the average company really gets social CRM. They understand that they can reach customers on social platforms, they dig for customer insights, and they invest in and value customer relationships. But this just isn't the case.

Amid the business landscape, many companies pay lip service to these ideas but don't really employ the tools and tactics they could. To avoid this problem, consider the following best practices as your business incorporates social media into its customer service:

- **Know your business goals before you develop your social customer service tactics.** Sounds logical right? But, many companies rush headlong onto social platforms without understanding what their goals are. This is a real waste of resources. For example, if you don't have consistent messaging between Facebook and Twitter, you'll confuse your customers, and they will leave.

- **Understand that you can't fake customer relationships.** The French novelist Jean Giraudoux is credited with the famous quote, "The secret of success is sincerity. Once you can fake that you've got it made." Joking aside, we all know that one of the hallmarks of social media is authenticity. Now that a customer can tell everyone on Facebook that your customer service is a joke, feigning sincerity is out the window. People know the real thing.

- **Your business must constantly monitor the web, because you must be alert to potential problems.** Plan to check in on your social platforms much more often than once a week. If you don't assign one or more employees (depending on company size) to constantly monitor your social media accounts, you're penny-wise and pound-foolish. If you're the last to know about some terrible problem with your product or service, it might be too late to save your reputation.

✔ **To provide customers with the content they need, learning where your customers consume information, read reviews, and follow news.** This follows the old adage, "fish where the fish are." You can't expect to change your customers' long-established online habits. If they communicate on Twitter, you aren't going to get them to come to your website's newsroom to read boring press releases.

✔ **To know what your customer wants, your research and communication must be ongoing. It's not a one-time thing.** Social media takes time. When you add it as a layer to your CRM, you'll need to take the time to make the data make sense. Don't be frustrated that you don't immediately know how to value it. (But when you're ready, Chapter 14 can help you start analyzing data.)

Also, just in case you're still not convinced that customers really value customer service, the 2012 American Express Global Customer Service Barometer found that consumers say they'd spend 21 percent more with companies that offer great customer service.

The American Express survey also found that customers use social media for customer service because they want the following:

✔ To receive an actual response from a company.

✔ To praise the company for a positive experience.

✔ To share information about their service experience with more people.

✔ To vent frustration about their experience.

✔ To ask other users how they could have gotten better service. Customers want to pay you more, if you'll just treat them right!

Encouraging customer engagement

Another way to look at the value of social customer service is to look at it from the customer engagement side. In other words, how does great customer service increase your customer's dedication to your company? To understand this, it's helpful to look at the Engagement Pyramid developed by consulting firm Groundwire in 2010.

The Engagement Pyramid consists of six different layers of engagement that a person can have with your company, (one being the lowest and six being the highest). As you read the descriptions, see if you can think of specific customers you know in each category and how they impact your business.

The levels of the pyramid are as follows:

✓ **Level One: Observing**

The customer is simply aware of the company and periodically looks at its messages.

✓ **Level two: Following**

The customer allows you to use her e-mail address or other contact info so that she can learn about your offerings.

✓ **Level three: Endorsing**

At this level, the customer endorses your products and allows you to identify her as an advocate.

✓ **Level four: Contributing**

The customer actively spends time or money to help your organization. For example, she might participate in forums or sponsor events.

✓ **Level five: Owning**

The customer now transforms into someone with a deep commitment to the company who does things like invest or join the board.

✓ **Level six: Leading**

The customer volunteers to lead initiatives to help support the company's major goals.

Most customers will never advance beyond level four. However, identifying customers who are moving up through these levels can be a huge benefit to your company. By understanding the continuum, you can help create situations that will encourage customers to move ahead.

Don't let your customers' engagement flag. Once a customer has endorsed your product, you may consider approaching him as a guest at a planned event. The next time, you could approach him to assist with sponsorship of that event.

Dealing with complaints

We all complain about something: the weather, our workload, or our lack of time off. The home for complaints used to be customer service department. Now, complaints have lots of places to go via social media, which amplifies a complaint's negative message. Complaints are on Facebook, in your Twitter feed, and all over review sites. Regardless of where you find them, complaints take two general forms, as follows:

Buy less, so you don't need a bigger bag

One of the funniest examples of bad customer service Stephanie has seen is worth a mention. On a clothing checkout line at a retail store, a customer ahead of her had several purchases and intended to make several more. The cashier started to pack her purchases into a too-small shopping bag, tightly stuffing in the merchandise. Seeing this, the customer said that she'd like a bigger bag. She didn't want her clothing crushed and rumpled.

The cashier replied that she couldn't give her a bigger bag because, due to several thefts in the store, management had instructed cashiers to offer only smaller bags. Management's concern was that the larger bags were accommodating theft. The customer threatened to abandon her sale. Only after much discussion was she given a larger bag.

Think about how the store manager, in his attempt to curtail thefts, was also encouraging shoppers to buy less — clearly an outcome he didn't intend!"

✔ **Complaints with a clear resolution:** Your customer service reps and social media responders encounter problems that need solving. For example, a customer might say that the product must be returned, the fit is wrong, or he ordered a blue one and got a green one. These are the types of issues that support people hope they'll find every time they pick up the phone or respond to an e-mail, chat, or social media comment. The rep is clear on what kind of response is needed to solve the problem and satisfy the customer.

✔ **Complaints without a clear resolution:** The second form of complaint is much more difficult to deal with in today's always-on web. Perhaps the customer is irate, writing negative online reviews, and there's no clear problem to solve immediately. But solve you must. A knee-jerk defense could make things worse. For example, we've seen restaurant staff reply to irate customer reviews by writing insulting replies to the customers. This is your worst nightmare. Your reputation could hang in the balance.

Collaborating with the customer

We know the new social customers expect to be heard — and their concerns acted upon. Some companies are known for their ability to listen and react to customer feedback. When these companies can demonstrate that to the customer, they likely have a customer for life. Some companies have specifically developed programs to solicit customer ideas and opinions online, because customers who feel they have a hand in shaping a product will be more likely to champion and buy it.

For example, Starbucks came under fire in recent years because customers felt that the company wasn't responsive to their needs. To fix this and demonstrate a real desire to hear from consumers, Starbucks launched My Starbucks Idea (`http://mystarbucksidea.force.com/ideahome`), shown in Figure 10-1.

The site allows customers to offer their own ideas about how to improve Starbucks products, experiences in the stores, and social involvement. According to the site, Starbucks has implemented over 200 ideas gathered there. In this way, Starbucks opened a channel for the voice of the customer to be heard.

Clearly, almost everyone who took the time to participate on the site was either interested in what Starbucks was doing in their neighborhood or with its products. This was the audience that Starbucks wanted to reach.

The real value to the company is not only the PR factor, but the opportunity to collect vast amounts of data about who these customers are, how they use the products, and what they want to see in the way of improvements. This data would be hard to collect from small focus groups or surveys. Think about how you can use this type of site to gather the information you need about your customers.

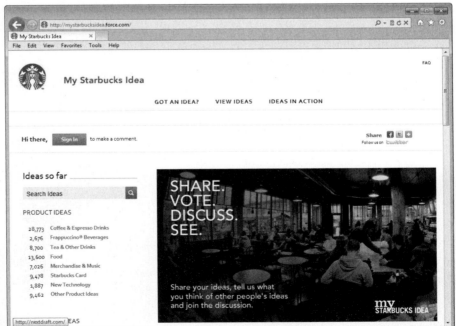

Figure 10-1:
My
Starbucks
Idea.

Starting to serve your social customer

The state of social customer service should remind us all of Malone's Laws of Technology, created by Michael S. Malone, former editor of *Forbes ASAP* and the author of *The Guardian of All Things: The Epic Story of Human Memory* (St. Martin's Press). The law states, "All technological revolutions arrive later than we expect, but sooner than we are prepared for." Such is clearly the case for social customer service. It's here, but most companies aren't ready for it.

If you're just getting started in formulating your social CRM plan, consider the following:

- ✔ **Use the right platform for the type of complaint — fast versus slow.** If your product demands quick answers (in an industry such as information technology, for example) integrate a platform like Twitter that allows you to monitor customer concerns in real time. Customers will appreciate that you understand the urgency of their questions.

- ✔ **Use video or step-by-step documentation in help and support areas on your website.** Create quick videos or step-by-step documentation based on your FAQs to help those who learn better using different formats. Seeing the answers in action satisfies customers.

- ✔ **Be generous with service.** I know this one is obvious, but sometimes it's ignored in favor of cost cutting. If anyone questions whether this strategy works, just ask Zappos. (They quickly built a multibillion dollar online shoe company by strictly focusing on customer service.)

- ✔ **Make sure employees understand that responding to negative comments in kind is forbidden.** One customer's negative comments can become a war of words with employees. Shut this one down before it happens. It becomes a food fight and everyone but your company will enjoy the play-by-play. Share a set of clear commenting guidelines with anyone in your company who responds to customers.

- ✔ **Give enough information online so that customers can make the right buying decision the first time.** One easy way to get this done is to assign yourself the task of buying one of your products. On your website, look around, check out the data, look at shipping information, find out how to return an item, and so on. The key is to do it yourself. The further away managers get from the actual shopping experience, the more likely they will be out of touch with the concerns of the customer.

 Make sure that you understand why your customers use social media to connect with you. Guessing why is a mistake. A study by IBM called *From Social Media to Social CRM* found that the top two reasons why consumers interact with brands on social media are for discounts and purchasing links. Companies, on the other hand, put those two reasons on the bottom of their list. It's important to have the facts before you create your promotions.

Correlating your engagement type to your financial performance

It's always fun to compare your own company to others. When it comes to social media, the stakes are high. In 2009, Wetpaint and the Altimeter Group did a study called *Engagement: Ranking the Top 100 Global Brands.* They looked at the social engagement of the top brands to see whether their participation in social media impacted revenue. They found that the brands fell into one of four engagement profiles. Why not see how your company compares? Here are the profiles:

✔ **Mavens:** These are brands that are engaged in seven or more social channels (the term *channels* refers to platforms like Facebook and Twitter) and that have a high engagement score. (A high score means that they actively monitor and communicate through these channels.)

✔ **Butterflies:** These brands are engaged in seven or more social channels but have a low engagement score.

✔ **Selectives:** These brands are engaged in six or fewer channels and have high engagement scores.

✔ **Wallflowers:** Brands labeled Wallflowers are engaged in six or fewer channels and have low engagement scores.

The most important finding in the study was that financial performance correlated with engagement. Brands that had higher social engagement with their customers had higher revenue returns. That's a great incentive to increase your social engagement right now. Nobody wants to be a wallflower.

Now that you're formulating how your social CRM program will work, you'll want to think about what key social metrics you should capture. According to Debra Donston-Miller in The BrainYard, an InformationWeek publication, you should consider several social metrics, including the following:

✔ **Quality of fans and followers:** This is a key distinction. Sometimes managers use the number of followers as their only measure of how well they're doing. This is half the picture and won't bring the returns you hope for. You may have acquired followers by virtue of one blog post or one offer, and they'll never return again. You want to evaluate how much engagement your followers display. A smaller active list trumps a large cold list.

✔ **Social demographics:** Understanding your customer demographics is a must for any business. We add psychographics to this list. Psychographics tell you about customer attitudes and opinions. Knowing who your customer really is ensures that the content you create and the offers you make will hit the mark.

✔ **Most popular pages, posts, and tweets:** Examining the response to your content is another must-do. Your content is the foundation for all your revenue-generating efforts. For example, if you see a great response to an article or topic, you may want to consider how to monetize it. By that we mean that if customers are very excited about several articles you've written about a topic, perhaps you want to create an expanded e-book or training course for sale.

✔ **Conversions:** This one is everyone's favorite goal. It's the one that keeps the lights on. But conversions don't only refer to purchases. It could be anything that turns an observer of your business into a participant.

These are a good start. You'll want to add several others as you get more familiar with how you can integrate your social data with your standard CRM data. Remember that metrics must be meaningful to your business. If they're not, find ones that are.

Reviewing the actions of the big brands

The major brands don't get everything about social media right. We all know that. However, there are some brands that really excel when it comes to social customer service, and their customers let them know it. By looking at what they're doing, you might get some good ideas about what you can do. According to the readers of MSN Money's 2011 Customer Service Hall of Fame, some of the winners include these companies:

✔ **Amazon:** This site (www.amazon.com) does something that's the envy of most other online retailers. They make buying simple. The user is one click away from purchasing any product. Instead of offering myriad support options after you purchase something, they make buying (or returning) so easy that customers are constantly delighted. Another really effective service is Amazon Prime. It allows you to get reduced pricing on shipping, among its many other features. Of course, one of the reasons that customers like Amazon is that you can buy so many different products from one place.

✔ **Apple:** No one is surprised when Apple makes the list of best in customer service. If you look at their support portal (www.apple.com/support), as shown in Figure 10-2, you see that they have a substantial self-serve area that includes video tutorials, manuals, tech specs, downloads, and online communities. Their stores have a Genius Bar, and they offer support through AppleCare and other sources. The thing that makes Apple support stand out is that they prize their service to customers. Stories about how Apple store personnel have gone the extra mile to support customers can be found on many review sites.

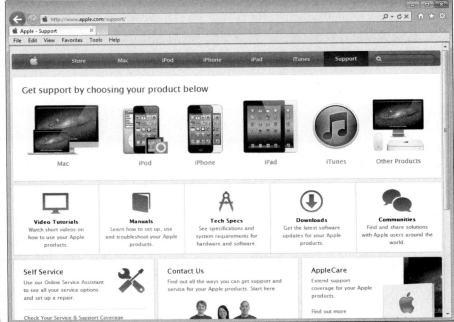

Figure 10-2:
Apple's
customer
support
portal.

Apple Stores (Apple's bricks-and-mortar retail outlets) take advantage of something that researchers have uncovered about shopping: If you hold a product in your hand, you are more likely to buy it than if you just look at it. There's a method to their madness at Apple.

✔ **Nordstrom:** This retailer set out to provide the best possible customer service available, in stores and online at http://shop.nordstrom.com, and they succeeded. Their service is legendary. They knew that if they wanted to compete with other upscale retailers, they would have to distinguish themselves. Employees are trained that nothing trumps customer service.

Also, they're always trying to upgrade their service. They recently gave handheld units to their sales associates so that they could check company-wide inventory while assisting customers. This ensures that if they have the merchandise in any store, they can sell it to customers without delay.

✔ **Publix Super Markets:** Publix (in stores and at www.publix.com) takes a different approach when it comes to providing customer service: They say they focus on treating their employees so generously that those employees are then motivated to provide excellent customer service. They also pride themselves on good prices. Apparently, customers agree.

> ✔ **Trader Joe's:** This company (online at http://traderjoes.com) does two specific things that stand out. The first is that it has an engaging theme, calling shopping at Trader Joe's an "adventure." In order to differentiate themselves from the competition, they stock unusual items and provide enthusiastic service. In addition, like Publix, they claim that their employee benefits are superior. These benefits include medical, dental, and vision coverage for all employees (full time and part time), retirement plans, and an employee discount on all purchases.

Listening to the Social Customer

By definition, a social customer is one whose voice will be heard. But are you really listening? Listening to customers takes time and resources. You need to allocate employees who monitor social networks in real time and let them build rapport. You have to have faith in the strategy and let it build over time.

It's easy for employees to appear uncaring when all they have is 140 characters. But by educating your staff and letting them build customer relationships, you're helping to ensure the future health of your company.

Social networks provide a wealth of information and can be a source of real revenue for your company if you understand the value of the social graph.

Understanding the social graph

Understanding what the social graph is and how it's plotted is key to understanding your customer's social relationships and how to leverage them. The term *social graph* refers to the networks of connections among people. The theory is that all people in the world are connected by six degrees.

The cultural trivia game Six Degrees of Kevin Bacon uses the concept of the social graph. In the game, you have to link from Kevin Bacon to someone else in six steps based on your connections to each other.

The idea that six degrees is close can be misleading. When we think of connecting to people who matter to us, six degrees is a long stretch. Paul Adams, in his book *Grouped,* says that we really can have a meaningful connection to only those people who are within three degrees. If you look at a social graph, you can see how distant three connections really are.

To visualize what a basic social graph looks like, imagine if you were to draw a circle with your name in it in the middle of a piece of paper. Then draw circles linking back to you that represent your closest online friends. Then add friends of your friend's friends. This picture you created would show you the beginning of your own social graph, as shown in Figure 10-3.

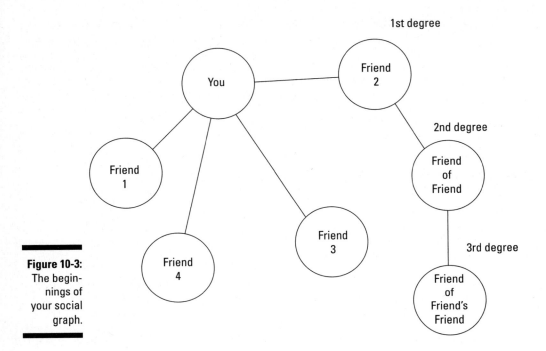

1st degree

2nd degree

3rd degree

Figure 10-3:
The begin-
nings of
your social
graph.

You see your friend one degree away, a friend of a friend as two degrees away and a friend of a friend's friend as three degrees. That's really getting distant.

So how does this relate to social networking platforms? A deployment of a social graph you may instantly be familiar with is the use of Search plus Your World from Google. If you sign up for a Google+ account, you're connected to the following:

✔ **Information shared by all your Google+ followers**

✔ **Information about the searches you do**

✔ **Your search history**

If you want to view this information when you search with Google, you simply click the link that says Personal Results, as shown in Figure 10-4. When you click that, you'll see information that's specific to you and your connections.

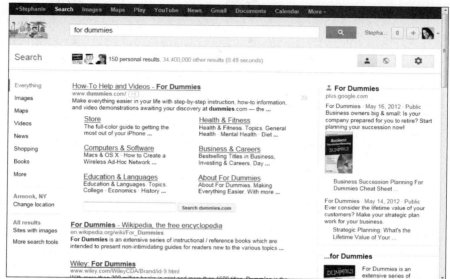

Figure 10-4:
Personal
results link
in Google.

There are several ways to leverage the social graph for your company's benefit. They include the following:

- **External networks:** Leverage the relationships of fans that connect to you from their social platforms or social bookmarking sites. They might tweet a blog post of yours or put it on Digg, a social bookmarking site. This will help you find connections that your company might never make on its own.

- **External networks:** Use an API like Facebook Connect that lets you link your company's application with your customer's Facebook network. This means that users can log in to the application using their Facebook account. Since you're tying your application to a habit your customer already has (logging into Facebook), you're making it more likely they will use the application.

- **External networks:** Leverage your employees' networks outside the company — to their relationships on social platforms. If employees participate in the company's social outreach, they can help the company reach new people.

- **Internal networks:** Leverage your employee's relationships within your company to effect better employee performance and leadership roles. It's important to remember that employees have relationships with people in different departments. When the company makes it easy for those employees to communicate, they help foster collaboration.

Recognizing the power of viral

Viral tweets, videos and posts have the power to bring corporate executives to their knees. If you think that's an overstatement, think about the following viral customer service catastrophes that befell two major corporations:

- **Bank of America's interest rate scandal:** In 2011, Bank of America decided to double the interest rate on Ann Minch's loan. Not willing to pay such an outrageous increase, Minch unleashed a self-proclaimed "Debtors Revolt" on YouTube. As a result of the furor caused by her video, she was asked to make an appearance on a network TV news show. The PR was awful, and Bank of America relented, but not without a lot of bad press and a tidal wave of consumer protests. To date, the video has been viewed over half a million times.

- **Too fat to fly:** In 2010, Southwest Airlines told movie maker Kevin Smith that he was "too fat to fly," as he humorously depicts in Figure 10-5. Airline staff insisted he exit the plane in which he was seated, citing safety concerns and a Customer of Size policy. He had originally purchased two seats, but got on an earlier flight that had only one remaining seat.

  Smith wasn't going to take that sitting down. Unfortunately for Southwest, Smith is also a comedian with a huge Twitter following. After several nasty and funny tweets went viral, the airlines issued several apologies and offered Smith a $100 voucher.

  As you may expect, the offer was met with much derision and more funny tweets. All the major media outlets picked up this story of bad customer service, and Southwest ended up looking like a bully. Their handling of the situation clearly showed that they weren't ready for a social media onslaught. Some thought about handling this type of fiasco was in order.

Of course, not all stories that go viral are bad ones. Most people who plan marketing campaigns hope that their stories will go viral and bring recognition and revenue raining down upon them.

That's certainly what happened to Susan Boyle, the *Britain's Got Talent* TV-show contestant whose audition stirred the hearts of millions of viewers, but nothing about her video was planned. It was a happy accident, and many viral incidents are just that. The power of viral is a force to be reckoned with. It's difficult to remember that YouTube launched in 2005, which isn't that long ago. What did marketers and consumers do without it?

Figure 10-5: Kevin Smith's own "too fat to fly" photo.

Monitoring your social reputation

The power of viral reminds us that our social reputations can be influenced by the smallest actions. To ensure your customer service is hitting the target, use online monitoring tools. These tools help you know what people are saying about your brand in real time. When your brand is mentioned, you want to know.

Following are some reputation-monitoring review sites to consider:

- **The Consumerist:** The tagline of this site (www.consumerist.com) is "Shoppers bite back." Its staff has an irreverent attitude and presents columns like "Customer Disservice" and "What in the What Now." This site, affiliated with the publisher of Consumer Reports, accepts tips from consumers about bad service or products. Staffers research stories and provide information that they believe will empower consumers. The site doesn't accept advertising.

- **PlanetFeedback:** This site (www.planetfeedback.com), shown in Figure 10-6, enables consumers to post letters addressed to the companies with which they have customer service issues. The letters are published online, and everyone can add a comment. (See Chapter 9 for information about two other customer review sites — Yelp and Epinion.)

Figure 10-6:
Planet-
Feedback's
home page.

Following are some free monitoring tools to consider:

- **Social Mention:** You start by putting a search term in the search box at `www.socialmention.com`. The search engine then returns mentions of the term on Twitter, StumbleUpon, and more than 100 other social media sites.

  What's useful about this search engine is that not only does it return the search results, it also provides these content measures:

  - *Strength:* The probability that your topic will be mentioned
  - *Sentiment:* Positive versus negative results
  - *Passion:* The probability that the respondents will repeatedly mention you

- **Addict-o-matic:** Promises the "latest buzz on any topic," as shown in Figure 10-7, at `http://addictomatic.com`. Their searches cover blogs, articles, and social platforms, including YouTube. The key benefit of this site is the Bookmark tool, which allows you to save your searches and come back to them.

Figure 10-7:
Addict-
o-matic's
search box.

✔ **Google Alerts:** This tool (at www.google.com/alerts) allows you to set up automated keyword searches that alert you when content has been updated. They are very easy to set up, and you can have a multitude of them. You can put in your company name, names of industry influentials, or any other searches you do on a daily basis. Google searches its database and returns the results to you via e-mail or in Google Reader.

Also consider using these fee-based tools as necessary:

✔ **Radian6:** This tool is popular among enterprise users and is now owned by Salesforce.com. It's easy to scale, has a solid dashboard that shows you conversations across the web, and offers a unique feature that allows you to tag workflow. You can find more info at www.radian6.com.

✔ **Trackur:** This is an affordable tool (you can choose from several tiers) that allows you to track your brand mentions on the web. What's different about this tool is that in addition to returning search results, Trackur makes it easy for you to see who influences your brand. Find out more at www.trackur.com.

- ✔ **Sprout Social:** With this web application (available at `http://sprout social.com`), your company can customize its social media monitoring and create good-looking reports from the results. You can analyze your influencers and compare yourself to your competitors.

- ✔ **Wildfire's Social Media Monitor:** More of a comparison site (`http://monitor.wildfireapp.com`) than a tracking site, but it's very useful. You can compare Twitter feeds or Facebook pages on the fly. For example, you can compare your company to your competitors — based on Twitter or Facebook accounts — or check out the leader boards to see how the big companies compare.

Using Community-Based Support

If you've been in business for a while, you probably have some passionate customers. Are these customers willing to help others using your products? That's a key question you need to ask yourself when you're considering developing a community-based support site.

These kinds of sites run the gamut from a few users who informally answer questions, to sites that require major resources and monitoring by your company. To decide what's right for you, look at what successful communities are all about.

Building the community-based support site

In their book, *The Hyper-Social Organization,* Francois Gossieaux and Ed Moran list four elements of all successful communities. They are as follows:

- ✔ **Members share a passion for the topic.** A cohesive group can be formed only if people truly care about the topic and want to share that information with others. We've all visited forums where no one but the forum owner has posted anything. For a group to thrive, the members really need to care. This creates a commonality of purpose and sharing becomes automatic.

- ✔ **The content includes both user-generated content and professionally produced information.** The content should be of the highest quality. Companies should considering outsourcing material from experts who can add value. In addition, the community should feature user contributions.

- ✔ **Access to member profiles is available.** Members join communities to find connections and learn more about the topic. If you facilitate that by helping them share information about themselves, you'll help fulfill their need to find like-minded people.

✔ **Navigation is easy.** We use the term *navigation* here to refer to things like finding information or meeting a new member. If it's hard to move around your site and find what you came for, you will discourage people from returning.

Growing your community

Management traditionally has a difficult time figuring out the value of social media initiatives. With community-based support forums, the case is clear. It's a benefit.

The support costs decrease because of the contributions of unpaid members, and the productivity of the paid staff rises. This is a win-win in any manager's mind. But creating a successful community is hard work. If you build it, they may not come.

So what do you need to think about when creating your community? Here are some things to consider:

✔ **Software platform:** Search for an easy-to-use software platform that provides your members with easy access to all the functions they need. Don't try to cobble something together. Part V introduces several platforms and helps you start your search.

✔ **Rewards:** Most people who come to these communities and share are there for the intrinsic value it provides. Rewarding them is icing on the cake, but doing so lets everyone know that your company values its most active customers. Creating something like a leader board that shows who is most active can be very inspiring.

✔ **Member interaction:** Make it easy for members to meet each other online and share information. This will strengthen the bond among community members and your company. This is a huge benefit because you're on your way to creating customer evangelists.

✔ **Knowledge base:** Devoting some money to building up the knowledge collected in this forum will help cut support costs. You can see what problems users experience when using your products and turn the knowledge base entries into the precise information they need. Real-time problems that crop up can be swiftly handled.

A great example of a thriving community site is the SAP Community Network (http://scn.sap.com/welcome), as shown in Figure 10-8. It's run by SAP, a market leader in CRM, to support its vast array of products and services. Once you become a member, you can write a blog, answer forum posts, and meet other members. The community is very robust and includes employees, users, vendors, and mentors.

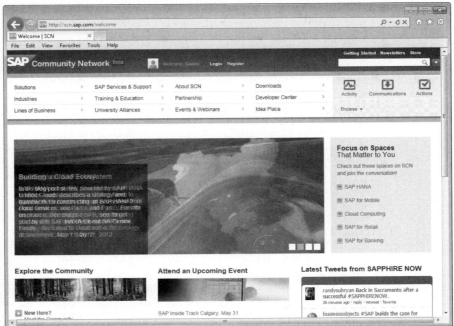

Figure 10-8:
The SAP
Community
Network.

Member communities are very influential. The Nielsen study *Global Faces and Networked Places* says that member communities reach more Internet users (66.8 percent) than e-mail (65.1 percent). That's quite a reach. Member communities can be a corporate asset if done correctly.

Creating Goals for Social Customer Service

Almost every organization will tell you that they want to provide a good customer service experience. No one sets out to disappoint and drive customers away, but it happens every day.

One way your company can dramatically improve social customer service is to let customers serve themselves. Now, of course that doesn't mean that you abandon phone support or ignore customer requests in favor of self-service.

What it does mean is that with the current technology available, every company can provide ways for the customer to get the information they need 24/7.

Benefitting from a self-serve portal

Both you and the customer benefit from providing self-serve portals. Following are some of the tangible benefits for your customers:

- **Ease of navigation:** Customers see a complete listing of the help you offer: FAQs, catalogs, product descriptions, specs, and so on.
- **Shared information:** Customers see what other customers are saying and doing in regard to your products.
- **Access to status of reported issues:** They can review their support tickets 24/7.

Here are some of the tangible benefits for your company:

- **Access to customers' real thoughts:** Customers provide feedback, so you can see how effective each part of your site is.
- **Visibility of current promotions:** You can make sure customers see specific documents or promotions.
- **Cost cutting:** You cut down on costly tech support calls to a live operator.
- **Increased call center staff productivity:** Self-service increases the productivity of your call center staff. They can focus on higher-priority calls.
- **The latest info on customer trends:** Reports from your social CRM provide key information about what topics are hot.
- **Less work for staff:** Self-serve portals provide assistance without requiring costly phone support.

Integrating a self-service portal

Integration of self-serve options can be challenging. You'll want to make sure that you're adding value to your system, not just adding a layer of complexity. It's not a sexy project, but one that has lasting value.

Just like the undertaking of any technical project, consider the following when you plan your portal:

- ✔ **Set expectations for everyone, communicating what's possible and what's not.** Employees may have different ideas about the use of self-serve portals. Some see it as a big opportunity; others see it as a waste of time. When you begin, make sure that each employee knows all the benefits and cost-saving value your company will accrue.

- ✔ **Evaluate staff responsibilities.** Make sure you understand which employees will be impacted and who will have direct responsibility. You need to get buy-in from all involved, from top management to staffers.

- ✔ **Evaluate resources and costs.** Know what you need to spend to get the portal that meets your needs. Establish a budget and be realistic about costs.

- ✔ **Think about scalability.** One of the main reasons why some tech projects go wrong is that growth isn't considered. Right now, you may need a small portal, but consider how you will support it if your company grows in size, adds products, and has to serve more customers.

- ✔ **Set a timeline.** Many IT projects start with an unrealistic timeline. The dates are either driven by management expectations or a lack of understanding about complexity. Be realistic. Wishing won't make it so.

- ✔ **Make sure you identify the data and metrics you want to use.** We look at examples of metrics earlier in the "Starting to serve your social customer" section. You determine success metrics for your self-serve portal ahead of time.

- ✔ **Make sure everyone knows about launch plans and follow-through.** There's nothing worse than hearing a support person say, "They never tell us what's happening." We've all experienced that. It makes us feel helpless and resentful that our time is being wasted. Make sure everyone knows when things launch and how to use the information to assist customers.

Defining the social knowledge base

Social knowledge bases can be financial assets. You can use them to capture vital information from both inside and outside the company. Some knowledge bases take the form of business wikis. A *wiki* is a database that users can edit. People can add new content and modify entries as needed. The most common example of a wiki is Wikipedia (at www.wikipedia.org).

We categorize social knowledge bases in organizations as follows:

✓ **Internal knowledge base (may also be a wiki):** Companies have a wealth of information stored in the heads of their employees. They also have product information, manuals, documents, and a host of disparate information that gets lost in the clutter. In order to optimize the use of this content, companies create wikis that employees can use to input and search for important data. Examples of this include information about specific ongoing projects or company policies. Companies most often use a wiki for this type of database because it gives them the ability to extract important knowledge from employees.

✓ **External knowledge base (may also be a wiki):** These kinds of wikis are accessed by customers, product advocates, and departments to provide essential information for their customers. An external knowledge base can be part of a self-serve portal or a community-based site, or it can stand alone. Examples of the information collected here include product information, FAQs, help information, and manuals.

American Express has made great use of a social knowledge base (not a wiki), which you can check out at `http://americanexpress.com/knowledge center`. It's even more valuable if you're a member. As a member, you can log in and see both your own personal information and the knowledge base that can be used to grow your own business.

Another company lauded for its use of a knowledge base is Autodesk. Its site is called WikiHelp (`http://wikihelp.autodesk.com/enu`), as shown in Figure 10-9. It boasts a large active community of participants and over two million contributions to its database.

If you'd like to create your own knowledge base, here are some vendor platforms to consider:

✓ **MindTouch:** One of the most well-known wiki vendors. Their products are cloud-based, enterprise contact management systems. You can find out more about MindTouch at `www.mindtouch.com` as shown in Figure 10-10.

✓ **Microsoft Office 365:** This is one of the big boys associated with knowledge-management systems. They are cloud-based and can be set up in Sharepoint. Find more info at `www.microsoft.com/en-us/office365`.

✓ **MediaWiki:** This one is free and open source. Check out `www.media wiki.org/wiki/mediawiki` for more details.

Figure 10-9:
Autodesk
WikiHelp.

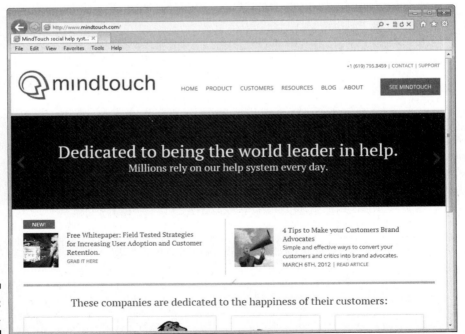

Figure 10-10:
MindTouch.

Recovering from Social Media Uproars Like a Pro

As we discuss in the earlier section, "Recognizing the power of viral," comments posted on social media sites can get out of hand very quickly. Some companies bring the negative feedback upon themselves, and some are victims of circumstance. The following are examples of companies who recovered from disasters and went on to improve their customer service.

✔ **Comcast:** We mention Comcast in our opening paragraph for this chapter. The 2006 YouTube video of the service rep falling asleep on his customer's couch while on hold with the service department is classic. You can watch it here `http://bit.ly/VlqSYM`.

Needless to say, Comcast was humiliated. The press had a field day. Comcast was at a crossroads. They either had to improve their customer service or watch their company take a slide in revenue. The stakes were high. Comcast publicly committed itself to improving. So to paraphrase the constant refrain of former Mayor of New York, Ed Koch, "How are they doing?"

The American Customer Satisfaction Index in 2011 shows that Comcast continues to rise and is beating several of the competitors. Customers have actually praised their service. They had to put in several years of hard work to turn it around.

They invested a reported two billion dollars in the last few years to overcome their abysmal record. They did such things as

- *Outfit their field staff with handheld devices for better communication.*

- *Set up a portal for internal troubleshooting.*

- *Establish listening posts on social media, like this one on Twitter* `https://twitter.com/comcastcares`.

✔ **Dell Computers:** Another case in point is Dell Computers. Dell's reputation was on a downslide. Proof came in the form of a University of Michigan study that showed Dell's service was a cause for great concern to its customers. Popular blogger Jeff Jarvis chimed in with a harrowing tale detailing his efforts to get his PC fixed. Social media started picking up on it, and media like *Newsweek* got interested in the story.

Just like Comcast, Dell had a decision to make. They could either ignore the reports or confront them head-on. They decided to take action. One of the things they did was create a place on their website to receive customer suggestions. This wasn't an easy choice. It's a very public way to handle criticism. But Dick Hunter, Dell's head of customer service, wanted to show they were serious. When Michael Dell returned to lead the company in 2007, efforts were accelerated.

So how are they doing today? Customer surveys have shown that Dell really has improved. They are committed to social customer service, and in 2010, they opened their Social Media Listening Command Center. This effort continues to help them improve their service through social channels.

Remember these examples in case your company has a PR fiasco. You can rise from the ashes. In fact, if you ask these companies what they think about these incidents now, each might say the problem was an important turning point for the company.

Chapter 11

Supporting the Age of Mobility

· ·

· ·

Got your smartphone handy? If you're like almost 50 percent of wireless device owners, you probably do, according to a Nielsen study. We use our smartphones and other mobile devices like actual companions that assist us in navigating our day.

In marketing, mobile is known as the third screen. We've gone from the first screen (TV) to the second screen (the computer) and now on to the third screen (the mobile device). If anyone is concerned that the previous screens would disappear, they can stop worrying. Mobile users have figured out how to enhance each of the other screens by using them in tandem.

For example, if we're watching a TV show, we may look up the actor's bio on our smartphone. If we want to visit the museum we read about while sitting at our desktop computer, we can get directions while we're on the way from our mobile device. If we want to find a new restaurant, some of us ask Siri (iPhone's mobile assistant) or other smartphone review apps for a recommendation.

Armed with this knowledge, business owners need to make decisions about how to integrate this behavior into their social media strategy. In this chapter, we look at how pervasive mobile devices have become and how they impact your business. As a social CRM user, you can't afford to ignore it. As former CEO of Google, Eric Schmidt has said, "Put your best people on mobile."

Looking at Consumer Trends in Mobile

It appears that mobile devices are always with us as we go through our day. Research from Microsoft Tag tells us that Americans spend 2.7 hours per day socializing on their mobile device, be it a tablet or a smartphone.

The shocking part of that statistic is that, according to the folks at Microsoft Tag, "it's twice the amount of time they spend eating and one third of the time they spent sleeping each day." In fact, they predict that by 2014, the global use of mobile devices will overtake desktop web use. (Microsoft Tag is the group that developed the Tag app to produce QR codes and 2D bar codes used in consumer magazines. Find out more at `http://tag.microsoft.com/home.aspx`.)

The mobile web experience is varied. Some content is hard to see and some has been created to be viewed specifically on a mobile device. To understand how businesses should look at the use of mobile devices, a distinction needs to be made about these two different kinds of mobile experiences:

- ✔ **The mobile web:** This term refers to the Internet viewed from a mobile device. This includes things like surfing the web from a browser or reading a blog. The content may or may not be optimized for a smaller touchscreen device. Either way, the links and scrolling work just as they do on any web page.

- ✔ **Applications for mobile devices:** These are custom software programs designed to assist the customer in viewing specific content. They help access data in a pleasing way or engage with brand content. These applications are specific to the device's operating system. For example, iPhone runs the iOS operating system, and programs have to be written specifically for that system.

Because of this distinction, businesses have to decide how much effort they want to put into massaging their content for access on mobile devices. Some may elect to create custom apps. Others may decide that their mobile presence doesn't require the extra expenditure because they push much of their content through social networks.

Understanding the needs of the market

To get a clear understanding of your customer's mobile needs, it's helpful to view the results of a study done for Yahoo!'s 2011 white paper, *Mobile Internet – Delivering on the Promise of Mobile Advertising*. This study (the first in a series) breaks the categories of mobile use into seven identifiable modes and the amount of time each day spent in that mode.

In Table 11-1, we also include a Mindset column. The study linked mindset to each mode. Of course, the consumer could have more than one mindset while using their mobile. The one cited is the most pervasive, according to the study. In the next section, you find out more about how to best reach your customer based on the pervasive mindset.

The information in Table 11-1 gives you some idea of how to approach a customer who's engaged in a particular behavior (mode). For example, if you're planning to advertise, you may want to avoid placing the ad near GPS data (GPS users are in Navigate mode and tend to be irritated) unless you can really help smartphone users get where they need to go!

Table 11-1		Seven Modes of Mobile Usage	
Mode	*Time per Day*	*Example*	*Pervasive Mindset*
Connect	38%	SMS (text), IM, e-mail, social networking	Sense of happiness
Search	18%	Search engines	Exploring
Entertain	15%	Games, movies, radio	Involved
Manage	10%	Banking, scheduling, health records	Sense of purpose
Inform	9%	News, audio, video, blogs	Exploring
Shop	7%	Purchasing, price comparisons, discounts	Concerned
Navigate	3%	Maps, GPS	Irritated

Using consumer behavior to develop mobile campaigns

As a businessperson, you need to figure out how to use the different modes of behavior and the attendant states of mind to reach your customers as they go through their day. For example, if you're a health care provider, you may want to help your customers schedule appointments using their mobile devices. You'll also want to know if your customer demographic uses a mobile device as often as predicted. According to a Nielsen Wire article posted on September 26, 2011, 62 percent of 25–34-year-olds own a smartphone. If that's your demographic, you need to pay attention to mobile.

You can't create new behaviors in your customer; you want to fit in with what they're already doing. Customers can't even change their own behavior very easily, so trying to change them for your brand is nearly impossible.

Here are some of the behavior modes and how they relate to your mobile strategy:

- **Connecting:** It's no surprise that connecting is the main way people use their mobile phones. They text, send e-mail, check into their social networks, and instant-message their friends. Your main goal should be to make sure your message is appropriate for the platform.

  For example, if you want to engage customers while they're on a social platform, you would send out a different type of customer message than one you send to a business e-mail address. The underlying message would be the same; only the tone and format would be different.

  A key takeaway for your campaign: Make sure that your messaging is consistent across platforms. You don't want to confuse your customers. Remember that sales trainers always say, "a confused mind always says no."

  Even if you have permission to contact a user at his professional e-mail address, remember that he might look at the message from a mobile device, so make sure the experience is good and doesn't waste his time.

- **Searching:** Searching can be even more important to a mobile user than it is to someone sitting at his desktop. Search results could determine which location he heads to next. In 2011, Google published results of a study, The Mobile Movement, that includes this information: 77 percent of users go to a search engine first when picking up their mobile device. (For more on this topic see Chapter 7.)

- **Viewing:** When you're creating content for mobile users, you have two choices. You can either develop an app that works specifically with your content or you can make sure your site is maximized for mobile viewing and provide a link to your original site. Check out how your site looks in the major search engines, including Yahoo!, shown in Figure 11-1.

  A key takeaway for your campaign: Optimize your site for mobile viewing if at all possible. Make sure customers don't have to go to a competitor's site because they can't adequately view yours.

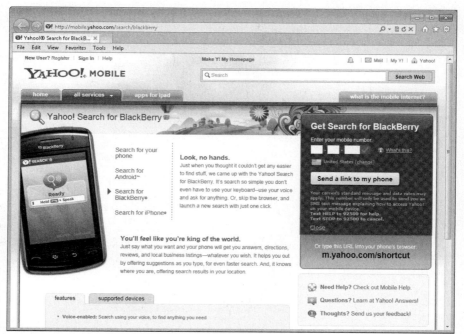

Figure 11-1:
Yahoo!
Mobile
Search
for the
Blackberry.

✔ **Entertaining:** Mobile users love to entertain themselves while on the go. Standing on a long line at the grocery store doesn't inspire the boredom that it used to. Obviously, major TV and movie content producers will have the bulk of your customers' attention, but users can always text or play a game with a friend. Your business should consider the use of mobile games and contests to help your customers engage with your brand, like Elle Magazine does (`www.elle.com/Sweepstakes`), as shown in Figure 11-2.

A *key takeaway for your campaign:* A game or contest with the right message can draw your customer's attention when they want to engage with your brand.

✔ **Managing:** When users are managing tasks on their mobile devices, they most often have a sense of purpose. Being able to accomplish something while they're out running errands goes a long way to making them a loyal customer.

A key takeaway for your campaign: If you can, help your customer accomplish a task very easily, such as scheduling an appointment or looking up a record of their data. If they can't do it easily, you defeat the purpose of making it available to them.

✔ **Informing:** When customers look for news or other types of current information, they may not have a specific topic in mind. It's up to you to help surface the most important content, like Alltop does (`http://alltop.com`), as shown in Figure 11-3.

A key takeaway for your campaign: Try to aggregate your content so that people can easily scan it for the topics that interest them most. Perhaps you can group your most viewed blog posts together or surface breaking news.

✔ **Shopping:** There was a time, not that long ago (in the mid 1990s), when people feared buying something from the web. Shopping carts were faulty, and there were no entities like VeriSign to verify the credibility of an online business. Many shoppers felt that punching in their credit card number online would be chancy at best. Not so today. Thanks to sites like Amazon, shopping can be a care-free affair.

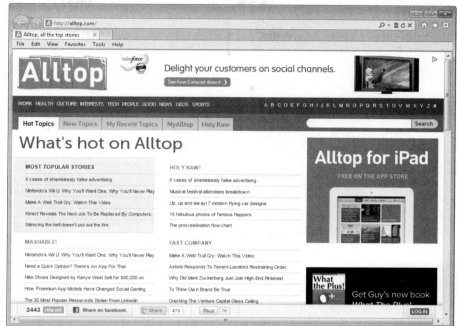

Figure 11-3:
Alltop's most popular posts on the iPad.

A key takeaway for your campaign: Make sure that comparison-shopping sites have your data. Mobile shoppers most often access these sites. They take their mobile devices into the stores and use an app that lets them scan bar codes or take a shot of the actual product and find pricing information online. For instance, consumers can use the Google Shopper app (www.google.com/mobile/shopper), as shown in Figure 11-4, to compare prices quickly while they're on a shopping trip.

Another way that buyers can comparison-shop is by using their mobile browser to visit sites like Bizrate (www.bizrate.com).

One key to shopping behavior online is the type of technology available. One of the technologies currently under consideration by communication companies like Nokia is *near field communication* (NFC). It's a delineation of standards for companies creating mobile shopping technology for smartphones that requires the phone to tap or be close to the source of the item. What that means is you can complete a transaction by touching or tapping something. Some people call it *tap to pay*. Technology experts predict wide use of this technology by 2016.

Figure 11-4:
Google
Shopper.

✔ **Navigating:** You know that being found is the lifeblood of any local business. If you rely on foot traffic, look into companies like Foursquare (see the next section for more about Foursquare) to help you reward customers for stopping by.

Key takeaway for your campaign: Make sure that your business's physical location is correct on all popular mapping services, including Google Maps, Yahoo! Maps, and MapQuest. It may not be. If this is the case, alert customers to how they can revise their GPS or other maps to find you. Don't take anything for granted when it comes to mapping. You should also submit the corrected information to the mapping service. They will be happy to correct it.

A recent Nielsen study found that shoppers use their smartphones differently depending on what type of store they're in. Does this surprise you? Probably not. Each type of store requires you to put on your consumer hat to figure out the way to get the best deals. In grocery, department, and clothing stores, smartphone users typically check for mobile coupons. In electronics stores, they read reviews, compare prices, and scan QR codes. (For more information on this topic see Chapter 9.)

Not in my store!

Recently, retailers have been struggling to combat a shopping behavior they call *showrooming* — looking at products in bricks-and-mortar stores and then purchasing them online (through another company) at the best price available. No one can argue with their logic, but retailers don't want to sit still and allow their stores to be elegant showrooms for online retailers.

After much consternation, some retailers have figured out a few ways to combat this behavior. According to an interview in Mobile Commerce Daily, Martin Hayward at Mirror Image Internet says that retailers are testing these techniques:

✔ **Free shipping:** Offering free shipping to people who purchase from their app while they're in the store

✔ **Coupons:** Providing a coupon that can be scanned at checkout when they buy in the store

✔ **Reduced prices:** Providing special terms for items purchased in the store

If you're a retailer plagued by showrooming, you may want to try some of these tactics.

Locating the location-based device

Location figures prominently in the use of mobile devices. If a user is willing to share her location, an app can show her a variety of suggestions about what to do in her current location. She can, of course, also find her way using online maps and GPS apps.

There are four main ways the consumer uses a mobile device with respect to location:

✔ **Checking in:** Local retailers are using online check-ins as a way to generate foot traffic to their stores. To check in, a customer logs into one of the location-based services, such as Foursquare (http://foursquare.com). This service allows retailers to reward their customers for not only acknowledging when they're in the store but for engaging with others who also frequent the store. Rewards include badges, discounts, and points.

✔ **Finding local information such as news, weather, and movie schedules:** Some businesses provide information specific to their location. If you're a customer who wants to see a movie or attend an event, it's critical for you to get those times in advance. As a business owner, you want to make sure that customers can, on impulse, find your schedules and make plans. To optimize your online presence for mobile users, make sure your site displays information that's relevant to the users' location, such as showing movie times at the closest theater automatically instead of making customers hunt for that information on your site.

✔ **Getting recommendations:** The web has become a recommendation engine. Friends, family and people you've never met tell you their opinions. Most people rely on the recommendations of others (not an establishment itself) to choose a restaurant or hotel.

Google has replaced Google Places with Google+ Local (`www.google.com/+/learnmore/local`), as shown in Figure 11-5, as a way to get specific recommendations about businesses in your area. For restaurants, they include Zagat ratings so that you can see what other patrons have to say.

✔ **Shopping and discounts:** As we discuss earlier, location is one of the key ways that people find products and view them. Offering in-store discounts via mobile phones has become a way of life for local stores.

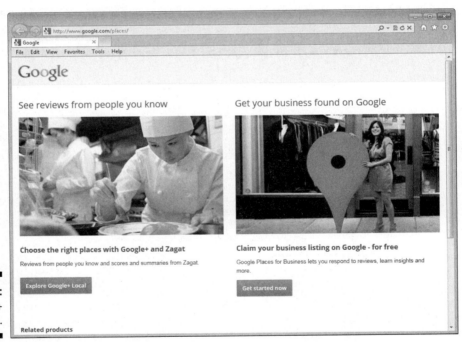

Figure 11-5:
Google+
Local.

Navigating the Mobile Enterprise

Mobile device use has a strong hold on the enterprise. Your company must become mobile friendly because both your customers and employees already embrace it. The good news is that mobile social CRM has a positive effect on all aspects of customer service in the broadest sense.

During the evolution of mobile devices, several forces came together to make the mobile enterprise a reality, including the following:

✔ The creation of apps and use of the cloud

✔ The development of smartphone technology and web standards

✔ The need to integrate social media and other real-time data

Most people agree that business functions can be enhanced by pushing them out to mobile devices. What they disagree about is which functions and devices should be deployed.

In this section, you look at the issues involved in deploying mobile devices across the enterprise and how that impacts social CRM. The following list looks at what companies are doing with mobile devices to impact social CRM:

✔ **Training employees in the field:** Employees used to have to attend a training class at a specific physical location, which might be far away. Now they can get on-the-spot training using iPads or other tablets any-where they have an Internet connection. This saves time and money.

   How this enhances social CRM: Employees have the skills necessary to serve the customer without long trips away from where they're needed.

✔ **Finalizing sales and pricing with the customer:** A salesperson would often have to go back to headquarters to get the latest prices, contracts, and approvals. In many cases, the employee can now find that informa-tion using a mobile device from a customer's location.

   How this enhances social CRM: Customers are better served by their salespeople and can get their purchases in a more timely fashion.

✔ **Managing documents and accessing them from remote locations:** If an employee was traveling and needed specific documents, she might have to log on with her computer. Now she can access these documents from a smartphone or tablet without having to lug a heavy computer through airports.

   How this enhances social CRM: Customers can have access to documents and other material that will help them use products and services.

Defining the mobile enterprise

When an enterprise goes mobile, it has an impact on every part of the organization. In an AT&T white paper, "The Mobile Enterprise: Moving to the Next Generation," AT&T lays out these six functions that are affected by mobile usage:

- **People:** Obviously every employee is impacted. An employee who's given a mobile device has many more options for how he works.

- **Processes:** Work flow and the types of functions that employees can accomplish at various locations are impacted.

- **Operations:** This includes not only internal functions but also affects the way the enterprise works with partners, vendors, and so on.

- **Systems:** Systems affect all the data collected in a variety of databases and any applications created specifically for mobile use.

- **Assets:** This refers to the devices themselves and the materials and people that support them.

- **Customers:** Employees can improve customer service and respond to social network data in real time.

Benefitting from mobile

In the case of social CRM, there have been advances in the adoption of mobile devices for sales teams. Companies like Salesforce.com have led the way in developing mobile device applications. Benefits to the mobile enterprise are as follows:

- **Employees can work more efficiently and productively.** Employees can develop productive habits and schedule work as necessary. Employees can use apps that have been developed by outside vendors to enhance their productivity. For instance, Nuance Communications offers an app called Dragon Dictation, shown in Figure 11-6, that converts your spoken words to text on your smartphone.

- **The enterprise saves money.** Employees can work in places where working used to be off limits, such as the doctor's waiting room. The enterprise can realize savings from staffers who can work anywhere and at any time.

- **Collaboration is easier.** Working with teams halfway around the world used to be an impediment. Now employees can work closely with both internal teams and external partners.

✔ **You have access to data and analysis regarding your social media accounts.** Your customers are on social media platforms talking about your products. Effective collection of data can be analyzed to increase sales and customer loyalty.

✔ **Real-time interactions with customers are possible.** Customers can interact with employees to get the kind of customer service they need.

✔ **Competitiveness can be improved.** If your competitors can't react to customer behavior as quickly as you can, you have an enviable competitive edge.

✔ **You can create a faster sales cycle.** When your salesperson can instantly produce a contract and your customer can sign on the dotted line, your sales cycle is dramatically improved.

Using mobile with your employees

Employees are heavily impacted when mobile devices are part of the workplace. Companies are also heavily impacted. Therefore, your company has to create guidelines to minimize risk to the company.

As affordable mobile devices for personal use became available, managers and IT policymakers had to decide how to accommodate employees who brought them into the workplace and accessed company systems with them. This gave birth to the concept called *bring your own device* (BYOD). When an enterprise has a BYOD policy, it means that employees can get approval to use their mobile device on the network. This brings up a host of issues.

When an employee connects his or her mobile device to the company network (or more likely, asks someone in IT do help connect the device), that employee is *provisioned* (connected) to the network. When an employee is provisioned, the device that he's issued becomes a node on the network, and he's subject to the restrictions and security demands of the company. These considerations include the following:

- **Platforms and devices:** In order to be provisioned onto the network, employees must use sanctioned devices, most likely paid for by the company. The employee is typically responsible for keeping the mobile account in good standing.

- **Security requirements:** Each company sets its own security standards, based on its IT needs and capabilities. The security system may require employees to use specific types of passwords and locking algorithms on their devices. When a device is lost, presumably this security should prevent outsiders from accessing data. In addition, mobile data is encrypted so that if the device is broken into, the data doesn't fall into the wrong hands. Companies are constantly monitoring these issues for changes.

- **Company data:** The enterprise decides what kind of data the mobile employee has access to. For instance, a company might allow a sales team but not a marketing team to access pricing data.

- **Diagnostics and repair:** If a device fails in some way, employees have explicit instructions about who is authorized to repair the device. If a unit needs to be replaced, the company spells out the guidelines for that.

- **Conditions for connection to the network:** Employees are given the conditions under which they may deploy their devices. Overseas trips and other special conditions are spelled out. If the enterprise believes there is a security risk, employees are denied access.

So how do employees really use their mobile devices? It's fun to speculate and imagine that they spend all their time on social networks, but the facts don't bear that out. According to Symantec's 2012 State of Mobility Survey, Table 11-2 shows the major ways employees worldwide really use their mobile devices:

Table 11-2	The Way Enterprise Employees Worldwide Use Mobile Devices
Function	*Percent who use this function*
E-mail	86%
Web browser	80%
Contacts	80%
Calendar application	75%
Instant messaging	73%
Office applications	71%
Task and project management	63%
Social media applications	62%
Line-of-business applications	59%
Sales force automation or CRM	51%

Can small businesses compete?

It's not surprising that small businesses have also embraced mobile devices. They don't have to grapple with the many issues that face the mobile enterprise.

For small businesses, the issues of productivity and savings loom large. Mobile devices are a great tool. In addition, mobile devices help small businesses level the playing field. They can create their own apps and interact with customers on social networks as well as or better than larger companies.

According to the AT&T Small Business Tech Poll 2012, when small business owners were asked to rate the importance of mobile technology for their small business, 66 percent said they couldn't survive without it. In a very short time, the mobile device has become a necessary adjunct to any computer. But what do small business owners say about bringing on mobile devices?

In 2012, Web.com Group reported the results of its Small Business Mobile Survey. The report found these three primary motivations for small businesses to use mobile technology:

✔ Providing better service to customers

✔ Attracting more local customers

✔ Gaining a competitive advantage

If you're a small business owner and can't deploy all the mobile marketing tactics you want to, you're in good company. According to the Web.com survey, 64 percent of the small business owners surveyed have a one-person marketing team, thus preventing them from doing all the mobile marketing they would like.

Part III
Developing a Social and Collaborative Business

The 5th Wave   By Rich Tennant

"The sensor in my running shoe is transmitting information and encouragements to my iPod. Right now, Lance Armstrong is encouraging me to stop running like a girl."

In this part. . .

Part III explains how social CRM impacts the whole
business — not just sales, marketing, and customer
service. When you implement social CRM, internal
collaboration becomes even more important, too. You
discover strategies for helping employees work across
departments. You then learn about the tools and
technology that can help facilitate internal collaboration.

Chapter 12

Building a Social Organization

*I*f you're wondering if social media adds a new layer of complexity to corporate policy, wonder no more. Just like everything else in its wake, social media impacts corporate governance. Even if a corporation has corporate governance guidelines in place now, it still needs to revise them to include social media guidance.

If your corporate leaders forbid employees from using social media as part of their sales and marketing strategy, they're missing out on a powerful tool. Just like every other iteration of Internet tools — for instance, websites and e-mail — social media techniques must become part of the fabric of a brand's strategy.

For your social strategy to succeed, your business needs to foster a collaborative environment among employees. That is ultimately the resounding message of this book. Collaboration is absolutely essential when you're building a successful social CRM model. In order to fully utilize all forms of information, it's important that your internal units work in a collaborative way.

In this chapter, we explain how to build consensus among the leadership within your company. We also highlight some of the key ideas surrounding effective communication between business units using internal social networks.

Defining the New Internal Ecosystem

Ecosystem collaboration can be defined as the "new business reality." Edelman Digital explains the new internal ecosystem as the new business reality and identifies the following three truths that explain this reality:

- ✔ **Create more efficient and effective information management processes.** Harness the massive amount of available content and data to rethink and reequip business operations.

- ✔ **Innovate at faster speeds.** Focus business efforts on innovation rather than continued improvement in order to stay relevant.

- ✔ **Empower employees.** Equip employees with the right data at the right time in order to increase brand impact.

Ultimately, this business environment is about empowering every aspect of your business to work more efficiently. Isn't that what collaboration is all about? In practice, this new reality also means that requirements are changing drastically for companies all over the world. This change will be easier for some employees than for others. Some people and organizations are naturally more prone to collaboration. You may know the team players, as well as the ones who seem to struggle with collaboration or managing change. To show employees your effort to foster collaboration is sincere, be sure to lay the groundwork for what we call *true collaboration*.

True collaboration goes well beyond meetings, training, and committees — although those activities can certainly jumpstart collaboration. True collaboration takes place when your business has the following:

- ✔ **All the environmental factors are present.** This means appropriate people are in place, and everyone sets aside personal agendas, stakes, goals, and egos. We talk about gaining the support of upper management and employees in the upcoming section, "Meeting the Needs of a Social Organization." Also refer to Chapter 5 for tips on choosing the right person to lead your business's social strategy.

- ✔ **All involved are committed to meeting the desired outcome, no matter what.** For instance, when brainstorming runs off on a tangent, the facilitator must loop everyone back to the common goal and desired outcome. Simply asking, "What does this have to do with our desired end result?," can often get things back on track toward true collaboration.

The camaraderie that occurs in true collaboration resembles a true community, too. The "We did it" attitude can positively impact other initiatives within the organization and the community, and it starts with the leadership meeting the needs of a social organization.

Meeting the Needs of a Social Organization

Today's corporate leaders are faced with changes coming from all sides of the enterprise. To understand the needs of the changing social organization, you'll find it helpful to look at the factors that are creating that change:

- ✓ **New technology that impacts customers as well as employees is frequently introduced.** When consumers change the way they shop, your business needs to be ready. For example, your business needs to respond to the way smartphones, tablets, and other devices enable the customer to comparison shop.

- ✓ **Massive amounts of data (also called *big data*) flow into the organization.** Corporate leaders are tasked with analyzing real-time data efficiently so that they can make better decisions. They can't afford to miss something that could change the tide for the corporation for better or worse.

Changes in data management and technology dramatically affect how the social enterprise functions.

Most leaders agree that technological changes are the most difficult to tackle because they produce the most rapid changes. The following list shows some of the most important and most rapidly evolving technical issues that play a role in enabling social business and social CRM:

- ✓ **Use of mobile technology:** Mobile technology frees up the workforce to maximize their time working. It also impacts how customers can receive marketing messages.

- ✓ **Impact of social media:** Representatives can hold a dialogue directly with customers and pass customer feedback about products and services to employees. In turn, the employees can mold the products and services to more effectively meet customer needs.

- ✓ **Development of real-time applications in the cloud:** Using the cloud to store data gives a company several advantages. For example, when a company stores data in the cloud, employees can access fresh data every time they search sales data, and they can use that data to develop more effective sales and marketing techniques. The key is to have the social CRM systems that make this analysis meaningful.

So, now that you understand the challenges and benefits of today's rapidly changing technology, you're ready to consider how you can help the key players in your social CRM strategy leap over the obstacles and head toward the benefits.

Getting the CEO on board

The capabilities of the CEO make a huge difference in the corporation's ability to adapt to technological and other changes. At no time in history has the ability of CEOs to understand these changes been this front and center. Your CEO needs to possess a good understanding about how technology affects every part of the organization. If a technologically savvy CEO leads your business, the leadership he or she can provide is a wonderful asset to implementing social CRM.

Unfortunately, current leaders may not have the training and experience to make effective use of these technologies. Indeed, given the speed with which technology is implemented, it's unlikely that most C-level executives have this training and experience.

 If your CEO doesn't have the requisite knowledge of how the mobile technology, social media, and cloud-based data impact each function of your business, others in the company need to compensate by helping your CEO understand the benefits of investing in social CRM.

Kristin Zhivago, of Zhivago Management Partners, offers some ideas on how to handle this situation. At the 2012 Optimization Summit (as reported by Daniel Burstein on the Marketing Sherpa blog), Zhivago introduced seven CEO personas that help you get buy-in from your CEO. Each CEO persona characterizes the one area in which a CEO is typically most comfortable. The seven personas are as follows:

- ✔ **Sales:** Competitive, controlling, and easily influenced
- ✔ **Technical:** Logical, inclusive, and process-oriented
- ✔ **Finance:** Can be elitist or exclusionary
- ✔ **Legal:** Can see both sides; weak on process
- ✔ **Marketing:** Visionary and customer driven
- ✔ **Operations:** Always focuses on process first
- ✔ **Serial entrepreneur:** Behavior influenced by background

Zhivago says that once you identify your CEO's style, you can determine what information you can provide to help that executive champion the technical changes that drive social CRM. Consider where your CEO falls along each of these continuums:

✔ **Reactive versus visionary:** Do you need to provide feedback from your CEO to your direct reports so that these managers can understand the leadership vision?

✔ **Stress versus process:** Does your CEO need you to suggest a process to handle a project or activity? If you can help keep momentum going, you can alleviate the stress felt by everyone involved.

✔ **Company-centric versus customer-centric:** Would your CEO rather talk to customers or staff only?

✔ **Stats versus stories:** What information is most valuable to your CEO as he or she forms opinions: statistics, customer anecdotes, or operating stories?

Challenging chief marketing officers to support the social enterprise

Moving on from our discussion of CEOs, we next tell you about chief marketing officers (CMOs) and their preparedness for social media and changing technology.

Social media has really thrown CMOs a curveball. Previously, they were the ones who owned the marketing campaigns. They could dictate what was needed from other departments and decide when campaigns would start and stop. That's not possible today.

For one thing, many social media campaigns don't have ending dates. They evolve from one type of outreach to another. For example, a social media campaign might start out as a promotion offering a discounted product and end up managing an ongoing user community.

In addition, salespeople might have their own campaigns running on a specific channel — perhaps LinkedIn — that don't directly involve the marketing department. To add to the complexity, data streams in from other departments that bear on the decisions that the CMO needs to make. The current CMO role is fraught with confusion. Many aren't sure where to place their emphasis.

In IBM's 2011 study, *Today's CMO: Innovating or Following?,* CMOs were asked, "Do you plan to increase or decrease the use of the following tools and technologies over the next three to five years? You can see the results of the survey in Table 12-1.

Table 12-1	Change in Tool and Technology Budgets	
Tool/Technology	*Increase Spending*	*Decrease Spending*
Collaboration	67%	27%
Customer analytics	67%	24%
CRM	65%	25%
Social media	64%	27%
Content management	61%	31%
Data management	51%	35%
Reputation management	55%	35%

What's really surprising about the statistics in Table 12-1 is the percentage of CMOs who plan to decrease spending in areas like social media and CRM. These two areas are critical to the organization's future growth.

The CMOs inability to see the potential in those areas doesn't bode well for their organization as a whole. Most analysts agree that spending should increase to accommodate rapid changes in technology (discussed earlier in this section) and employee needs (which we discuss in upcoming sections). The CMOs who don't see that will be caught short.

Supporting business units

The leadership of the company is just the first stop in convincing the company to integrate a social CRM strategy. Other management positions need to be developed into social CRM rock stars! Each business unit will have its own goals for engaging socially across multiple channels.

Integrating a socially charged ecosystem within the company has many benefits associated for each department, as highlighted in Table 12-2. The system incorporates the idea that every policy, every system, and everything your business does will impact the outcome of the company. It's important to understand the benefits for each department when implementing a social CRM ecosystem within the company.

Table 12-2	Social CRM Benefits to Each Department
Department	**Benefits**
Human Resources	Using the employee base to recruit with a deeper understanding of candidates and ecosystem needs
Marketing	Obtaining information from business development to produce more meaningful marketing
Product Development	Working with the marketing team to harness customer interactions within the community to discover new product opportunities
Business Development	Using information obtained from marketing and product development to understand opportunities for further engagement of prospects
Customer Service	Tapping into employee- and customer-generated solutions within the community and seizing escalated/ unanswered questions to provide support to community members using internal information

Table 12-2 is by no means a full view of how social CRM reaches each department, but this information can help get the social business wheels spinning.

Make sure that every department understands the importance of implementing an internal social strategy. It's hard to change, and the leaders within your organization must be prepared to implement the solution — because with the benefits also come the challenges of integrating software within your company.

Realizing the social challenges

All the benefits sound great, right? If integration were easy and without challenges, we'd all have embraced it fully by now. Full integration is the perfect ideal, the goal. You need to strive for it, and with hard work you'll reach your goals. But if you make a step toward integrating your internal systems with the customer at the forefront of your strategies, you're sure to realize many payoffs.

Challenges are made to be met and overcome. With some awareness of and preparation for the challenges ahead, you'll be better equipped to rise above the obstacles. Here are some of the challenges that you can expect when you're building a collaborative environment:

✔ Keeping social CRM out of a customer service only silo

✔ Sharing a full view of customer profiles without compromising privacy

✔ Getting buy-in from all departments and decision makers

✔ Implementing drastic organizational changes

✔ Discouraging employees from using social media inappropriately

✔ Avoiding inconsistent measurement

The challenges discourage many enterprises from taking the plunge. It's true that embarking on a truly collaborative ecosystem will take time, energy, and resources, and the payoff may not be realized for years to come.

Establishing an Internal Social Network

To boost the collaboration process, many businesses have looked to internal social networks. Instead of using the power of social networking only to brand and market the business, businesses have uncovered the value of idea sharing within a secured internal network.

For instance, Facebook offers closed and private groups that require an invitation to join. It's a free way to connect employees on a platform that fosters idea sharing, collaboration, and communication. It doesn't require an appointment invitation, weekly meeting, or knock on the door to get brainstorming activities started.

Also, IBM Connections offers a software solution for businesses to establish their own internal social network, unaffiliated with an outside site. This gives the enterprise more control over how to configure the site. Aside from engaging employees, businesses using an internal social networking site can also invite partner and vendors to the site for collaboration activities and file sharing. Members of an internal network can upload and share files within the network.

Social networks, when used with true ingenuity in mind, offer a powerful tool for idea sharing and collaboration. Here's a list of some of the things that your organization can do with these tools:

✔ Start conversations.

✔ Recruit talent.

✔ Harness innovative ideas.

✔ Earn customer trust.

✔ Engage communities.

✔ Inspire business evolution.

✔ Foster brainstorming within areas of expertise internally.

✔ Offer accessibility to senior-level employees.

✔ Provide mentoring opportunities.

Shall we go on? Here's a challenge: add at least five more collaborative opportunities to this list.

Internal social networking can create a corporate culture that leads to a competitive edge at every turn. Knowledge is meant to be shared and leveraged, and collaborative social networks are an exciting way for your organization to evolve with the times.

Chapter 13

Enabling and Empowering Your Employees

*T*he idea that social media platforms allow employees to speak directly to customers brings a chill to most corporate legal department staff members. On the other hand, businesses that have succeeded in making social media an asset have taken the time to train employees and provide them with clear guidelines and information.

As we explain in this chapter, the key to using social media effectively is to anticipate problems, create the right policies, and mentor employees tasked with communicating directly with the public. Without involving the whole organization, you will impede your efforts to be prepared.

Gaining Your Customer's Trust via Social Media

Consumers have continued to embrace social media. They feel that it's a trusted source of information about a company. If you bypass it, you're missing an opportunity to make the case for your products and services.

In the *2012 Edelman Trust Barometer* study, respondents were asked, "How much do you trust each of the following places as a source of information about a company?" The choices were traditional media, online multiple sources, corporate information, and social media.

The results were compared with the previous year's results, and the findings were

- Traditional media jumped 10 percent.
- Online multiple sources moved up 18 percent.
- Corporate information rose 23 percent.
- Social media rose a whopping 75 percent.

This study highlights that people are increasingly turning to social media for trustworthy information. Given this trend, can your business really afford to miss out on gaining the trust of your audience by restricting your participation in social media?

Another interesting finding for the marketers from the preceding study: People need to hear something about a company three to five times before they believe it to be true.

In the sections that follow, you explore how these trends impact the way a business enables employees with social media.

Changing role of the new social employee

Now that we've looked at how critical the management role is, we turn to what is termed the *new social employee*. The social employee's role has shifted in many cases from being behind the scenes to interacting directly with customers. Therefore, we need to consider new ways to help social employees succeed in that role.

Previously, most employees were invisible to customers. Now given the opportunities social platforms offer, many more employees in support positions interact directly with customers. For example, in the past, employees handling shipping were unseen. Now if a customer has a question, the customer can contact the department's staff directly for clarification.

When examining ways to empower social employees, we begin by using two specific measures to evaluate the direct contribution they can make on social media platforms. From within the organization, employees can contribute by doing these things:

✔ **Talk directly to customers and provide excellent service that encourages word-of-mouth recommendations.** We know that customers talk about the service they receive, so employees who provide meaningful experiences can make a huge contribution to positive word-of-mouth marketing. Previously, when an employee or department provided inadequate service, they could remain virtually anonymous. Now their names and bad deeds can be recorded by unhappy customers on social media for all to see. That makes employees who provide positive experiences even more powerful and important to the organization than they were in the past.

✔ **Talk to each other to facilitate customer service and effective collaboration with one another.** Technology has made work flow processes more transparent. Therefore, they're more closely scrutinized than they've ever been. Employees who facilitate work flow and find ways to improve collaboration make an important contribution to organizational growth.

There is another way, in addition to the two measures listed previously, that employees can contribute. They can use their personal connections on social platforms outside the organization. We deal with that aspect later in this section.

Both measures listed previously are of equal importance to an organization's health. When the employee's potential is used in both ways, the impact on the enterprise can be substantial.

In his book *The Conversation Company* (Kogan Page), Steven Van Belleghem lays out the four possible outcomes for your company based on the degree to which you can encourage both employees and customers to participate in conversation. The following bullets introduce the range of participation your company may have from employees and customers:

✔ **Low to high participation from internal stakeholders (employees)**

✔ **Low to high participation from external stakeholders (customers)**

Given these continuums, here are the four possible outcomes, the impact of each outcome, and ways to improve upon each outcome:

✔ **Your participation from both employees and customers is low.**

Designation: A boring company

When you have low participation from everyone inside and outside the corporation, you have what is bluntly designated as a boring company. When you look at this company through the lens of either social media or effective collaboration, you find it's a veritable ghost-town.

No one is inspired to say anything about it or work together to do anything innovative. In a word, it's boring. It has the potential to fade as competitors move more authoritatively along both measures.

Improvement tactic: If your company fits this designation, you need to amp up activity within the employee base to get the conversation started. You have to reward employees for providing the kind of service that they are eager to talk about on public channels. You also need to encourage customers to tell you what they think. Your company or brand is invisible. That's the worst situation you can face on social media platforms.

✔ **You have high participation from employees and low participation from external stakeholders.**

Designation: A proud company

A proud company designation is usually a result of the fact that employees are really excited about working for this company and provide tons of examples to customers of their quality work. This is great, but is such a closed system that customers feel they aren't invited to comment.

Improvement tactic: In this situation, you need to encourage employees to invite customers to discuss their experiences and highlight the value your company has brought to them. This means that customers talk about how well *they* are doing as a result of working with your company.

✔ **You have low participation from employees, but high participation from customers.**

Designation: An adored company

If you are considered an adored company, your managers are often reluctant to change anything. That's because on the whole, this is a desirable designation to have.

Improvement tactic: You are so beloved by customers that employees don't feel the need to participate in the discussion as often as they might. If you encourage more employee participation, you will increase their satisfaction, but clearly you are in an enviable position.

✔ **You have both high participation from employees and customers.**

Designation: A conversation company

This is the most desirable designation. When you have both high participation from employees and customers, you are clearly doing something right.

Improvement tactic: None. Keep doing what you're doing to encourage a high degree of participation from both employees and customers. Your company has the most potential for high growth in the future.

An example of a conversation company is Burberry (find Burberry online at `http://us.burberry.com/store`). What makes Burberry interesting is that this high-end clothing retailer isn't given to offering big discounts. However, Burberry's Facebook Page has over 13 million likes. The company provides beautiful photographs of its merchandise to entice readers and has a very interactive community.

It is well known that Steve Jobs believed that the best ideas are generated when employees chat together in informal settings. The building he helped design for Pixar had an atrium in the center, where employees lunched and engaged in other interactions. He believed that the interactions employees had with each other in that setting made for a much richer environment. The quality of movies Pixar developed suggests Jobs was definitely onto something.

Using employees' outside connections

Employee participation can be especially valuable to a company when employees are permitted to draw on their own social media connections outside the organization. This can be controversial. It requires the corporation to evaluate the extent to which they will allow employees to make connections for the company when they speak to their own online networks. This is an interesting issue because employees with excellent connections have always been considered great assets to a corporation. The reason this becomes an issue now is that these employees may communicate with their connections on social networks that are visible to everyone.

If an employee creates an online paper trail that suggests the appearance of inappropriate sharing of information, the corporation may be liable — even if there was no impropriety whatsoever. The issue then becomes one of determining when and how employees can identify themselves as working for the company or speaking on their own. Some companies ask their employees to include the following on their personal Twitter feeds: "The views expressed here are my own and do not reflect my company."

We explore how to balance these issues in the upcoming section, "Creating a Social Media Policy."

Valuing the social employee

Looking at ways to value employees instead of treating them strictly as cost centers has become a hot topic in this fluctuating economy. Employers began to realize that there is only so much they can do to cut costs without harming the integrity of the company.

New ways to monetize employee performance were fostered when employees began to use their own technology to accomplish tasks in their private lives and brought that over into their work lives. It changed business's ability to increase performance and changed the business's expectations about how employees should be allowed to do their work.

In February 2012, Forbes published an article, "The Empowered Employee Is Coming; Is the World Ready?" In it, John Hagel, Suketu Gandhi, and Giovanni Rodriguez trace the shift from considering employees as cost centers to value centers. To understand how this shift is evolving, the article's authors suggest that businesses consider these three factors in the following order:

1. **People:** Because of issues with the economy, organizations did everything they could to cut costs. They shrunk the workforce, sent jobs overseas, and eliminated any other costs they could find related to employees. When they couldn't find any more ways to cut the budget, they were forced to turn to the idea of finding value by enhancing the role of employees.

   In your business, look at how you can empower the employee to serve the customer. Can you give him a smartphone or other tools to help him provide better customer service?

2. **Performance:** If employees could provide value by increasing performance, they could become valuable assets. They could be given opportunities to succeed, to create even more value. New technology facilitates this new way of thinking. Such things as training and focusing on employee development become a wise business decision.

   The Forrester Enterprise 2.0 User Profile supports the article's argument. The Forrester research shows that 51 percent of employees feel more productive when they use social software.

   In your business, think about what employees really need to know to do their job. Develop training and make it convenient to attend. Supply the kind of information that makes employees better at what they do every day. This has a two-fold benefit. It shows employees that you're investing in them and it adds to their skills, making it easier for them to do their jobs.

3. **Place:** The entrance of new technology that serves to empower the employee to work in a variety of environments causes employers to begin looking at their work environments as important links in the performance chain. By improving workplaces and allowing employees to use new gadgets like smartphones and tablets, businesses can help employees succeed in decreasing their workload and getting better results.

   In your business, consider looking at how your offices are laid out. Does it have rows and rows of cubicles? Consider opening the environment up to allow better collaboration.

The article's authors are in no way implying that this shift to viewing employees as value centers is a done deal, but they do see how the tide is turning and wonder if corporations will seize the opportunity.

As many people already know, the author William Gibson famously quipped, "The future is here — it is not very evenly distributed." As companies see the benefits in valuing employees, they will likely jump on board. Time will tell.

Creating a Social Media Policy

Before you construct new policies from scratch or revise them, it's helpful to figure out how your company is currently handling its social media engagement. Is the workflow dictated by upper management or does it happen on its own? By answering this question, you can see how to integrate policy changes most effectively.

In this section, we look at three critical elements of developing a sound social media policy that conforms with the needs of the enterprise. They are as follows:

- **How models of customer engagement affect policy:** When you understand how social media is handled in your organization, you can make necessary changes to policy or develop it further.

- **Additional concerns that social media brings to policy creation:** You need to understand how social media impacts current policies so that you can make revisions that keep you on track and out of the courts.

- **Some best practices for implementation of social media policy:** It's always helpful to see what others consider to be best practices so you can learn from their efforts. It's also important to revise them to suit your company's needs.

Reviewing how organization affects policy

It's likely that your company's way of dealing with social media wasn't planned. Things probably evolved as requests came in and problems were handled. Obviously, this isn't the best way to deal with such a critical issue.

Figuring out how to organize the enterprise to deal with social media is a topic that's discussed by several well-regarded social CRM experts, including Jeremiah Owyang and Adam Metz — Owyang specifically in his Building Your Social Strategy: Prioritizing Efforts for Scale presentation at the Bazaarvoice

Social Commerce Summit in 2011, and Metz in his book *The Social Customer* (McGraw-Hill).

As you think about how your organization can improve its ability to handle social media, it's helpful to look at the five customer engagement models Owyang developed. These organizational models are as follows:

- ✔ **Decentralized:** This model develops *ad hoc*. The process is very dis-organized because no guidelines dictate processes or spell out how to respond to customers. Each department deals with its own issues. In the absence of any governance guidelines, this model usually applies.

- ✔ **Centralized:** This model has one designated leader, and all policies and governance flow from that person — like a standard organization chart. This model is inefficient because only the leader can formulate policies and solutions. The leader has no chance to learn from the employees on the front lines about what's working and what isn't.

- ✔ **Hub and Spoke:** This is the model that Owyang recommends you shift to as soon as possible. There is a central hub, but all the spokes can share information and develop policies together. If you start here, you can sort out all the issues that arise without missing out on the group experience.

- ✔ **Multiple Hub and Spokes (also called Dandelion):** This model has one central hub that flows out to smaller hubs and spokes.

  Metz suggests that this model works for consumer brands and large enterprises that have different products and services that operate independently.

- ✔ **Honeycomb:** Picture a honeycomb with all the cells operating in unison. All the departments provide assistance and support to the good of the social media organization. The negative here is that everyone has to be made aware of what everyone else is doing at all times.

Obviously, not every organization can quickly pull off a Hub and Spoke model, but awareness of the models makes it easier for you to evaluate what your organization is doing now and how it can plan to improve in the future.

Understanding the importance of revising social media policies

Any corporate legal department staff will tell you that their most important mission is to save the corporation millions of dollars in lawsuits and license breaches.

They'll also tell you that vigilance is the most important aspect of their job. They have to constantly monitor the changing legal environment and protect the corporation from exposure. Some people argue that their zeal can get in the way of innovation, but no one denies the legal department's importance.

In their excellent book *Social Marketing to the Business Customer* (John Wiley & Sons, Inc.), Paul Gillin and Eric Schwartzman outline several reasons why your company shouldn't simply revise current policies for social media. They recommend that your business create specific social media policies from scratch. The reason for this is that social media may change the definition of such things as soliciting and disclosure of information.

Here are some of the areas that they recommend any business engaged in social marketing consider:

- ✔ **Public disclosures:** Updates on social media can in some cases be considered a public disclosure, so make sure your policy covers it. (An example of a public disclosure could be the expression of a budget number or other information that may affect the stock price.)

- ✔ **Company property:** Make sure your policy about not using company property for personal gain clearly spells out what employees who manage social platforms can and can't do.

- ✔ **Confidential information:** Online resources need to be clearly defined so that even if something is found online, an employee can easily distinguish whether it is public or private.

- ✔ **Technical services:** A clear definition of where confidential information can be posted should include the use of online platforms like Google Docs and other tools that include cloud storage.

- ✔ **Inappropriate solicitations:** In many cases, social media qualifies as a solicitation of information. The policy should be written to spell out inappropriate solicitations.

- ✔ **Passwords and security:** People who run your company's social media accounts may lay claim to the followers as their own if they leave the company. Ensure that your policy includes statements about who owns the passwords and accounts and what security measures will be taken to protect them.

- ✔ **E-mail:** Make it clear as to what information can and cannot be in an employee signature. This will clarify whether they can list their social media accounts in their e-mail signature.

As you go through the above list, you can see that rewrites from scratch are critical. That's why it's so important to evaluate and clarify your own policies before you're forced to confront an unpleasant situation.

When creating your policies, you can find very helpful collections written for a variety of different industries for you to model. They are compiled by the following people:

- **Eric Schwartzman:** He has created a social media policy template that you can use as a guideline.

  ```
  http://ericschwartzman.com/pr/schwartzman/social-
               media-policy-template.aspx
  ```

- **Chris Boudreaux:** He compiled a list of policies at his Social Media Governance blog.

  ```
  http://socialmediagovernance.com/policies.php
  ```

- **Dave Fleet:** You can find his list of resources at his blog, Conversations at the Intersection of Communications, PR and Social Media, as shown in Figure 13-1.

  ```
  http://davefleet.com/2010/07/57-social-media-policy-
                 examples-resources
  ```

Figure 13-1:
Dave Fleet's
resource
list.

You can also find a social media policy tool wizard to help you fill in the blanks at this page:

```
http://socialmedia.policytool.net/welcome/wizard
```

Folding social media policies into the organization

Because social media technologies continue to evolve, it can be hard for managers to get their arms around all the issues related to social media governance. It can be helpful to look at the UBM Techweb Technology Brief *Information Governance: Taming the Data Wild West*, in which UBM Techweb outlines these best practices for implementing an information governance policy:

- Check that your in-house counsel and department heads agree with policies.
- Decide which policies and what types of information take priority.
- Decide which technologies best suit the policies you put in place.
- Make sure that employee training is available when you roll out policies.

The good, bad, and ugly of superfans

Almost every business owner dreams of attracting a large group of adoring customers who love whatever they do and tell all their friends to buy their products, but there are two sides to that coin. In her 2011 presentation Building a Brand Superfan, Baochi Nguyen of Boingo Wireless looks at the other side of having superfans (as she calls them) who love your company. What about the overzealous fan who says things about the company in a way that makes it seem as if he's a paid representative? Can there be too much of a good thing?

Apparently so. Nguyen provides cautionary tips for making sure you deal with the legal issues that may arise. When it comes to governance, you want to be prepared for problems from any quarter. Her tips include making sure that

- **Your legal department documents the superfan relationship.** You want to make it

clear whether the fan is speaking for herself or the organization.

- **You follow FTC blog disclosure rules.**
- **You don't turn fans off by engaging in ways that seem superficial.**
- **You aren't too heavy-handed in your encouragement of fans.**
- **You don't drag your fans into controversy and make them defend your brand.**
- **You don't pay too much attention to the superfans to the exclusion of others.**

If you're interested in reading the government's rules for blogger disclosure, you can download them here: `http://ftc.gov/os/2009/10/091005revisedendorsementguides.pdf`.

By taking a slow and steady approach to making the necessary changes, social media governance can become manageable.

Dealing with Communication Crises

We're all familiar with the companies that have faced PR disasters and lived to tell the tale — for example, Comcast and its sleeping representative. (See more about this incident and Comcast's recovery in Chapter 10.) Many of those disasters occurred when social media was new, and few companies were prepared to handle the ramifications of an inappropriate response.

Surprisingly, even though we're about five years into using this technology, many companies are still unprepared. According to Deloitte's *2010 Ethics & Workplace Survey,* 40 percent of executives report that their company doesn't allow access to social media sites at work. Other companies ignore the issue and hope their current policies will suffice. Either approach does the business a disservice.

The rewards of engaging your business in social media far outweigh the risks. For example, according to comScore's white paper *It's a Social World,* you can reach 82 percent of the worldwide online population through social networks. Can your company really afford to restrict communication with that many potential customers? That said, the risks are real. In the following sections, we explain how your company can prepare for a problem and thus position itself to recover from a crisis.

Setting expectations for social media responses

Can you really avoid PR crises? Case studies on the topic suggest that at the very least you can mitigate them, but first let's look at what we deem a *social media crisis.* Clearly, corporations have faced bad publicity in the past, so what makes social media disasters particularly frightening to managers of all levels?

Here are a few ways social media has changed the way businesses handle their PR:

✔ **Your company must react more quickly because PR crises on social media spread quickly.** In the past when something happened to a person, it was unlikely that she or others around her would have a camera ready to take video of the whole incident. Now with the presence of smartphones, cameras are always available.

✔ **Social media gives people with bad news about your business a broader audience.** In the case of an airline when it loses your property or does something disrespectful to a passenger, it's more likely to be a big embarrassment.

✔ **Social media makes employee blunders with confidential information more public.** Now, it is just as likely that a blog post or a Facebook comment could release the information before the corporation is ready.

These are just three differences. There is the potential for so many more. With this in mind, your business must prepare to face any kind of PR disaster without much warning. To do so, make sure your business has policies and procedures in place and trains employees in following these measures.

A study by Jeremiah Owyang of Altimeter Group called *Social Business Readiness* offers some insight into how your business can prepare. In the study, companies that prepared ahead of time and trained their employees were able to avert a majority of the potential crises they faced.

The companies (dubbed advanced) in the study identified the following four internal requirements that led to the successful handling of a crisis. These requirements are worth considering when you're evaluating your own crisis response readiness:

✔ **Baseline governance and reinforcement:** Make sure your policies outline what employees can do and how to do it in a professional manner.

✔ **Enterprise-wide response processes:** Your processes should define the workflow for engaging in social media, responding to a crisis, and determining appropriate responses to customers.

✔ **Ongoing education program and best practices sharing:** Based on the success of companies in the study, your company will be better prepared for a crisis if you encourage sharing of effective procedures throughout the organization.

✔ **Leadership from a dedicated and shared central hub:** In defining your social media processes, establish a central hub that guides the entire organization in following best practices for social media engagement.

Training employees

As we note in earlier sections on the new social employee, improving employee performance is a good financial decision. In an effort to find the most cost-effective training methods, managers have placed more emphasis on training in the field.

Cloud technology makes training affordable and doesn't diminish the quality of the training. Employees don't need to be summoned to far-off training centers, incurring major travel costs. They can operate from their home base and still get the training they need.

In the case of social media, employees need specific training on how to avoid PR disasters, but the training shouldn't be narrowly focused. In addition to preparing employees to deal with disasters, trainers should teach employees how social media tools help the company thrive. (See Chapter 7 for more on social media stories.)

When you're thinking about creating or obtaining training for employees on social media, some specific training content for PR disasters includes these items:

- ✓ **Create written guidelines.** Make sure to document policies and make sure that everyone knows where to find them. Let everyone know the name of the person or department that is responsible for them.

- ✓ **Keep an up-to-date knowledge base.** Use knowledge base software to keep updating and refreshing the information employees have access to. As employees become more practiced in their use of social media, you want to make sure that they share that knowledge with everyone who could benefit. You find more details about keeping a knowledge base in the next section.

- ✓ **Assess your employees and do training updates.** Don't assume that one training session will keep your employees informed. It's the corporation's responsibility to keep employees abreast of changing policies and procedures.

- ✓ **Use visuals to assist work flow.** Don't underestimate the power of a flow chart or other visuals that show employees who's responsible for what and how the workflow proceeds. Keep that current so that if people leave or change departments, you don't render the chart meaningless.

- ✓ **Make sure you're in touch with your audience.** No amount of social media training will prevent a disaster if you're out of touch with your customers. If you don't know what they think, you'll be blindsided by their reactions.

Contributing to the Internal Knowledge Base

The purpose of a knowledge base (KB) is to share information that's already known to others in the organization or included by subject matter experts.

When you provide a database of collected wisdom, employees don't have to reinvent the wheel. They can go into the KB and see how a procedure or tactic should be implemented.

A knowledge base cuts down on support costs and can be the source of quality information. (See also Chapter 10 for more about knowledge bases.) You can construct internal KBs that can then be converted to KBs for external (customer) use.

The KB can contain more than just text. It can include screenshots, audio, video, and so on. Incorporate anything that will help the employee or customer solve the problem.

Don't worry if you feel you've added too much information. If you used the information to solve the problem, it's worth including in the knowledge base entry.

Before you start writing a KB article, you can prepare yourself by following these tips:

✔ **Follow the simple structure most often used for knowledge bases.** Most knowledge bases state the problem and then the solution. If the solution has steps to follow, include those next. If you need to include information from a subject matter expert, be sure to get that ahead of time so that it's integrated into the article.

✔ **Conform to the KB conventions.** Don't confuse users who are reading more than one article at a time. Use the same terminology in all KB articles. When you're unsure of which terminology to use, make an effort to scan the KB for the correct term, consult the KB documentation, and if you still aren't sure, ask the KB point person.

✔ **Write in the same style, format, and tone as other articles.** Don't be too familiar if the rest of the KB is formal in tone. You don't want the reader to be put off by too many different styles.

✔ **Use an accepted format for KB articles.** Look at how other articles are formatted and fit in. You could choose an FAQ style, a tutorial, a steps list, or other format that's recognized and easily read.

Most knowledge bases use software that formats the articles as you write them. If you're starting from scratch or don't have a way to format the information, you may want to consider using a fee-based tool called Bloomfire (available at www.bloomfire.com). It's a content-management tool that allows teams to input, retrieve, and manage key information.

Most KB software indexes every word in the text, which means that if the word is there, the search engine will find it and return it in the search results. But it's still important to use tags so that users can search the text by known topics set up by the KB administrator.

✔ **Familiarize yourself with the software you'll use to write the article.** Make sure you know how to use the software to input your article. Input some sample copy just to ensure that when you put in the real article, it won't disappear into the ether. Also, make sure the entire database is continually backed up so you can restore it in case there's a database meltdown.

Using SEO to Deflect Questions and Calls

When you read about the importance of SEO (search engine optimization) and optimizing content, you aren't likely to see much information about its impact on customer service. That's mainly because it's easy to understand how picking the right keywords will help customers find information about your products and services but not as easy to see how it affects customer service.

When it comes to SEO, most emphasis is placed on making sales. Managers are focused on meeting revenue projections. They aren't generally concerned with eliminating tech support costs. This can be short-sighted. A reduction in tech support calls can have a substantial impact on the budget.

So what about saving money by helping customers find your support information instead of e-mailing or calling you? In this section, we look at how SEO plays a role in deflecting questions and calls, benefitting both your company and your customer.

Although SEO techniques have been around a relatively long time (in Internet years), they aren't well understood. For most managers, SEO is a necessary evil that's handed off to someone who's willing to do it. It doesn't figure into their big-picture thinking about how to reach customers using social media.

But everything a customer does online to find information about a brand flows through the search process. Therefore, keywords play a critical role in the process.

To clarify how keywords and customer service work, the following example shows how customer support can be enhanced using keywords on a social platform like Twitter. On Twitter, your customer has at least the following two search choices to find support for a particular brand:

✔ **Your customer can run a search with the company name to find a Twitter account that offers support.** When you do this search, you'll find all the brand names that fit that search, as shown in Figure 13-2. To help customers with this type of search, make sure that your brand name accompanies any content that you create for customer support.

Figure 13-2:
Search for a
brand name.

✔ **Your customer can search for the name of the product.** When you do this, you'll find all the tweets that contain that product name, as shown in Figure 13-3. Again, to help your customer find the answers they need, make sure that product keywords are included in all your support materials.

In addition, if your customers know that your product or company has breaking news as they search, they can look at the Trends list on the left side of the page, as shown in Figure 13-4. Notice that the trends are listed as keyword phrases. Your customer could also use those same terms to search directly on a search engine.

Okay, those are easy examples. It's likely that whomever is doing your SEO work will use your brand and product names, but what about specific support topics? If your customer makes a search for some topic contained in your knowledge base, are they likely to find it?

If you take the time to place the very keyword phrases your customers use to search for your specific support information in your tweets, you could help them find answers to their product questions. (See more about the customer search process in Chapter 8.) This immediately increases customer satisfaction and cuts support costs.

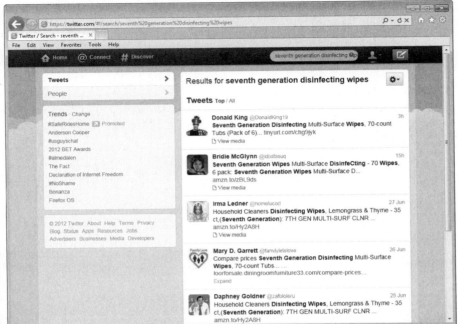

Figure 13-3:
Search for
a product
name.

Figure 13-4:
Twitter
Trends.

You may think this too, is obvious, but think about it more carefully. If you have a Twitter account dedicated to customer service, do you also create informational tweets that contain keywords and links to support information without having to be asked for it? Probably not, but you should. So when your customer searches Twitter to find a specific topic that's related to support, you have to hope that someone has already asked it.

Go to your support area now and see if the content is so clearly set forth in chunks with keywords that when it gets segmented in a search engine, the right keywords go with it. This can be a surprising exercise. You may find yourself revising your help and support areas to include the right keywords to ensure that your content is found on social platforms.

Part IV
Measuring the Impact of Social CRM

The 5th Wave   By Rich Tennant

"So far our social media presence has been pretty good. We've gotten some orders, a few inquiries, and nine guys who want to date our logo."

In this part. . .

This part is for the number-crunchers, the people who track campaigns, the ones who want to figure out the ROI. Because social CRM emphasizes relational goals over transactional goals, figuring out how to define metrics for social CRM can be tricky. The massive influx of data you can pull for social media sites can seem daunting as well. In this part, we help you sort the wheat from the chaff. Decide what social data your business needs to pay attention to based on your goals. Then discover strategies for using these metrics in your company's analytics.

Chapter 14

Analyzing Data to Drive Results

In This Chapter

▶ Realizing that data can be extracted from social media

▶ Understanding that data goes beyond the numbers

▶ Leveraging data to build deeper customer engagement

▶ Planning for the ever-evolving social data

*T*here's no shortage of information and data created through social media. Nearly every move we make online is traceable, and trackable. Every time a user likes, shares, or comments on a piece of content on Facebook, it generates a data point for Facebook itself, and for the content originator. Twitter users know when their tweets are retweeted, and Twitter provides analytics for reach and penetration.

For businesses, this data is a jackpot of insight into the social customer. This social data illustrates a customer's preferences, behaviors, views, ideals, and so much more. CRM 1.0 involved collecting basic customer information: address, phone numbers, birthday, place in a sales cycle, and so on, but social CRM data gives new life to your understanding of your customers. You get to know them on a more attitudinal and emotional level. You learn their sentiments.

In this chapter, we show you the best ways to harness the massive amounts of customer data generated in social media, and we help you identify ways to filter the good information from the less relevant data points. Finally, we show you ways to leverage gathered data to enhance customer experiences with your brand.

Understanding the Social CRM Data Storm

Information flows in many directions in social business. It isn't just companies shouting through a bullhorn to customers. Consumers engage brands on customer-preferred platforms, and then other customers, vendors, partners, and employees join the conversations. This provides a very different view of customers, one that is closer to a 360-degree view.

This is all great news for business, albeit at times a bit overwhelming. A tremendous amount of data is gathered every day, and not all of it is useful.

In order to sort through all the social data available and turn it into useable metrics, businesses need social CRM monitoring and reporting tools. These solutions allow businesses to harness their data and translate it into a greater understanding of the social customer.

 Filters and processes can help you sort what's relevant from what's not. To do that, take a moment and think about what you would want to know about your customers, in a perfect world with no data restrictions. Identify the key traits or features that you need to get a clear and accurate picture of your social customers. This varies by industry, and may change within your own business. For instance, consider the following examples:

- ✓ When you're rolling out a loyalty program, you may want to know who your most engaged customers are. You could look at how many sales can be attributed to current customers, or how many times customers share your messages in social media.

- ✓ During back-to-school season, you might then want to know how many customers have children, and their ages.

- ✓ When you open a new bricks-and-mortar location, you'll need to know which customers live in that area.

All this information is available through social channels. You just have to know where to look, and how to get it.

Plenty of tools can help businesses mine data from the social chatter. Your options include the following:

- ✓ Each social network has its own innate reporting capabilities, such as Facebook Insights.

- ✓ Social CRM solutions, which we cover in Chapter 16, also include reporting.

✔ Sites like MediaVantage (www.mediavantage.com) and Track Social (www.tracksocial.com) have taken data collection and analysis to a new level. These sites can pull all the data into one place and enable businesses to customize analytics and reporting formats for their needs.

No matter what tools you use for reporting and data analysis, make sure that you're looking at data within the context of your business structure. Determine relevant metrics to help you reserve resources and focus on the social conversations that hold the greatest value.

Teaching the Different Parts of Data

When determining what data you want to corral, it's important to keep in mind the different types of data and what they can teach you. Many businesses use historical data to take an educated guess at future performance across similar metrics. Forecasting, budget planning, and sales goals are often based on historical analytics data, but this approach can be limiting. To capture a well-rounded historical view for planning, it's important to understand the difference between *descriptive analytics* and *predictive analytics*.

✔ **Descriptive analytics:** This type of data identifies past events and the perceived or real factors that played into creating the events. The idea is to look for indicators of success and failure in past initiatives. It's a reactive strategy to marketing planning — looking back, reacting to discoveries, and adjusting future plans to meet the past conditions.

✔ **Predictive analytics:** This is a mathematical model that accurately predicts future results and outcomes based on hard facts. It's easier (and typically more affordable) to keep existing customers than to generate new ones, which is why predictive modeling often leads marketing initiatives for promotions and offers. Taking what you know customers prefer and reaching them with what they want falls into predictive modeling.

Keep in mind that the past can't always predict the future. Both descriptive and predictive modeling have their limits, in part because the following factors make tomorrow (or next year) a little different from yesterday (or yesteryear):

✔ Today's marketplace is ever-evolving and complex.

✔ You're gathering a lot of data at a rapid pace in social CRM.

✔ Markets are moving targets that you can't always accurately predict.

However, if you analyze historical data in the right context, you can develop a more tangible approach to planning. But it's vital to distinguish the types of data you're gathering and analyzing first, as we outline in Table 14-1. After you know what you have, you can draw conclusions and translate that data into actionable metrics.

Table 14-1	Key Differences between Descriptive and Predictive Analytics
Descriptive Analytics Modeling	*Predictive Analytics Modeling*
Perceived outcome based on historical data	Accurate prediction of outcomes based on past outcomes with the same factors in place
Relational	Equation-based
Rearview	Future-focused
Reactive	Precision planning

Combining Business Intelligence with Social CRM

Taking business data and turning into actionable knowledge is *business intelligence* (BI). It's seeing your organization for what it really is and what it has the power to become by considering all the data available. BI technologies aim to empower an organization with better decision-making processes, using the power of knowledge at its fullest to create a competitive edge for your brand. In many ways, it's the precursor to the kind of data we have access to through social CRM.

BI technologies provide historical, current, and predictive data for any number of business purposes. Here are a few ways that you can use BI to direct and affect brand initiatives, along with social CRM:

✔ **Reporting:** Say your marketing team is leading a campaign in order to launch a new product. Your social CRM or BI system can pull data about online conversations, such as retweets, while your BI system tracks sales. In this way, you can see the success of the campaign through social CRM and BI together.

✔ **Forecasting:** The same marketing campaign mentioned in the preceding paragraph can also be used to predict the success of another new product launch later in the year. Descriptive analysis will tell you what types of messages were shared more often, and social conversations can be tailored accordingly for optimum reach.

✔ **Strategic planning:** To determine what your business's next new product should be, look to predictive analytics to determine what consumers want. By looking at the questions customers asked during the most recent launch, you can get a clear picture of what features customers were hoping for the first time around.

✔ **Performance measurement:** Make BI and social CRM reports easy to consume, with clearly outlined goals and metrics. To continue with our product launch example, you might set a goal of 100 retweets (RTs) and 1,000 units sold on day one. You can then easily track this and report on performance through BI and social CRM.

Structuring Data Collection and Reporting

Before you begin gathering customer data, be sure you're moving with purpose. Avoid wasting time and resources by targeting your data collection and reporting efforts. Ask these questions to guide what reporting you truly need:

✔ **What targets do you want to track for your business?** Consider whether you'd benefit most from looking at all your customers, or just a core group.

✔ **How much flexibility and customization do you need in your reporting?** Decide whether you'll be interested in the same metrics every day, month, or year, or if it varies seasonally.

✔ **Will you use reporting to gauge employee performance?** Evaluate whether you can or will tie social metrics to specific employees. For example, if coworker Matt is mentioned on Twitter, how will you use that information?

✔ **How often do you need to update reports?** Think about what types of data you can realistically compare. Daily data is a lot to digest, but yearly is too long to wait. Many businesses find it helpful to look at summaries weekly and full reports monthly or quarterly.

✔ **What is the best way to disseminate the data and intelligence?** Identify who needs to know what, and when, as well as the best way to present information. Some information may be helpful for everyone, while you should reserve other information for management.

✔ **Who needs to be abreast of data reporting?** Appoint a few people to analyze the information and disseminate the reports they create. Not everyone needs to see the raw data.

✔ **Do you need to set threshold alarms if certain changes occur with data points?** Imagine the best- or worst-case scenario. What would you want to know the moment it happened, without waiting for a weekly or monthly report?

✔ **How quickly do you want reports generated?** Create a timeline that works with the cadence of your reports. For example, a weekly report will need to be available more quickly than a quarterly report.

✔ **What amount of time is reasonable for employees to spend generating reports?** Allocate time efficiently. Reporting is important to track your company's health, but not at the expense of work that leads to trackable data.

Make sure you're collecting and storing only the data that's most relevant to your business goals. Determine what you need most and shape processes to fit that efficiently.

Translating Social Media Data Into Metrics

When many of us first think of data and analytics, we think of quantitative results suited for spreadsheets, and we can yield powerful insights by analyzing quantitative factors. The number of RTs on Twitter can tell you how many people found a piece of content interesting, and the number of likes on a Facebook Page provides a good indicator of people who want to engage or associate with your company.

However, numbers aren't the whole picture of circumstances or economic environments. What about valuable words within text? Next we tell you about the value of text analytics and text mining.

Defining text analysis

The process of deriving high-quality information from text is often referred to as *text analysis* or *text data mining*. Patterns and trends are applied to text to identify a value. Spam filters exemplify a widely recognized use of pattern recognition and text mining. Your e-mail service provider taps into linguistic features that typically indicate an unwanted bulk message.

In social CRM, sentiment analysis looks at the text of a customer's message to determine if it's positive, negative, or neutral. Like spam filters, sentiment analysis isn't 100percent accurate, but it can provide a strong indicator of trends. A sharp spike in negative messages is worth looking into, even if the exact number of messages is off slightly.

Text mining is a complicated process that goes on behind the scenes of most social CRM solutions. It starts with a classification system using statistical, linguistic, and algorithmic techniques to analyze text. The information gathered from that text is then arranged in a format that's easy to read and provide metrics on.

Turning textual data into high-quality information combines a set of guides for relevance to the entity conducting the text mining. Here are the typical ways text is consumed or identified for text mining:

- ✔ **Text categorization:** This is putting textual terms into similar groups or classes.

- ✔ **Text clustering:** Here you outline a set of rules or characteristics for grouped (clustered) words.

- ✔ **Sentiment analysis:** This is similar to text clustering. With sentiment analysis, you presume a feeling or emotion within the text.

- ✔ **Summarization:** This derives a condensed statement or indicator from the entire document or block of text.

- ✔ **Named entities:** Here, text mining considers a relationship between a name and accompanying text in the source.

Depending on your goals and the metrics you're using to track them, you may or may not be interested in every type of text mining, but know that any social CRM solution with text mining capabilities can offer multiple types of text sorting.

In this next section, we talk about how to leverage text mining to generate useful business insights. With text mining, you close the gap where quantitative data leaves businesses wanting a fuller view of analytics.

Using data to enhance customer interaction

Knowing how and why customers interact with your brand is vital to fostering long-term relationships. You need to stay up to date on the trends among your customers in order to maintain engaging conversations with them. So, if you have 2,000 Facebook fans, you'll want to stay on top of what they're saying, whether they're commenting, and whether they're sharing you content.

Analyzing the content that's produced through social media channels can help you answer these questions accurately. Instead of acting on a hunch or on what you think is happening, you can use analytics to get real data from numbers and text. (Look at Chapter 16 for some social CRM solutions to check out.) Then you can prepare for more-targeted interactions with your customers.

Determining what metrics matter for social CRM

The central theme for social CRM is customer loyalty, but identifying it can present a challenge for many marketers. Just about everyone can agree to what customer loyalty is: a strong affinity for a brand that results in a desired customer behavior. Where the challenge exists for marketers is defining that desired end result, which is customer loyalty.

As we mention in this chapter, you'll first need to identify what you want to know about customer loyalty — which metrics — before you can start to extract data to measure. Behaviors beyond transactions and purchases can indicate customer loyalty. Perhaps a loyal customer will share your Facebook post or mention your brand in a post of her own. That can indicate loyalty as well and be rewarded as such.

 Your data can help you reward customers for loyalty if you segment your customers based on level of affinity. There are many ways to look at your customers based on your brand's determination of value of loyalty. Here are a few ideas on segmentation using social CRM:

✔ **Likely to recommend your services:** Look for fans or followers who frequently post positively about you, or share your messages.

✔ **Likely to repeat purchases:** Combine traditional CRM sales information with social information about their habits and lifestyle.

✔ **Likely to purchase additional products or services:** Gather information on life events, such as marriage and new babies, as well as demographics, to predict future behavior.

✔ **View your brand to be superior:** Use text mining to track positive posts, as well as sharing behavior. You can also look at other brands a customer is connected to (or not) in social media.

✔ **Wouldn't ever purchase a similar product from a different brand:** Identify so-called superfans through text mining and volume of posts about you. Sometimes these customers even mention your company in their bio information or handle, such as MacFan4Life.

✔ **Communicates actively with the brand:** Tally posts that mention your brand, and social media conversations with your social media representatives, to find your most vocal customers.

How you measure and segment your customer loyalty can be based on short- or long-term goals. Just keep in mind that outside factors may impact some of the situations outlined previously, and they don't always correlate to customer loyalty. For example, an increase in a certain behavior could be the result of a specific promotion. Customers may stick with your brand because it's too difficult to switch, rather than because they like you. Ask yourself, are there really other options for them? Utilities especially are often faced with this situation, as customers may not be loyal to their cable or power company but they don't have many other options. Be sure to look at customer loyalty beyond transactional numbers and consider the layers of customer loyalty.

Measuring the importance of advocacy

Value exists in brand advocates, particularly in the social realm. *Brand advocates* are the customers who tout your brand to their network. In this way, the power of one customer can exceed their single purchase as they share their views with many people online — more than they could reach without the help of social networks. This is great for businesses. Even better? Social media enables us to the see the reach of our customers. The very public characteristics of online social networking opens us up to insights we never had before about our customers' spheres of influence.

We need to consider the emotional relationship customers have with our brand and how they demonstrate that — directly with us and also to their network. Are they likely to recommend our brands, or are they actually going out and actively recommending our brands right now? Tapping into text mining can reveal the true sentiment of our customers to determine the power of advocacy.

Realizing the Net Promoter Score

Net Promoter Score (NPS) is a metric (and registered trademark of Bain and Satmetrix) for customer loyalty, specifically evaluating the likelihood of a customer to recommend your brand. It's widely adopted by many Fortune 1000 businesses but can be a powerful measuring tool for small- to medium-sized businesses as well. The score identifies customers in these three categories based on asking a simple survey question: How likely are you to recommend this brand?

- ✔ Promoters
- ✔ Passives
- ✔ Detractors

Businesses use the results of the Net Promoter Score to direct (and measure) employee and company interactions with customers. With insights into this metric, you can identify customer service issues and see where you aren't delivering your desired brand experience. You can then adjust your communications to meet the needs of your customers. For example, if a detractor shares negative comments about your brand, you would address that person much differently than you would your best customers: your promoters.

An official NPS score can be measured only using the NPS proprietary system, but that doesn't mean you can't approximate by looking at social CRM data or designing your own survey. Use text mining to see who often speaks positively about your brand, and connect with those people to keep their positive conversations going. Identify those who post negative comments and see how you can fix the issues they saw, and turn them around. And finally, brainstorm ways to turn passive customer conversations into positive ones.

Finding a Social CRM System to Meet Your Needs

Now that you know how you can turn social data into metrics, you can begin to determine what information is most important to you now, and think about what may be important in the future. Knowing all the capabilities of social CRM systems will open your eyes to the vast amount of customer information available to you.

Think about what you want to know, and what you'll do with that information. Are you looking, for instance, to create brand advocates, get feedback on new products, or compare against competitors? Knowing what you want will help you find the social CRM solution that's the right fit for your company.

But how to choose? There are many social CRM systems available today, and more will likely be added as social media use continues to increase. In Chapter 16, we identify the top ten enterprise-level social CRM solutions you should look into, but don't stop there. We encourage you to do your own research as well to determine the best system for your business, your employees, and your customers. What works for one company may not be the best solution for a similar company in the same industry. Look for free trials and compare various solutions on data collection, reporting capabilities, and user experience.

Analyzing the Future of Analytics

Marketing and PR initiatives have their own set of metrics. What works for those avenues toward customer engagement can't be applied with a blanket over social media. Each tool used to reach and engage customers requires its own set of metrics.

To make social media analytics deliver the metrics you need, you need to define your standards for measurement. You can build an analytics framework that you can apply to various social media platforms. What works for your industry may not work for the next. Here are two metrics that you can use across multiple channels and for many industries:

✔ **Engagement:** At what level do your customers interact with you, your brand, your employees, and your community?

✔ **Word of mouth:** How far is the reach of your customers and what sentiments are they sharing with their network?

Capturing a deeper understanding of our customers in our social CRM systems is gold. With predetermined standards for measurement and the ability to segment affinity levels, you have more than sufficient knowledge to adjust your business's communications to meet social customers when, where, and how they want. Remember that social CRM aims to enhance customer experiences by creating a corporate culture that fosters customer-centricity in every facet. This has to be true as you look for metrics and goals and analyze customer interactions.

Chapter 15

Keeping Up with Evolving Technology

Social CRM technology offers the promise of a 360-degree view of a customer, information that reaches every department of the business. It ties every department together with the same goal of providing an outstanding customer experience.

As social media platforms evolve, the technology we use to capture customer data will have to evolve along with them. The transactional data captured by CRM 1.0 is complemented by a deeper view into our customers with the advancements of technology for social CRM.

Many of you reading this book are most likely thinking, "Man, we were just getting used to our original CRM software. Now social media has us running just to keep up." You're not alone.

Educating on the Future Technology

Have you ever worked at a company and felt lost when it rolled out a new initiative or software development? It's an unsettling situation, and one that can lead to less than ideal job satisfaction. Employees don't like to feel like they aren't prepared for something or that they don't understand what their role is within the organization.

Educating and training employees on future technologies is vital to company-wide adoption of new and ever-changing software, tolls, and platforms. Employee training for social CRM and any related technology or culture changes will help you retain talent and increase job satisfaction. When you have a good training program, you increase your recruiting opportunities as well. People want to know that they'll be empowered to do their job well and will have the knowledge to meet organizational expectations.

Developing your current employees' skills with ongoing training and educational opportunities demonstrates how much you value your employees. It's wise to reassure your team that you're willing to invest in them. You can foster long-term retention and put loyal team members on a career path for growth within the organization.

Social CRM is all about the customer, and your employees might be your most important customers. Invest in their education and training in order to keep up with the dynamic technologies affecting how you do business.

Changing the employee outlook

Not everyone is quick to accept change. In fact, some people become overwhelmed with the fear of the unknown, especially when they don't clearly see their place in the changes. When introducing new technologies, be transparent with your employees and focus on how it will help the company achieve its goals, and what that means for them. When you incorporate employee sentiment into your technology evolution, consider how you can convey the following to your employees:

- ✔ **Demonstrate a healthy balance sheet.** Most technology changes and integrations require some financial investment from companies. A healthy balance sheet can show your employees that you have the financial means to invest in the future of the organization.

- ✔ **Improve employee confidence in the company.** You can show your employees that you're staying in front of technology changes. This can demonstrate to your team that you have an edge over competitors.

- ✔ **Show your team that you have long-range plans.** When you make an investment in technology and strive to keep ahead of market changes, you show your team that your long-term plans can evolve with the times, that you're in this for the long haul.

Evolving with the customer

The social customer changes daily, and the technology that companies use to interact with them changes at the same pace. It's important that you stay in tune with the changing social ecosystem, from Facebook to Pinterest to the next social channel on the horizon, and watch for mobile marketing to take the spotlight as more and more customers rely on mobile devices to stay connected.

Customers have more options for how they can communicate with your brand than ever before, and with those options come varying customer preferences. Companies must listen and adapt to customer preferences to keep up with the evolving social customer. Missing the target on a customer's communication preferences can result in a lost customer, and disregarding what they've clearly stated to you could cause them to quickly become frustrated and unlikely to do business with you again. If you frustrate customers in these ways, you can bet that they won't recommend your brand to anyone else either.

Social CRM technology helps you stay on target with the wide range of preferences across your customer base. It's a lot to keep straight, but plenty of technology options are available to help you. In Part V, we review several software and cloud-based solutions on the market that help you evolve with the social customer.

The key to keeping your marketing messages in front of your customers is to stay true to the permissions and the preferences that your customers express. When you reach customers where and how they prefer, you must provide relevant content! Be sure that you make it easy for customers to obtain useful information. Each channel — e-mail, social media, blogs, and so on — serves different purposes for each customer. You need to craft your messages appropriately for each channel you participate in.

The most effective marketers in the ever-evolving social landscape will research, read up on trends, monitor social media conversations, use data analytics, and quickly adjust messaging. Marketers have to stay on their toes to keep up!

Unraveling the Future of CRM

Traditional CRM aimed to gather essential data to move customers through a buying cycle and gain incremental revenue from existing customers. The customer data collected was somewhat flat compared to the robust information now available through social media.

Evolving social CRM platforms capture the same types of information that companies are used to, but with a wider view of customers, including information like the following:

- **Transactions:** Just like traditional CRM, social CRM provides a historical view of customer transactions and those in the pipeline.

- **Conversations:** Beyond scheduled appointments and recaptures of previous interactions with your company, social CRM can provide insight into the content of every conversation a customer has ever had. This helps to paint a broader picture of their likes and dislikes.

- **Influence:** Here's big piece of the yummy social CRM pie! Social media and the CRM solutions that capture social conversations dig into the reach of an individual customer based on his or her network and sphere of influence.

- **Demographics:** Social CRM tools can tap into networks like LinkedIn, allowing automatic updating of demographic information. With traditional CRM, keeping up with customer demographics required manual updates.

- **Feedback:** Customer feedback through social channels can be categorized and captured, and then used to drive product evolution.

- **Customer needs:** Social media monitoring tools can identify key conversations taking place online where your brand can step in to provide needed information and meet customer needs.

- **Relationships:** Many people use social media to announce life moments like marriage and the birth of a child. You can track and help celebrate these milestones the way their friends might on these sites.

- **Preferences:** You can identify the types of conversations that take place on varying social media platforms and adjust your approaches to match your customers' preferences.

Building the customer module of the future

To build the customer module of the future, you must understand the customer life cycle. As mentioned in the previous section, CRM typically has tracked and managed the activities needed to move customers through a sales and buying cycle. The *customer life cycle* goes beyond a single transaction and seeks to manage the customer relationship for loyalty, retention, and even referrals.

The idea of the customer life cycle is to keep loyal customers moving through the buying cycle over and over again. The key is maintaining customer satisfaction along the way to earn the right to ask for the sale over and over again. Social CRM enables organizations to meet customers where and how they want, which increases your brand's chances of developing a longer-term customer life cycle.

Diving into the 360-degree view

The 360-degree view refers to the ability to completely see a customer, to have all-around insight into what makes that person tick. Reaching for the full view of customers means looking at how customers use and view social media, mobile technologies, and e-mail. Make sure that you understand each of these aspects of your customer interactions.

When you get the full view of your customer, you're empowered to craft more relevant messages and disseminate them with accuracy. The 360-degree view gives a more robust customer profile that incorporates past, current, and future touch points of the customer. These include, but definitely aren't limited to

✓ Purchase history

✓ Previous service issues

✓ Channel preferences

✓ Influences — past and present

✔ Life events

✔ Likelihood to recommend and/or repurchase

✔ Motivations for interaction

Pushing Mobility and Embedded Technology

Mobile technologies speed up the rate at which we do just about everything. From a single handheld device, we can search the Internet, fire off an e-mail, engage via text messaging, play games, pay bills, and access a huge number of applications. Social CRM technologies that incorporate mobility factors have a huge opportunity to increase customer interactions and accelerate customer service and transaction opportunities.

Bricks-and-mortar retail shops can take advantage of the power of mobile technologies, too. Consider the following possibilities:

✔ Tablets can enable customers to enter their own profile details onsite.

✔ Mobile attachments enable you to swipe credit cards. Instead of leaving customers waiting in line with time to reconsider their purchase decision, meet them at the point where they made the decision to buy.

✔ Inventory tracking can also benefit from mobile devices within the store, providing real-time data on inventory.

✔ Mobile devices also allow you to quickly communicate with your team to keep everyone informed of sales and promotions, or update stock of any items.

Empower employees to develop deeper customer relationships by providing mobile devices that fit with social CRM solutions. When employees have down time in the store, they can reach out to past customers with new product information, service information, and current promotions. You'll end up with more effective employees who are engaged the whole time they're on the clock.

Many CRM solutions today are web based, which makes it easy for employees to update the system from anywhere the Internet is accessible, often using mobile devices. For instance Siebel, an Oracle CRM solution, provides mobile access to its users. The mobile version has the same capabilities and functionality as the desktop version.

A social media plan or strategy that doesn't take into account customer use of mobile devices is missing a big piece of the social picture. Anyone with a smartphone can accomplish just about anything on his device that he could on a computer, especially when it comes to social media. Mobile device users can send e-mail; upload photos; and engage on Facebook, Twitter, Pinterest, and LinkedIn. The list of mobile applications that connect users goes on and on, and it's growing every day.

Keep in mind that businesses must remain agile and in tune with how people connect online, especially with their mobile devices. The building of a new social data set is extremely important to the future of social CRM and requires careful consideration of mobile trends.

Part V
The Part of Tens

The 5th Wave   By Rich Tennant

"Good news, honey! No one's registered our last name as a Twitter handle yet. Helloooo @HaffassOralSurgery!"

In this part. . .

Every *For Dummies* book ends with a Part of Tens. This book offers a social CRM top-ten extravaganza featuring our picks for social CRM vendors. We start with our list of enterprise-level social CRM tools. You then find customer service solutions, small-business vendors, and marketing and automation vendors. These chapters are a great starting point for your research into software that can support your social CRM. We also introduce you to ten thought leaders. Stay in touch with what these folks are doing and saying, and you'll be a step ahead in understanding the latest developments in social CRM.

Chapter 16

Top Ten Enterprise-Level Social CRM Solutions

In This Chapter

▶ Introducing top customer service CRM firms

▶ Checking out the strengths and weakness of the top CRM applications

*W*e all know that enterprise is different than small business. Each company must have a differing level of support when it comes to technology. In this chapter, we've compiled the following list of enterprise-level social CRM providers that you can use as a starting point for researching your own enterprise-level solution, if that's indeed what you need. We chose the providers listed in this chapter based on whitepapers, customer experiences, executive interviews, usage, and a little help from our friend Paul Greenberg. Remember him? The Godfather of CRM? Paul writes *CRM Watchlist,* an annual list of top-performing vendors at ZDNet. We recommend you check it out.

One more thing: research and define your overall strategy before diving head first into a software product. We want this list to be a guide, not the rule.

Oracle CRM

```
https://blogs.oracle.com/crm
```

It's hard to look at any enterprise CRM or social CRM list and not see Oracle somewhere toward the top. Oracle has dominated the CRM space since the early 2000s and continues to do so despite the extreme changes. With over 380,000 clients (including ZDNet), Oracle is at the top of the list covering sales, marketing, loyalty, and services.

Oracle is powerful in part because it has invested heavily in many different CRM product offerings over the past eight to ten years. The major investments have allowed Oracle to build the projects that enable businesses to track any human contact being made internally with your employees or externally with your customer base. Oracle brings a complete solution to its clients globally, and the majority of those clients are fond of the enterprise suite of products.

Oracle has truly built a CRM solution that coexists with all Oracle products from human capital management to supply chain management. And coexisting is key to advancement in the digital and technology world.

SAP

www.sap.com/crm

CRM Watchlist has touted SAP as one of the more "innovative companies" out of the top-performing CRM vendors. That's a major accomplishment. SAP, shown in Figure 16-1, has been able to meet the needs of enterprise-level clients with its ability to adapt and ride the growing social CRM wave. SAP has an innate desire to stay innovative by cocreating products with its enterprise-level clients. Check out SAP's Co-Innovation and Sales OnDemand as examples (you can find more information at http://bit.ly/QqKuIb).

Like many of the other companies on the list, SAP has spent a considerable amount of time, money, and brainpower to position itself as a "customer experience" company. With that experience comes a move (better late than never) to the cloud. And much like Oracle's suite of products, the SAP CRM application is built directly into the SAP Business Suite, which helps reduce cost and allows management to be more proactive with staff and resources across all channels of communication. SAP's social CRM solution coexists nicely with other SAP products.

SAP is also good at community management. If you need to manage a huge user community (externally or internally), SAP could be a good choice to explore.

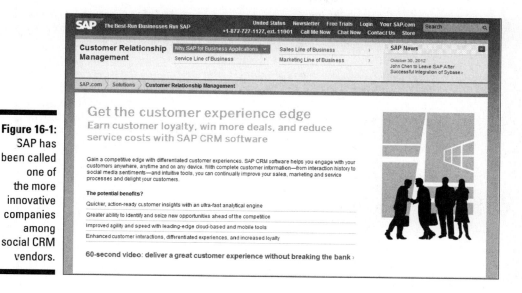

Figure 16-1:
SAP has
been called
one of
the more
innovative
companies
among
social CRM
vendors.

Microsoft Dynamics

http://crm.dynamics.com

What software or technology solutions list is complete without the undeniable power of Microsoft? Microsoft Dynamics CRM tends to focus on two key components: customer service and sales. As of this writing, Microsoft Dynamics has yet to place a considerable investment into the third component: social CRM. However, the speed at which change happens in this industry leaves Microsoft Dynamics wide open for investment and improvement. If we were gamblers, we'd place our bets on an investment.

According to *CRM Watchlist,* Microsoft Dynamics boasts a client list of 30,000 companies, with over two million users. This is one of the larger client lists in all of CRM. Microsoft is second to Oracle but still builds an impressive array of products to help the small to enterprise-level clients. That isn't exactly the 380,000 clients that Oracle's CRM solution has, but it's still nothing to laugh at.

Many in the CRM world are moving to the cloud, and like SAP, Salesforce. com, and Oracle, Microsoft has spent a considerable amount of money on its cloud-based ecosystem with the beautiful name of Windows Azure.

Salesforce.com

`www.salesforce.com`

"No software" is the leading theme behind the Salesforce.com revolution. And because of the Internet, actual boxed software doesn't matter in the world of social CRM. Salesforce is the leader in the downloadable software generation. The folks at Salesforce.com even coined the term *social enterprise* after building thought leadership behind the idea that one-to-one communication is king for businesses in the 21st century.

Salesforce is moving fast into the world of complete CRM and social CRM. It completed massive acquisitions in 2010 and 2011 with the likes of Manymoon, Radian6, and Heroku. Every acquisition positioned Salesforce closer to the idea of the complete social CRM system.

Salesforce.com classifies its social product set as the Social Enterprise, which includes the following products:

- ✔ **Sales Cloud:** This is a suite of products that includes all the CRM capabilities in a one-stop shop on the web. This tool helps drive proactivity among sales and marketing teams.

- ✔ **Service Cloud:** This product helps your customer service department implement social media practices. It allows you to assist customers in real time in the social media world.

- ✔ **Data.com:** Salesforce created a database with the leading B2B and B2C business data in the world. With Data.com, you can access the data directly from the Salesforce.com platform.

- ✔ **Chatter:** Think of Chatter as an internal and employee-owned Facebook for your company. This product allows for real-time conversation and helps make businesses processes social. Collaborate in real time from anywhere and with anyone from your company.

- ✔ **Force.com:** This platform allows for development of third-party (individuals outside of Salesforce) applications to help with the development of the Salesforce.com platform.

Are you looking for sales force automation and the tools to support your sales teams? Salesforce is the company for you.

SugarCRM

www.sugarcrm.com

SugarCRM, whose web page is shown in Figure 16-2, is a relatively small company that packs a large punch in the social CRM revolution. If your marketing organization needs to automate key processes and tasks ranging from lead generation to marketing campaign analytics, this company is for you. Like Salesforce, the SugarCRM platform is web-based, but unlike Salesforce, it has an open-source model.

What's the benefit of an open-source model? SugarCRM is offered under the Mozilla Public License and the GNU-GPL license, which means that SugarCRM's clients have complete access to the underlying code. This level of access enables clients to control the direction of the social CRM software package.

The company also offers several different deployment options, including on-demand, on-premise, and appliance-based solutions to suit customers' security, integration, and configuration needs.

If you're in Europe, SugarCRM may be of particular interest to you. According to the company's website, about one-quarter of its customers are located in Europe, and more than 30 percent of their downloads take place in Europe.

Figure 16-2: SugarCRM offers a range of services for businesses.

Jive

`http://jivesoftware.com`

According to CrunchBase, Jive is "the largest and fastest growing independent vendor in the Social Business market." Jive originally built its credibility upon its extremely powerful community software. Since then, Jive has made huge progress into the world of collaboration, social networking software, and social media monitoring.

Jive pretty much solidified its position within the social space when Jive acquired Filtrbox and renamed it Jive Fathom (a little creepy). Jive Fathom allows you to listen to, analyze, engage with, and act on conversations happening within the social space. Jive Fathom competes directly with Salesforce.com's Radian6 product.

On a side note, if you're ever in Portland, look for the Jive office. It is one of the best looking buildings in *Portlandia!*

Pivotal

`http://cdcsoftware.com`

This is almost an honorable mention, but we feel Pivotal is valuable because of the strength it built in 2010. However, 2011 didn't treat the company well. Pivotal was owned by CDC Software (which is now bankrupt), and will need a couple of financial quarters to transition back to an independent software provider. However, Paul Greenberg wrote a post over at PGreenblog (at `http://the56group.typepad.com`) in June 2011 describing Pivotal as one of the first and "real social CRM products." We agree with him.

Pivotal is styled after the Microsoft CRM interface (role- and task-based navigation), which should make it comfortable to use and reduce the learning curve and speed of adoption internally within the company.

Infor

```
http://infor.com/solutions/crm
```

Infor is worthy of mention in this list despite its lack of "premium social CRM tools." Infor made massive gains when (in 2011) it announced a partnership with Salesforce.com to combine the Salesforce.com CRM applications with Infor's ERP (enterprise resource planning) and financials applications. This combination gives you a complete, 360-degree view of customer information across the enterprise. And when we say *complete*, we mean completely across the enterprise.

Other than a social CRM tool offering, Infor offers a deep CRM suite, which includes customer service and sales channel tools as well as multichannel marketing capabilities, resource management, and e-mail enhancements.

SAS

```
www.sas.com/knowledge-exchange/customer-intelligence
```

SAS is a powerhouse. There's no doubt about that! Over the past couple of years, SAS has been investing in the social and CRM space by strengthening its tools for monitoring and response.

SAS defines its product as *customer intelligence* instead of using the ever-popular *CRM* acronym for customer relationship management. The company tends to focus on solid customer intelligence and an integrated "marketing management framework" or (in other words) tools for intense customer engagement. SAS is truly about optimizing customer experience.

What places SAS on this list are its social media and web analytics solutions, which supply you with the programs necessary to interact with people and conversations that are happening in the online environment. That's pretty social, right?

IBM CRM

http://ibm.com/crm

Honestly, where would we be without the "Big Blue Machine" of IBM? This company is a little hard to ignore. If you're looking for a CRM vendor that can manage every aspect of your business from supplier management to mobile marketing and cross-channel selling, the IBM platform may be for you.

IBM can literally handle any aspect of a customer service and/or relationship experience. IBM emphasizes personalizing what businesses can offer customers, as shown in Figure 16-3.

Figure 16-3: IBM has a robust social CRM solution.

Chapter 17

Top Ten Customer Service–Centric Social CRM Solutions

In This Chapter

▶ Introducing the top customer service CRM firms

▶ Checking out the strengths, weaknesses, and opportunities of each vendor

*W*e believe that all CRM is a function of the customer experience. Whether customers typically call into a customer support line or complain on Twitter, a successful customer service model is needed in order for any size organization to thrive. The competition is just too fierce. Customer service is the deciding factor of whether a customer will continue to be a customer.

In no way, shape, or form is customer service easy. However, when you're on the level of an Amazon or Best Buy, it can be fairly hard to answer thousands of phone calls, tweets, and e-mails per day, but you do have to manage it.

Here's where this chapter comes in: We've compiled a list of the top ten CRM packages available on the market. They all fit in the mold of the social CRM model, but they just happen to have deeper functionality in customer service and support.

Sword Ciboodle

www.sword-ciboodle.com

In addition to having an amazing name, Sword Ciboodle, shown in Figure 17-1, has been ranked among the top (and best in class) companies for process-centered CRM solutions. This means they kick butt in the world of complex call and contact centers.

Sword Ciboodle covers both sides of the equation, with Ciboodle Flow to Ciboodle Crowd, tracking and managing the customer experience. Whether you need live chat functionality or customer intelligence, Sword Ciboodle delivers on all levels of the customer experience. Its software offering is excellent, but the company also offers a direct approach to viewing client interactions and service.

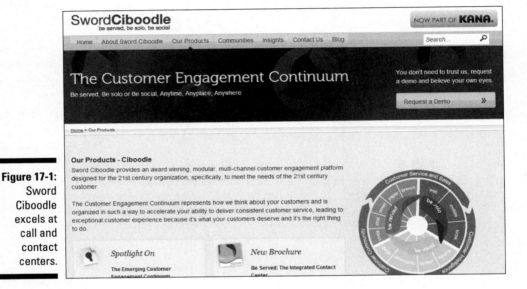

Figure 17-1:
Sword Ciboodle excels at call and contact centers.

Get Satisfaction

https://getsatisfaction.com

The name — Get Satisfaction — says it all, right? Not as cool as Sword Ciboodle, but it defines exactly what this company offers. Get Satisfaction provides online community and support software for the small to medium-size business, as well as enterprise-level clients. They also encourage user feedback for issues relating to bugs and different product features.

According to *Business Week,* the company's platform also enables "productive conversations between companies and their customers to provide social support experience, build products, increase SEO, and improve customer loyalty."

Attensity

www.attensity.com

You could lump Attensity into any group, but we believe the product belongs in customer support and engagement. When using Attensity, organizations have the ability to listen, use, and respond to the vast amounts of data stored in both internal and online sources.

Attensity follows the CEM (customer experience management) model; these solutions are built on an extremely reliable platform that enables listening, analyzing, and relating to the customer experience in the online environment. This is important to you, the reader, because it allows you to easily listen and analyze the different social media sites for tweets, Facebook posts, and other messages relating to customer service.

Parature

www.parature.com

Paul Greenburg said it best in his CRM Watchlist 2012: "Parature supports a solution and a platform for providing customer service in any physical environment." Parature is truly a good solution for the companies and organizations that don't have their own contact centers.

Parature, shown in Figure 17-2, has three core competencies within their environment: social channels, customer input management, and workload management. Their mission is simply this: "To be the expert in customer service, not just customer service solutions."

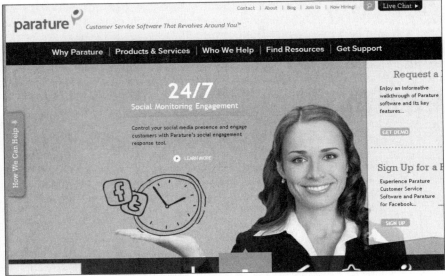

Figure 17-2:
Parature can provide customer service in a range of physical environments.

KANA

www.kana.com

If you haven't already figured this out, the world of CRM is filled with acronyms. We have another one for you. We aren't sure if KANA coined it, but it's still relevant. *SEM* (service experience management) means the convergence of CRM, knowledge management, analytics, and social media designed for customer service. Knowledge management is just one portion of the overall software package. This tool allows for management of different pieces of content and ideas from employees. With this tool, you can effectively manage the experiences and insight of your customers and employees.

The company has been through a fair amount of changes over the past six to seven years and has just started to make new leads in customer service management — nay, service experience management. KANA has built and manages a complete suite of products that include SEM Agent Desktop, SEM Web Self-Service, SEM Knowledge Management, SEM Experience Analytics, SEM Chat, Case Management, and the list goes on. These products are at the core of KANA's mission to transform customer service experiences.

Moxie Software

http://moxiesoft.com

Many vendors in the CRM, customer service, and social media space create offerings that tap into the knowledge base of both the employee and the customer. Moxie Software does it better than most, employing an understanding of social software that far surpasses that of most competitors. This is steeped in the history of the company as a social solution.

Moxie Software is one of the major customer service platforms that originally started in the social space. Since its creators started in the social media space first, they understand the concept of combining social media and customer relationship management better than their competitors. Many of their competitors went from old CRM platforms to customer service platforms.

Reach analyst firm Forrester believes that we're entering a new era called *the age of the customer*. This means that the familiar phrase, "the customer is always right" is more of a rule than a suggestion. It means the focus on customers takes priority. Moxie understands this and delivers with software that understands social media and CRM.

Back to Mr. Greenburg from CRM Watchlist 2012, "That's why the foundation apps aren't really apps but mostly portals called Employee Spaces which is organized around internal collaboration and Customer Spaces which is organized around communities and channels for customer outreach and participation."

Pegasystems

www.pega.com

If you're part of a growing business with multiple revenue streams (both new and old) Pegasystems might be something to look at. It's one of the leaders of BPM (business process management). I could give you an entire paragraph of jargon, but let's keep it simple. *Business process management* is a fancy way of saying, "We have the systems that allow you to automate almost any business process within your company." The software and systems allow you to scale your operations with surprising speed, from goal setting to business logic.

Pegasystems also offers what's called the *customer process manager* (CPM), which is built on its core software and customizable to industry-specific models, processes, and interfaces. The CPM process helps businesses manage every aspect of their customer-facing product, including marketing, sales, and customer service.

Astute Solutions

> http://astutesolutions.com

In late March 2011, Astute Solutions launched its SRM (social relationship management) offering, which advanced enterprise social media management by integrating the following capabilities into a single offering:

- ✔ **Monitoring:** Astute Solutions gives you access to customer feedback in real time. This matters to your CRM strategy, especially from a customer service perspective, because you can respond and turn that customer from a supporter to a raving fan.

- ✔ **Analysis:** Analysis of data that's pulled from customer feedback is paramount to any company's success. By analyzing data, you can change processes within the company from marketing to sales.

- ✔ **Engagement:** Monitoring is just the beginning in regard to social media. With Astute's social media management solution, you can engage customers who are sharing the buzz and positive sentiment in real time.

Astute provides a solution that includes not only natural language processing but also builds in a proprietary crawler. This crawler automates and manages searches over millions of different sites, forums, and social networks to track communication regarding your brand.

Contactual

> http://contactual.com

Contactual allows you to manage multiple aspects of your customer service experience, from call centers to virtual assistants. They also deal with an important aspect of service: the internal help desk. This helps your company scale (grow extremely fast) and still provide the same amount of support for your employees and customers.

Contactual is one of the only call center solutions within this list. It's important to understand that while social media is an important aspect of customer service, the call center is just as important. Honestly, we probably wouldn't have placed Contactual on this list if it weren't integrated with Salesforce.com and NetSuite, which gives them powerful allies in social CRM and CRM support models. Their multiple integrations allow them to synchronize with different social CRM platforms to provide an overall customer service experience.

Consona

http://consona.com

Last but certainly not least, Consona, shown in Figure 17-3, was one of the first companies to implement (successfully) knowledge-driven support (KDS), which integrates knowledge capture, reuse, and improvement directly into case management and support processes. This is more of an internal process for companies. Basically, a KDS gives contact center agents the ability and tools to quickly resolve customer service issues in all mediums from phone to e-mail to social media.

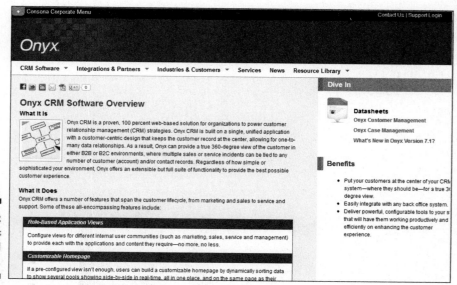

Figure 17-3:
Consona's
social CRM
solution.

One of the coolest Consona features is multi-way chat, which helps a company's analysts handle up to four chat sessions simultaneously and resolve issues faster. Consona also offers knowledge management solutions that allow for employees to work together to form a more social company.

One other thing to keep in mind is that Consona is the only CRM-based company that's focused entirely on service and support. This allows them to focus and perfect their software for this one need.

Chapter 18

Top Ten Social CRM Thought Leaders

*T*he world of social CRM would be a much different place without the leadership and guidance of the people listed on the following pages. Their guidance whether by phone, through writing, or e-mail helped form the contents of this book and the industry.

They are the preeminent thought leaders of social CRM and will continue to write, create, and lead the revolution of the social consumer. We recommend that you read, friend, and follow them. (Find each person's Twitter handle and website under his or her name in this chapter.) If you stalk them, we didn't tell you to do that.

Paul Greenburg

> @pgreenbe
> http://the56group.typepad.com

You want the scoop on CRM strategy, technology, stories, companies, and personalities? Paul is your guy. He's known widely as the Godfather of CRM. His writes about the world of traditional and social CRM, focusing on not only what CRM is, but also where it's going. His blog is shown in Figure 18-1.

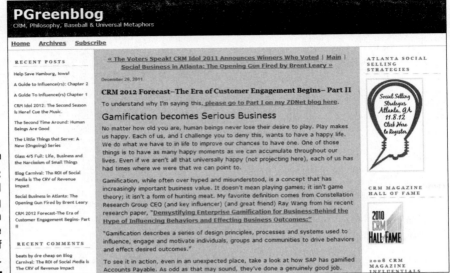

Figure 18-1:
Paul
Greenburg
is known
as the
Godfather of
CRM.

Adam Metz

@theMetz
www.adammetz.com

Adam Metz is considered an expert on the social customer. He's also touted as one of the first consultants in the social CRM space to devise a holistic social web analytics model for his clients (which we feature in this book).

R "Ray" Wang

@rwang0
http://blog.softwareinsider.org

Adam and Paul mention R "Ray" Wang multiple times throughout their writing, and literally hundreds of thousands of readers follow Wang's enterprise software blog, A Software Insider's Point of View. His blog, shown in Figure 18-2, provides insight into how disruptive technologies and new business models impact the enterprise.

When he isn't speaking all over the world, Ray Wang is Principal Analyst & CEO of the next-generation research and advisory firm Constellation Research, Inc.

Figure 18-2:
R "Ray"
Wang's
blog.

Wim Rampen

@wimrampen
www.wimrampen.com

Wim Rampen knows social communication. Period. He's especially sharp with anything pertaining to customer-facing departments and challenges.

When he isn't writing about customer relationship management, Wim is Manager of Customer Intelligence and Brand Management at Delta Lloyd Group.

Kate Leggett

@kateleggett
http://blogs.forrester.com/kate_leggett

Kate is a Senior Analyst Serving Application & Delivery Professionals at Forrester Research. She leads the charge in helping organizations establish and validate customer service strategies. You can find her research and writing all over the web. Her blog is shown in Figure 18-3.

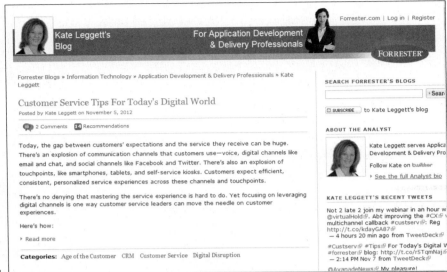

Figure 18-3:
Kate Leggett
writes for
Forrester
Research.

Esteban Kolsky

> @ekolsky
> http://estebankolsky.com

If you want to know anything about CRM, social CRM, social business, CEM, CX, or any other combination of letters that has *C* (for *customer*) in it, Esteban Kolsky is your guy. His blog thinkJar, shown in Figure 18-4, is one of the leading editorials focused on the world of social CRM.

Martin Schneider

> @mschneider718
> http://sharpmartin.com/tag/crm

When he isn't mixing things up at 451 Research, you can find Martin's writings over at CRM Magazine and other noteworthy CRM publications. Martin was previously at SugarCRM, where he started the CRM Outsiders, a blog and social media project that quickly became a destination for companies and individuals seeking insight into the new rules of social sales, marketing, and database development.

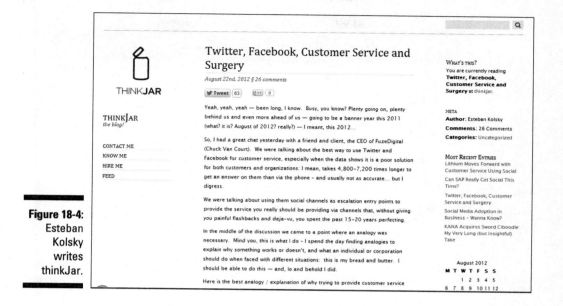

Figure 18-4:
Esteban
Kolsky
writes
thinkJar.

Mitch Lieberman

@mjayliebs
http://mjayliebs.wordpress.com

We enjoy Mitch's strong focus on customer experiences and next-generation CRM (social CRM). His day job is Vice President of Marketing for Sword Ciboodle. Mitch makes a point of reminding us that the hyper-connected, mobile, and localized customer demands simplicity and is less tolerant of business-driven organizational procedures.

What we love most about Mitch? His blog title, which is *Mitch Lieberman – A Title Would Limit My Thoughts. Touché* Mitch; *touché.* Check it out in Figure 18-5.

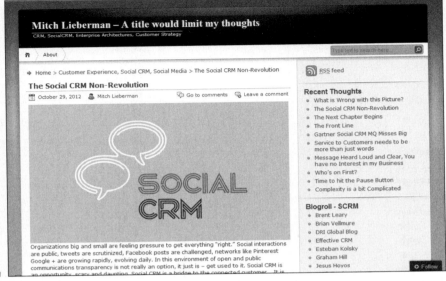

Figure 18-5:
Mitch
Lieberman
has no
limits on
his blog, A
Title Would
Limit My
Thoughts.

Bill Ives

@billives
http://billives.typepad.com

Bill is an academic psychologist who just happens to love the world of social business — and we love that he loves it! Bill rocks it over at the Merced Group, where he focuses on business strategy, program design, and implementation services in social business efforts. He's also a team member at Darwin Ecosystems, a content-awareness and discovery engine. You can keep up with what he's thinking via his blog, shown in Figure 18-6.

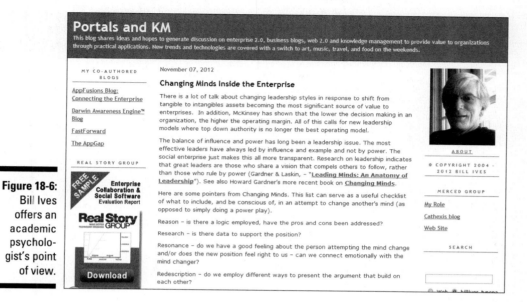

Figure 18-6:
Bill Ives
offers an
academic
psycholo-
gist's point
of view.

Marc Benioff

@benioff
http://blogs.salesforce.com/company/datacom

If you don't already know, Marc is the founder of Salesforce.com and one
of the top thought leaders in the world of cloud-based CRM solutions. He
revolutionized the way sales forces communicate with prospects and
customers. Benioff is regarded as the leader of what he has termed "The
End of Software," the now-proven belief that cloud computing applications
democratize information by delivering immediate benefits at reduced risks
and costs.

Chapter 19

Top Ten Small Business Social CRM Vendors

In This Chapter

▶ Introducing the top small-business CRM firms

▶ Understanding the strengths and benefits of each platform

CRM isn't only for the big dogs. Small- to mid-size businesses can also use it to manage, track, and build relationships with customers. This includes the social media world where, if used correctly, small businesses can cut costs on marketing and build a community of advocates for their brand.

This chapter is for the small business owners who need a detailed and concise solution to manage client interactions, lead generation, customer service, and social relationship management. When it comes to delivering the software, the companies you learn about in this chapter are at the top of their game. Their software can help staff at a small- and medium-sized company more deeply understand and engage customers.

Nimble

www.nimble.com

Nimble, whose website is shown in Figure 19-1, offers the small business solution that the world of social media and CRM has been waiting for. It helps you collect every piece of your online and offline relationships and store them in one place. With Nimble's social CRM software, you can send messages, add tasks, edit and download contact profiles, instantly find the social profiles of contacts, and view all activity — from e-mail messages to social conversations — with each contact. Nimble is one of those companies you just have to get to know.

Ken Hess, writer at ZDNet, said it best when be described Nimble in this way, "What makes Nimble different is that it is an all-inclusive workspace. It integrates your email, your CRM, your Sales Deals, your Contacts, and your Social Media connections in a single application."

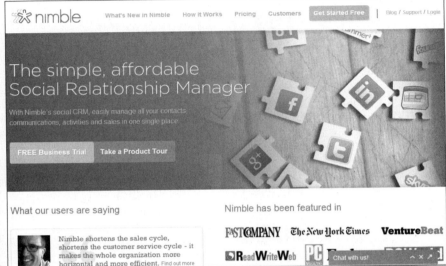

Figure 19-1: Nimble has a well-regarded social CRM solution for small business.

AddressTwo

www.addresstwo.com

Nick Carter — author, speaker and entrepreneur — started AddressTwo. It's a relatively unknown business based in Indianapolis, IN, but that doesn't keep it from being affordable and easy to use for the small business environment. And when we say easy to use, we mean it. While AddressTwo lacks the look and feel of the heavily funded CRM, it makes up for it in the easy layout and simple functions to get the job done. The software is perfect for individuals in the real estate, financial planning, or networking market.

Like most small business CRMs, AddressTwo costs about $10 to $15 per month.

Constant Contact

www.constantcontact.com

For those of you who don't know, Constant Contact is an ever-evolving e-mail marketing company that's making strides to build a complete engagement-marketing platform for small businesses, nonprofits, and member organizations. Constant Contact has a built a platform that gives the customer a robust set of tools to use in the social space.

The Constant Contact platform allows a business team to search, monitor, and connect with people across the web for business development, sales, and marketing purposes. With the Social CRM offering, Constant Contact also allows you to manage your marketing campaigns with social, mobile, local deals, events, and e-mail tools. With so many tools, the pricing is spread out over each offering. Check out their website for more information.

Zoho

www.zoho.com

Don't let the crayon-colored logo fool you. More than six million users work online with the social CRM Zoho. The software is a pretty straightforward, small-business CRM with capabilities such as calendar management, reporting, internal wikis, and document sharing. With Zoho, you can also create your own apps, which is a huge advantage for the more technically inclined user.

Zoho truly offers an entire suite of business-driven software products for smaller organizations. Zoho's tools include calendars, forms, e-mail, and invoices. Whether you're looking to automate processes, connect with your customers, or track your sales activities, Zoho manages to build and implement hardy web-based social CRM tools.

At the time of this writing, Zoho CRM is available at three pricing levels for customers. The enterprise level consists of the largest software offering and costs $25 per user per month. Zoho also offers a free version of the Zoho CRM for a business with less than three users. The professional plan fits somewhere in the middle, at $12 per month per user. The professional plan caters to the small business with 3–15 users.

Nutshell

`www.nutshell.com`

Nutshell's solution is valuable if you're looking for a system to manage the strict details of the sales process within your small business. While companies like Constant Contact, Nimble, and Zoho manage almost every aspect of your communication and business, Nutshell allows companies to significantly impact, drive, and manage sales activities of different teams across the organization.

The Nutshell pricing model is similar to that of the other vendors on the list, starting at $10 per month for each user. The company also has invested in several high-availability data centers to guarantee that service is always operational, and they have a fully staffed technical support team.

Relenta

`http://relenta.com`

Relenta's tagline says it all: "CRM for people who get things done." Relenta's software helps employees be more productive in their everyday work environment. The company is so enthralled with productivity that they implemented David Allen's Getting Things Done (GTD) principles within the software. Relenta helps small businesses view all activity with contacts and leads in a chronological order for a single client or prospect.

Relenta differentiates itself from the other solutions by emphasizing personal productivity. And when we say "emphasizing," we mean "almost religious fervor around productivity." The founder, Dmitri Eroshenko, even states in his bio that "Relenta is the result of my quest to take back my life." He also states, "You can always email me directly, and rest assured that Relenta will not let me lose your email in the shuffle."

Relenta offers a wide variety of pricing options for its customers, ranging from $25 to $250 per month. The differences in pricing depends on the number of users and contacts. Find more details at Relenta's website, shown in Figure 19-2.

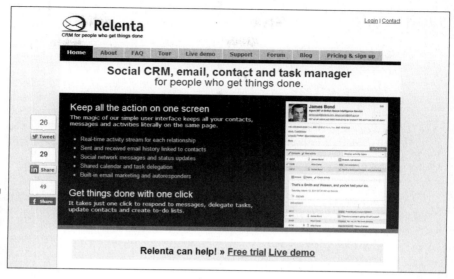

Batchbook

www.batchbook.com

If you're a sole proprietor or small business owner with a staff of three or fewer, Batchbook may have the best solution for you. Batchbook has created a social CRM offering that includes social media monitoring, communications tracking, e-mail forwarding, to-do lists, web forms, and sales tracking. Like many other social CRM companies, Batchbook is integrated with many small business tools, including Formstack and MailChimp.

Batchbook creates useful and user-friendly software for small businesses. The team has a background in programming and web usability, which helps in the creation and build-out of the software solution. Overall, Batchbook is fairly competitive in pricing ranging from $14.95 per month per user to $149 per month for up to 50 users.

JitterJam

http://jitterjam.com

Thanks to Jason Falls from Social Media Explorer for turning us toward the Meltwater Group's product called JitterJam. This software offering is a little different from the rest of the products on this list because the company focuses solely on the marketing, PR, and advertising agencies who service the needs of consumer-facing companies. Basically, JitterJam supports the small business marketer and agency.

The tool allows your company to import contacts like Facebook fans and Twitter followers and move them into one large database (much like you can with Nimble's social CRM software). You also can tag the contacts in order to organize them in a neat and contacts-oriented fashion. Remember, filtering is a necessity when you're building a powerful CRM tool and solution. Although the website isn't clear about how much the product costs, you can easily sign up for a demo for the service.

BlueCamroo

http://bluecamroo.com

BlueCamroo is one of the funkier social CRM software solutions on the list and not just because of its name. Although it's similar to JitterJam, BlueCamroo has a distinct marketing and positioning statement pertaining to social CRM and contact management. BlueCamroo tends to focus heavily on tracking web leads and web lead generation through visitors to your website. The software vendor believes that "every user visiting your website is a potential lead." The product's feature list is a mile long and contains every aspect of the lead-nurturing process.

BlueCamroo focuses on the following tasks: time tracking, invoicing, social media scouting, e-mail marketing, work flow rules, and security around employee external and internal communication. BlueCamroo is also priced competitively, with several packages ranging from $29 per month per user to $199 per month for 10 users. The package includes storage space in the cloud and an unlimited amount of cases.

Infusionsoft

`http://infusionsoft.com`

Infusionsoft's specialty is the small business that wants to combine CRM, marketing, and e-commerce all in one system. Infusionsoft combines CRM and digital marketing tools into a single online system that helps you automate and deliver valuable insights to your team.

The company tends to focus on three niche groups in the small business world: sales teams, service providers, and online marketers (with a focus on the e-commerce vertical). They allow you to find leads and shorten your sales cycle. One valuable upsell from Infusionsoft is that they allow you to spend more time with your customers because they automate many of the manual tasks keeping you in front of the computer. You can watch a demo of their product online, as shown in Figure 19-3.

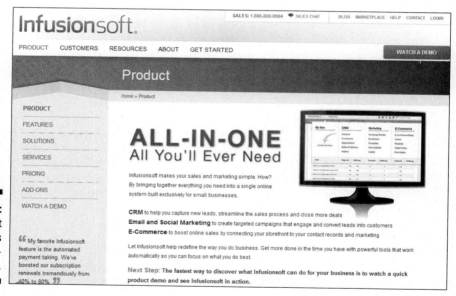

Figure 19-3: Infusionsoft specializes in an all-in-one system.

Chapter 20

Top Ten Cross-Channel Marketing Vendors

In This Chapter

▶ Exploring the top cross-channel marketing vendors

▶ Checking out the strengths and benefits of each platform

Cross-channel marketing vendors can help you manage every form of marketing within your company, from small to large. In addition to the actual CRM, CRM software packages can also help you control, manage, and implement entire marketing campaigns.

The software vendors listed in this chapter have the more robust offering when it comes to driving interaction with current, former, and future customers. It's imperative that a marketing system is either integrated directly into your social CRM solution or offered as part of the software purchase. Marketing automation is part of an overall CRM strategy and should be used as an add-on to your customer relationship management strategy as a company.

At the enterprise level, pricing can vary widely based on your company's needs. For pricing information for products from any of the vendors mentioned here, please contact the vendor.

Eloqua

www.eloqua.com

Eloqua tends to stay in the B2B space but has recently been moving into more of the consumer products and B2C marketing world. They were among one of the first B2B marketing automation products and still remains one of the largest in the world of revenue and employees. Although Eloqua probably doesn't fit the small business world, it does fit the mid-size to large marketing space.

Raab Associates recently published a Marketing Automation report that states Eloqua's strengths as "an advanced feature set including complex segmentation, real-time interactions, rule-driven content for email and Web pages, precise control over sales synchronization, extensive project management, detailed assignments and a fully extensible data model." As you can tell, a ton of stuff.

HubSpot

www.hubspot.com

HubSpot has reigned as one of the top social and digital marketing platforms for small business over the last couple of years. HubSpot offers excellent training on their products and marketing solutions. They create content that drives customer interaction and marketing automation success. The software vendor boasts that more than 6,000 companies in 45 countries use their software to attract leads and convert them into customers.

Their features include blogging support, social media monitoring and management, search engine optimization, lead-generation tracking, lead management, e-mail and marketing automation, analytics, and apps for third-party support.

Marketo

www.marketo.com

Marketo has been around since 2008 and usually aims to the small- or mid-sized marketing programs, as shown in Figure 20-1. However, the company is pushing into the corporate space as this book goes to press.

Marketo has an extremely robust platform that helps companies large and small track and manage leads for a variety of lead-generation strategies from e-mail to social CRM.

According to Raab Associates, "Marketo's major strength is its ease of use. Other particular strengths include integrated content testing, posting social media behaviors to the activity history, multiple scores per lead, and an API service for third-party support."

Figure 20-1: Marketo has been focuses on small- and mid-sized business but is moving into the corporate space, too.

Net-Results

www.net-results.com

Net-Results originally started as a web design firm that launched a variety of software products over the past decade. The company caters mainly to the small business world. If you're a small business owner looking for some advanced capabilities but would rather not deal in the Responsys or Marketo world, Net-Results is for you.

The Net-Results software boasts a pretty robust feature set that deals in lead scoring, unlimited segmentation of data, lead nurturing, e-mail marketing, list management, and CRM integration (just to name a few).

Experian CheetahMail

www.experian.com/cheetahmail/index.html

If you're looking for services and support to drive your digital marketing efforts, CheetahMail is for you. If you're looking for software that helps with building and creating a campaign, CheetahMail boasts one of the largest client services teams in the world and gives you the technology, too. Like Responsys and ExactTarget, CheetahMail is also recognized by Forrester as one of the top e-mail marketing vendors. The company also caters to the retail market, working with 75 of the 500 top Internet retailer vendors.

The company prides itself on its ability to service marketers with a full range of marketing services and capabilities, including digital marketing support, consumer data, and data management. Experian CheetahMail is also a valuable vendor mainly because it has built into the Experian structure, which gives the customer access to a variety of different tools offered by the company.

Neolane

www.neolane.com

Neolane is truly a cross-channel marketing platform, which allows users to organize and track one-to-one lifetime conversations with customers. More than 350 of the world's leading companies use the cross-channel marketing software.

Look into Neolane if you want highly sophisticated campaign management software. Neolane software can handle more of the financial, content management, employee interaction, and publishing controls than any other system on this list. However, even with a robust system Neolane makes it easy to use their software.

Silverpop

http://silverpop.com

Although Silverpop caters more to the e-mail marketer, the company does offer robust marketing automation software. Mainly focused on the B2B market, Silverpop's capabilities allow markets to efficiently manage leads and drive qualified sales opportunities through scoring and nurturing campaigns. Silverpop boasts a fully integrated suite of digital marketing solutions from social media to landing page management.

With the purchase of Vtrenz in 2007, Silverpop entered the marketing automation space and released a product called Engage 8. According to Raab, "Silverpop has strong email capabilities and supports powerful multi-step campaign flows, split testing and controlled user rights. However, they do limit their ability when it comes to project management."

Responsys

`http://responsys.com`

Responsys was founded in 1998 to provide software that would enable marketers to design, execute, and manage e-mail campaigns. Fast-forwarding to 2012, their Interact Suite provides marketers with a powerful, comprehensive set of applications to design, define, execute, and manage cross-channel marketing.

The company has built a reputation around the concept of "new school marketing," which reflects on the changing attitudes and behaviors of consumers using digital technology. This will give you a better idea of what they mean, straight from the Responsys website, "They fast forward through TV commercials. They've put down the newspaper. Old school marketing as one-way communication. The old power channels were TV, radio and print. Today the consumer has more options. Period." This is the new school of marketing. The website, shown in Figure 20-2, drives home the point.

Figure 20-2: Responsys has been around since 1998, but stays focused on the new school of marketing.

SalesFusion

`http://salesfusion.com`

Primarily a B2B sales automation tool, SalesFusion was officially launched in 2007 as an integrated marketing CRM solution designed to automate the entire lead-to-sales process. First Reef, LLC owns and operates SalesFusion.

If you're looking for lead generation and marketing automation software that's built extremely close to your CRM, SalesFusion may be for you. SalesFusion product features include e-mail marketing, landing pages, website visitors, lead scoring, social media, and event management (only to name a few).

ExactTarget

`www.exacttarget.com`

ExactTarget is global software as a service leader serving thousands of customers from London to Seattle to Melbourne, as shown in Figure 20-3. If you're looking for a system to run major marketing campaigns from social to mobile, this might be the technology for you.

The company has also been ranked as one of the top marketing automation software developers in the world and named time and again, by Forrester Research, as the industry's producer of the foremost cross-channel marketing software. Forrester found that ExactTarget's Interactive Marketing Hub product "brings the strongest current offering this year with intuitive campaign management, scalability, automated predictive models, collaboration tools and an open source technology platform that supports third-party developers. (Disclaimer: ExactTarget is Kyle Lacy's employer at the time of writing this.)

Figure 20-3:
ExactTarget
is a global
software as
a service
leader.

Index

• C •

• N •

• O •

• P •

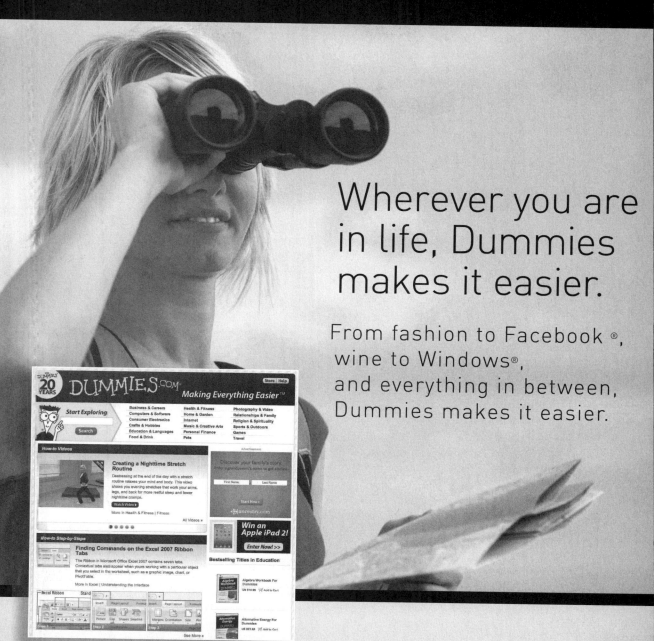

Apple & Mac

iPad 2 For Dummies,
3rd Edition
978-1-118-17679-5

iPhone 4S For Dummies,
5th Edition
978-1-118-03671-6

iPod touch For Dummies,
3rd Edition
978-1-118-12960-9

Mac OS X Lion
For Dummies
978-1-118-02205-4

Blogging & Social Media

CityVille For Dummies
978-1-118-08337-6

Facebook For Dummies,
4th Edition
978-1-118-09562-1

Mom Blogging
For Dummies
978-1-118-03843-7

Twitter For Dummies,
2nd Edition
978-0-470-76879-2

WordPress For Dummies,
4th Edition
978-1-118-07342-1

Business

Cash Flow For Dummies
978-1-118-01850-7

Investing For Dummies,
6th Edition
978-0-470-90545-6

Job Searching with Social Media For Dummies
978-0-470-93072-4

QuickBooks 2012
For Dummies
978-1-118-09120-3

Resumes For Dummies,
6th Edition
978-0-470-87361-8

Starting an Etsy Business
For Dummies
978-0-470-93067-0

Cooking & Entertaining

Cooking Basics
For Dummies, 4th Edition
978-0-470-91388-8

Wine For Dummies,
4th Edition
978-0-470-04579-4

Diet & Nutrition

Kettlebells For Dummies
978-0-470-59929-7

Nutrition For Dummies,
5th Edition
978-0-470-93231-5

Restaurant Calorie Counter
For Dummies,
2nd Edition
978-0-470-64405-8

Digital Photography

Digital SLR Cameras &
Photography For Dummies,
4th Edition
978-1-118-14489-3

Digital SLR Settings & Shortcuts For Dummies
978-0-470-91763-3

Photoshop Elements 10
For Dummies
978-1-118-10742-3

Gardening

Gardening Basics
For Dummies
978-0-470-03749-2

Vegetable Gardening
For Dummies,
2nd Edition
978-0-470-49870-5

Green/Sustainable

Raising Chickens
For Dummies
978-0-470-46544-8

Green Cleaning
For Dummies
978-0-470-39106-8

Health

Diabetes For Dummies,
3rd Edition
978-0-470-27086-8

Food Allergies
For Dummies
978-0-470-09584-3

Living Gluten-Free
For Dummies,
2nd Edition
978-0-470-58589-4

Hobbies

Beekeeping
For Dummies,
2nd Edition
978-0-470-43065-1

Chess For Dummies,
3rd Edition
978-1-118-01695-4

Drawing For Dummies,
2nd Edition
978-0-470-61842-4

eBay For Dummies,
7th Edition
978-1-118-09806-6

Knitting For Dummies,
2nd Edition
978-0-470-28747-7

Language & Foreign Language

English Grammar
For Dummies,
2nd Edition
978-0-470-54664-2

French For Dummies,
2nd Edition
978-1-118-00464-7

German For Dummies,
2nd Edition
978-0-470-90101-4

Spanish Essentials
For Dummies
978-0-470-63751-7

Spanish For Dummies,
2nd Edition
978-0-470-87855-2

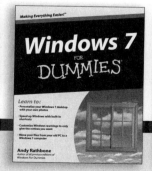

Available wherever books are sold. For more information or to order direct: U.S. customers visit www.dummies.com or call 1-877-762-2974.
U.K. customers visit www.wileyeurope.com or call (0) 1243 843291. Canadian customers visit www.wiley.ca or call 1-800-567-4797.

Connect with us online at www.facebook.com/fordummies or @fordummies

Math & Science

Algebra I For Dummies,
2nd Edition
978-0-470-55964-2

Biology For Dummies,
2nd Edition
978-0-470-59875-7

Chemistry For Dummies,
2nd Edition
978-1-1180-0730-3

Geometry For Dummies,
2nd Edition
978-0-470-08946-0

Pre-Algebra Essentials
For Dummies
978-0-470-61838-7

Microsoft Office

Excel 2010 For Dummies
978-0-470-48953-6

Office 2010 All-in-One
For Dummies
978-0-470-49748-7

Office 2011 for Mac
For Dummies
978-0-470-87869-9

Word 2010
For Dummies
978-0-470-48772-3

Music

Guitar For Dummies,
2nd Edition
978-0-7645-9904-0

Clarinet For Dummies
978-0-470-58477-4

iPod & iTunes
For Dummies,
9th Edition
978-1-118-13060-5

Pets

Cats For Dummies,
2nd Edition
978-0-7645-5275-5

Dogs All-in One
For Dummies
978-0470-52978-2

Saltwater Aquariums
For Dummies
978-0-470-06805-2

Religion & Inspiration

The Bible For Dummies
978-0-7645-5296-0

Catholicism For Dummies,
2nd Edition
978-1-118-07778-8

Spirituality For Dummies,
2nd Edition
978-0-470-19142-2

Self-Help & Relationships

Happiness For Dummies
978-0-470-28171-0

Overcoming Anxiety
For Dummies,
2nd Edition
978-0-470-57441-6

Seniors

Crosswords For Seniors
For Dummies
978-0-470-49157-7

iPad 2 For Seniors
For Dummies, 3rd Edition
978-1-118-17678-8

Laptops & Tablets
For Seniors For Dummies,
2nd Edition
978-1-118-09596-6

Smartphones & Tablets

BlackBerry For Dummies,
5th Edition
978-1-118-10035-6

Droid X2 For Dummies
978-1-118-14864-8

HTC ThunderBolt
For Dummies
978-1-118-07601-9

MOTOROLA XOOM
For Dummies
978-1-118-08835-7

Sports

Basketball For Dummies,
3rd Edition
978-1-118-07374-2

Football For Dummies,
2nd Edition
978-1-118-01261-1

Golf For Dummies,
4th Edition
978-0-470-88279-5

Test Prep

ACT For Dummies,
5th Edition
978-1-118-01259-8

ASVAB For Dummies,
3rd Edition
978-0-470-63760-9

The GRE Test For
Dummies, 7th Edition
978-0-470-00919-2

Police Officer Exam
For Dummies
978-0-470-88724-0

Series 7 Exam
For Dummies
978-0-470-09932-2

Web Development

HTML, CSS, & XHTML
For Dummies, 7th Edition
978-0-470-91659-9

Drupal For Dummies,
2nd Edition
978-1-118-08348-2

Windows 7

Windows 7
For Dummies
978-0-470-49743-2

Windows 7
For Dummies,
Book + DVD Bundle
978-0-470-52398-8

Windows 7 All-in-One
For Dummies
978-0-470-48763-1